VOYAGES

FROM TONGAN VILLAGES TO AMERICAN SUBURBS

Cathy A. Small

Cornell University Press

Ithaca and London

First published 1997 by Cornell University Press
First printing, Cornell Paperbacks, 1997

Printed in the United States of America

Library of Congress Cataloging-in-Publication Data
Small, Cathy.
    Voyages : from Tongan villages to American
suburbs / Cathy A. Small.
        p.   cm.
    Includes bibliographical references and index.
    ISBN 0-8014-3412-2 (cloth : alk. paper). —
    ISBN 0-8014-8436-7 (pbk. : alk. paper)
    1. Tongans—Social conditions.   2. Tongans—
United States.   3. United States—Emigration and
immigration.   4. Emigration and immigration.
5. Acculturation.   I. Title.
GN671.T5S63   1997   97-20598

Cornell University Press strives to utilize environmen-
tally responsible suppliers and materials to the fullest
extent possible in the publishing of its books. Such materials include vegetable-based, low-VOC inks and acid-
free papers that are also either recycled, totally
chlorine-free, or partly composed of nonwood fibers.
Books that bear the logo of the FSC (Forest Stewardship
Council) use paper taken from forests that have been
inspected and certified as meeting the highest standards
for environmental and social responsibility. For further
information, visit our website at www.cornellpress.
cornell.edu.

Cloth printing   10 9 8 7 6 5 4 3 2 1

Paperback printing   10 9 8 7 6 5

To my loved ones,
in Tonga and the United States,
here and beyond.

C O N T E N T S

ACKNOWLEDGMENTS

≋   This book was a product of the efforts of friends and neighbors, family and colleagues. Helpful suggestions, copyediting and proofreading, and thoughtful advice came from many sources: Anne Bromley, a poet; Jim Wilce, a linguistic anthropologist; Grace Everding, a neighbor and English teacher; Joseph Boles, a Women's Studies director; Edwina Small, my mother; Barbara Dapcic, a medical anthropologist; and Doug Duncan, a master's student in anthropology. I am thankful to Fran Benson, editor-in-chief at Cornell University Press, for subtitling this book and for being the responsive and caring professional that she is.

To the villagers of 'Olunga, I owe my deep gratitude for your many years of patience and kindness. To my Tongan family and informants—whose names I cannot offer—thank you for taking this work so seriously and making the time to read and correct the chapters of this book. My partner, who spent more than a year doing all our housework and putting up with my hermitage, allowed me the uninterrupted peace to write.

Thanks to all of you.

C. A. S.

AUTHOR'S NOTE

≋   The names of people in this book, as well as the Tongan village called "'Olunga" in the text, are pseudonyms. In a few instances, descriptive details relating to a person or event have been altered to protect the identity or the privacy of the people involved. Some photographs have been slightly altered (blurred, darkened, or cropped) so that the identity of particular persons described in this book could be protected.

In writing this note, I must also mention that I seriously question the efficacy of what I have just taken the trouble to do. At this point in history, no place in our writing can ever really remain anonymous and new questions arise about the effectiveness and appropriateness of the anthropological ethic that "protects" informants. I discuss issues and decisions about anonymity further on pages 211–212 of this text.

≋ V O Y A G E S

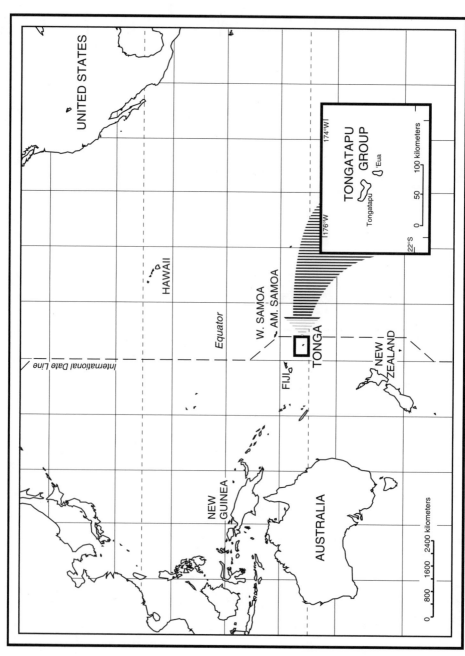

UNITED STATES

HAWAII

Equator

International Date Line

W. SAMOA
AM. SAMOA

FIJI

TONGA

NEW
GUINEA

NEW
ZEALAND

AUSTRALIA

0   800   1600   2400 kilometers

TONGATAPU
GROUP

Tongatapu

Eua

22°S

176°W   174°W

0   50   100 kilometers

Map by Ron Redsteer

I

DEPARTURES

≋ It is 1967. A teacher born in a thatched hut says a teary good-bye to her parents and eleven siblings. She will board an airplane and leave her island home for the first time. Her destination: the United States, where she will find work as a maid. In New York, in 1981, a student anthropologist boards another plane to go study gender and women's organizations in a village on an island in the South Pacific. She will collect data over three years for a book she will never write. Several years later a man from the outskirts of Salt Lake City loads a pony into a trailer and drives it to a family who arranged to buy the animal for their daughter's birthday. In front of the shocked seller, the pony is clubbed to death, and it becomes part of the feast to celebrate the child's birthday. The seller calls the police, and the incident appears as a small human interest item in the *Wall Street Journal*.

These three travelers, from different places and times, and with different purposes, are all on the same voyage. It is about this voyage that this book was written.

The pages that follow describe the pattern of global migration that is transforming the world. They could have been written only at this time, at the end of the twentieth century—a century that began with 70 percent of the world's peoples living in colonies and protectorates. As the century ends, 80 million migrants worldwide, many from these former colonies, are changing the face of the agricultural countries they left behind and the industrial countries to which they are turning. This diaspora is changing all our lives, our relationships, and our futures in ways that we may not even yet be aware of.

This book tells a global story that begins in an unlikely place: in a village on the main island of a country called Tonga, the only remaining independent kingdom in the South Pacific. Tonga is a small island nation of about 100,000 people, mostly farmers and fishermen. In the mid-1960s, after three thousand years in their island home, Tongans began leaving their villages and migrating to New Zealand, Australia, and the United States. What began as temporary migration in search of work and education steadily became permanent. By the mid-1980s, the overseas Tongan population was equal to one-third of the population of Tonga, and by the first years of the twenty-first century there will be more people of Tongan descent living outside Tonga than in Tonga itself. In the United States, many Tongans have settled in northern California, becoming part of America's new immigrant wave.

I tell a story of international migration through the eyes and lives of Tongan migrants. I open in Part I, "Departures," with a look at Tongan village life, showing what would prompt people to leave a place where starvation and homelessness are virtually absent and tradition and family are strong.

In Part II, "Arrivals," I then follow the first migrants in one Tongan family from their island home to their new home in northern California. You will hear of their first days in the United States, then see their lives twenty-five years later in a suburb of San Francisco, where they have raised their two American-born children. You will then meet another branch of this same family—who remained in Tonga for the same twenty-five years—and follow their journey in the 1990s from a Tongan village to an American suburb. You will hear from two sisters in this family, one who migrated and one who did not, and they will talk candidly about their lives and life decisions. In Part II, you will meet Palu, the one who migrated, and see her evolving view of herself as she becomes "an American."

In the third part of the book, "Returns," I go back to the village from which both families migrated together with the grown American children of the first migrants. You will see how village life looks a generation after migration began. You will hear Finau, the sister who stayed in Tonga, talk about her life and her decisions. Through the interactions of migrants and villagers, you will have an intimate view of how both now understand their family ties and the traditions that bind them together.

What happened to Tongan migrants and their American children, to the villages and relatives they left and the family ties they now maintain, holds many clues to the forces shaping the future. In the final part, "Travels Ahead," I try to make sense of these clues. Generalizing from the Tongan case, I paint a picture of the transformations occurring throughout the world as more and more people discover that their lives, their families, and their systems of loyalty and support cut across national and cultural borders.

By the end I hope to convince you that what you have read is not only a story of South Pacific island migrants but also a chapter in our collective history. In it, families are cross-cultural and transnational, long-held traditions are changing, Americans are reevaluating who they are, and science is questioning its own truths. Most important, in this particular chapter of our joint history we are all voyagers.

The Voyage Begins

A year after I first began anthropological fieldwork in Tonga in 1981, I was already writing books in my mind. In 1982 my mental book was about the difference between Western and Tongan ways. In 1984 the book was about the experiences of an anthropologist, based on my personal journals and my letters to family and friends. In 1987, after my dissertation on women's cooperatives was rejected by two publishers, I decided to rewrite it as a book about wider issues of social change. In 1988 it was a book about gender in Tonga.

I never actually completed any of these books. Every year or two, as I changed and as my relationships with Tongans deepened, the book I wanted to write evolved, and I was glad I had not written the one before.

I never started out to study migration, the main subject of this book. The topic of migration was a result of fieldwork, not an impetus. As happens to many anthropologists, what I thought was important changed.

Overseas migration was well under way when I first went to the village in 1981. My research focus was village women's cooperatives, and frankly, migration interfered with my work. My household censuses turned up uninhabited houses or households that kept changing numbers, depending on who was overseas at any time. Women's groups that I was tracing would lose members. Slowly I realized that migration was not simply an "outside" influence interfering with the culture I wished to study. Rather, it was a part of the culture I was studying, if I would just change my fixed notions of what culture was.

As I write this book, it is now fifteen years after my first fieldwork in Tonga. My informants have become my confidants, by which I mean the people I tell things to. I have been back to Tonga five times. Every time I return there are more people absent, more internal changes in the village as a result of their leaving.

People talk about this. It is part of their heartaches, their excitements, their life decisions. The events and relationships that villagers now consider important transcend national borders. Migration overseas has become a glaring fact of village life, inescapable no matter what one's academic interests or reasons for being in Tonga.

I was drawn even deeper into questions of migration's history and future when, in 1990, the people with whom I was personally closest migrated to the United States. Now "fellow Americans," we call one another regularly. I have come to know their family in California, who migrated a decade before they did. These personal relationships are reflected in what I write and also in how I write about migration.

But of course the personal is not really personal. My experiences as an anthropologist and a person would not have been the same at a different time in history. They could have happened only at the moment in history when the children and grandchildren of a colonial system began to seek their futures in the industrial world—and when the children and grandchildren of the earlier waves of migration, people like myself, were in a position to study the new wave of immigrants who have joined their national ranks. The personal is historical. This historical experience is part of a larger colonial legacy that has made the stories of America and of Tonga in the late twentieth century a joint story.

This is why, as the twenty-first century approaches, that in order to understand an island village in Tonga, one must leave Tonga, or why, in order to understand contemporary events in the United States, one must go back to places like Tonga, the former colonies and protectorates.

The New Migrants

"What is your book about?" an acquaintance asked me as I was in the middle of writing.

"It's about the migration of people from a South Pacific island kingdom called Tonga to the U.S. I'm trying to show the social history and the life histories leading up to why people left their homes and . . . "

"Don't we already know why people migrate?" the woman interrupted. The suddenness and force of her question surprised me.

"We do?" I asked back.

"Yes. Isn't it self-evident?" she continued: "to get a better life, to have more freedom."

It struck me that this is true in many ways, but it is not the whole truth, and at times in the lives of migrants it may not be true at all. In the United States, migrants are part of our identity as a nation. There is an American stereotype of the migrant—a well-worn groove—that determines who we think migrants are and what they will be. We expect our migrants to be special people, different from the ones who stayed behind. Their rugged individualism and personal drive led them to leave their homelands and break with their past. Here in the United States they will become Americans, creating stronger ties with other Americans than with their "people" in the old country, and becoming indistinguishable in one or two generations from other Americans. Again, this is a half-truth, and it is based on the experience of largely white European populations in an expanding industrial economy.

Since 1965, when U.S. immigration policy shifted, there has been an influx of non-European immigrants into the United States. The proportion of immigrants coming from developing countries increased from 12 percent in 1951–60, to 88 percent in 1981–90.[1] They are coming from Asia and the Pacific islands, Mexico and Central America, and there is much about their migration that is different from that of their European predecessors.

Most apparent, the conditions under which migrants are coming are different. The migrants are from former colonies and protectorates, and are often the legatees of several generations of colonial occupation. Many are nonwhite, and they are entering largely white, often racist industrial economies during a time when skilled manufacturing jobs are leaving these countries. For most migrants, the slots available are on the lowest rungs of the economic ladder, and they offer limited economic and social mobility.[2]

The new migrants are different in other ways, too. They bring over family members at four times the rate of European migrants. They maintain strong ties with those who stay at home, creating a new global phenomenon—the transnational family. Migrants send money and goods back home in such monumental amounts that the economies of many of their home countries have become based on these remittances. The new migrants often report a hybrid identity, defining themselves neither as "American" nor as people of the country from which they came.

The issues that "new migrants" raise for both host and home countries have become increasingly compelling in light of the fact that 100 of the world's 188 nations have economies that depend on either the labor or the revenues that migration supplies. Host countries are concerned that their national identity is changing. Only one-half of the nations in the world now have one ethnic group that makes up three-fourths of its population.[3] According to the 1990 U.S. Census, 14 percent of the population of this country speak a language other than English at home, and in California, the number one destination of new migrants and the state to which most Tongans have migrated, more than one-fifth of the population is foreign-born.[4] What is this doing to a sense of national identity? To feelings of patriotism? To the expectation that migrants will assimilate? Throughout the industrial world, concerns about these questions are expressed in xenophobia and rising nationalism.

Sending nations find that their economic future depends on the good will of migrants. The economies of some Caribbean and Pacific islands, including Tonga, would likely collapse without the continued support of migrants. Will migrants' sense of family connection and cultural loyalty persist? Will migrants maintain their stream of remittances and continue to bolster the home economy? Such questions, for both sending and receiving nations, have made migration, the global family, and transnational relationships central to an understanding of how the world of the twenty-first century will unfold.

This book offers a detailed, intimate local portrait of a complex global phenomenon. I proceed on the assumption that the story of people in a Tongan village, viewed contextually and historically, can tell us something about the nature and future of global migration processes. My agenda begs the question, is Tongan migration "representative" of the global migration phenomenon? The answer, to be fair, is no and yes.

Tonga is not representative of the experience of the former colonies that now send migrants because it was never really "colonized." While it became a British protectorate for purposes of Great Britain's foreign policy interests, it maintained local sovereignty. Tonga has always been 99 percent Tongan. Foreigners were never able to own land or become citizens.[5] Tongans were never conscripted as slave labor, nor was massive labor brought across Tonga's borders from the outside, as happened with its neighbor, Fiji. Tonga never had the natural resources such as gold or sugar that resulted in the forced appropriation of other lands and people. In short, Tonga escaped many of the greatest indignities and tragedies of colonization. As a result, it does not have the wealth differentials, the land concentration, the political volatility, or the extreme poverty that have been the legacy of many former colonies.

Nonetheless, Tongan migration is an unmistakable part of the "new migration" wave from agricultural to industrial nations. Tongans, like people throughout most of the developing world, live in a monetized economy where the perks and products of the industrial world are constantly being hawked through the media. Within the global cash economy Tongans are dirt poor; there are few opportunities for upward mobility without looking overseas to a university education or a well-paying job. Tonga, in fact, exhibits many features that are characteristic of migration elsewhere: the huge loss of population to overseas labor markets; the development of a remittance economy in which revenues from migrants keep the home economy viable; and the rise of transnational families whose resources, kinship ties, and loyalties cut across national boundaries.

Like stories of migration elsewhere in the world, Tonga's is about more than a movement of people; it is about a transformation of institutions and relationships. To explore this transformation, I take the anthropologist's tack and turn to writing about people's day-to-day lives in the hope that, through detail and intimacy, the stories of migrants and their families can lend insight into the legacy of international migration and, perhaps, provide foresight into our global future.

Writing about Migration: The New Ethnography

The story that follows is properly called *ethnography*. An ethnography is a descriptive account of a people's way of life written by an anthropologist who has conducted intensive long-term fieldwork within their culture. Ethnographic descriptions are the major data of anthropology. In telling the story of Tongan migration, however, I found that it was difficult to write the typical ethnography.

Standard ethnographies stay in one time and place. This ethnography is transnational and historical. It is a book that, in order to tell its story, must go back and forth in time and place. Standard anthropological writing adopts a tone of scientific distance. The author calls herself "the anthropologist" and the people she studies are anonymous "informants" who provide cultural information that is used to write objectively about cultural ways. I found that my scientific tone did not always work well in conveying what I wanted to say.

Writing an ethnography in the late twentieth century presents a sort of chicken-and-egg problem because the theoretical and methodological tools we have for doing ethnography (including the anthropologist as observer) are being changed by the same forces that we as anthropologists are studying.

The last ten to fifteen years have seen a critical reexamination of anthropological method and theory, expressed in recent theoretical writings on ethnography.[6] It is no accident that the academic lens is scrutinizing the nature of anthropology and ethnography at the very same historical moment when worldwide migration is occurring. It makes sense that this should be so.

Ethnography has long operated on the belief that culture is a separate, bounded, and integrated whole that can be grasped through a key informant who "knows" it and by an anthropologist who observes it at a fixed moment in time. What happens, then, when half of the people who belong to one's "cultural group" live across an ocean and in a different country? When "traditions" change within the course of a single lifetime? When the once-colonial countries of anthropologists and the once-colonized cultures of informants are changing their political relationship? When the people written about can read and critique the ethnographies written about them? Or when those who study and those who are studied have come to belong to the same nation? It is clear that ethnography—both practically and theoretically—must change. It must reexamine assumptions. It must ask new questions.[7]

In reflection, many of the most basic assumptions in anthropology— everything from how anthropologists make their arguments to whose voice should be heard in an ethnography to how to define traditions or culture— are on shaky ground, given the realities of our world. Anthropologists, accordingly, are experimenting with new ways of writing about cultures— such as postmodern ethnography—grounded in different assumptions.[8]

Parts of this book read like a standard ethnography. The first chapter, for instance, is based on the work I did as an anthropologist in the Tongan village of 'Olunga between 1981 and 1984, and it sounds just like my notes. As I continued the story of Tongan migration out of the village over time, and back to my own country, my relationship to Tonga and Tongans changed. As this happened, the words and tone I wanted to use to represent the story of Tongan migration changed too. The "Tongan People" became particular persons with life experiences and opinions that were individually unique. Individual life histories became an important part of the book, and many different Tongans now "talk" within it. "The anthropologist" changed to "I," and the anthropologist's story became part of the ethnography as well. My writing became less formal.

You may find that some people contradict one another or me. I do not edit out these contradictions or attempt to resolve them. You may meet people and then meet them again at different stages of their lives; their life histories may not always read in sequence; some people tell their personal histories with little interpretation or editing, so the style and consistency of writing vary somewhat from chapter to chapter. And in chapters where people talk about themselves, Tongan informants later read what I had written and edited the chapters along with me.

All these changes are experiments toward finding a more appropriate way to talk about people and culture—more appropriate to the times we inhabit and the relationships we are creating. Like many "new ethnographies" in anthropology, this one experiments with and informs about the strategies needed to represent changing relationships in the world.[9]

This book, then, is many things it did not start out to be. Although I have never considered myself a new or experimental ethnographer, I ended up using several experimental devices to write this ethnography. Although I was not initially interested in migration, it became the focus of the book. And although I did not set out to examine issues in anthropology—such as cultural relativism, informant anonymity, or the audience of ethnography—I did so in the end because these questions were raised by the process of writing and reflection.

As a result, this book about migration is about Tongan islanders and Tongan-Americans; it is a little about me, a little about America, and a little about anthropology. These disparate subjects belong together in the same book because they are all part of the same phenomenon, the metamorphosis of social relationships in our world: relationships between migrants and nonmigrants, between Tongans and Americans, and between anthropologists and informants. I think of these evolving relationships metaphorically as the "voyages" of our times. This is an ethnography of those voyages and their implications for the analytical constructs anthropologists use to view the world, and for the way each of us, both Tongan and American, views ourself.

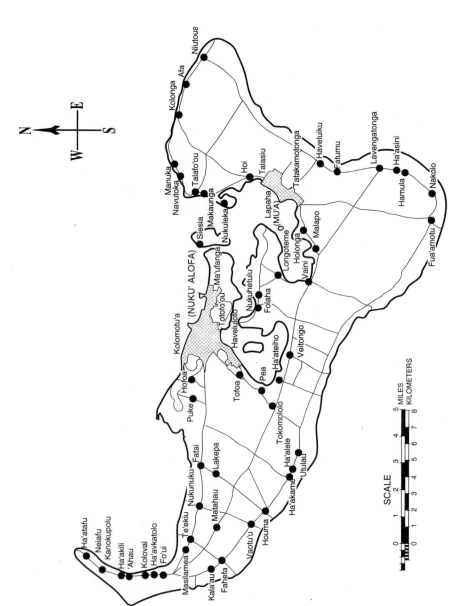

Major Towns and Villages of Tongatapu (Tonga's Main Island).
Map by Ron Redsteer

1

Portrait of
A Migrating
Village

♒︎ They came from the West.[1] The groups that eventually were called Polynesians settled the Tongan islands by canoe about 1500 B.C. They left a trail of distinctive Lapita pottery from the islands of Melanesia to Fiji to their first homes in Tonga and Samoa.[2] The entire migrating population probably arrived in two or three canoes, and they settled on the edge of the lagoon that cuts into the island on its northern side. As the population grew, it spread outward along the coastal areas and to 36 of the north-south string of 150 islands that make up the Tongan archipelago. These voyagers of Western Polynesia were later to settle other Polynesian Islands.[3]

By the first millennium A.D., Tongans had evolved the basic form of social organization in Polynesia—a stratified chiefdom consisting of high chiefs, lower chiefs, specialists including warriors and craftsmen, and common farmers. The first supreme chief of Tonga—called the Tu'i Tonga—was historically in place by A.D. 875. According to Tongan oral history, his name was Ahoteihu and he was the son of an earthly woman and a god. After Ahoteihu's jealous half-brothers, sons of goddesses, murdered and dismembered him in the sky, his godly father reconstituted him. Ahoteihu was returned to earth as its high chief. In retribution, his four half-brothers were ordered to return with him as his lower chiefs and ceremonial attendants— called the Four Houses—their lines to serve the high chief and his descendants for the rest of time.

The village of 'Olunga—where the twentieth-century story of migration begins—became the home of the Tu'i Tonga and the Four Houses. The ancient capital was moved there sometime around A.D. 1150 because, it is said, the daughter of the eleventh Tu'i Tonga was disturbed by the crashing of the waves on the cliffs at Heketa, the far eastern tip of the island where the Tu'i Tonga resided. She asked her brothers to build her a house along the quiet shores of the 'Olunga lagoon, and after their father died, the brothers followed their sister to 'Olunga. Every Tu'i Tonga since that time has lived in 'Olunga. It is more likely, as the historian I. C. Campbell suggests (1992: 10), that the sheltered lagoon of 'Olunga was a more practical location for a regime that had come to rely on long-distance voyaging by canoe and that was about to expand its chiefdom outward.

From 'Olunga, the Tongan empire was extended to Samoa and Fiji, and to the smaller outliers of Western Polynesia. Typically, younger brothers of Tongan high chiefs married into these outlying areas, setting up their sons as the areas' ruling chiefs while incorporating new island territories into their political and kinship system. As the Tongan chiefdom grew geographically, so did its long-distance trade, its warfare, and its internal stratification. Archaeologists can read the growth of this stratification by the widening differences in the way commoners and chiefs and high chiefs were buried.

The terraced burial mounds, or *langi,* that distinguish graves of the Tu'i Tonga line were first built during the reign of the eleventh Tu'i Tonga. When his sons followed their sister to 'Olunga, they built what has been called the first of the remarkable terraced tombs for their sister, Fatafehi. The eldest of these brothers became the twelfth Tu'i Tonga, but he died childless, unable to pass on his title to a son (or daughter), as was the Tongan tradition. According to Tongan oral history, his brother Talaiha'apepe, wishing to be the thirteenth Tu'i Tonga, devised a plan to inherit the title in a way that would preserve the appearance of patrilineal succession. He cut a block of wood from the tou tree and installed it as the thirteenth Tu'i Tonga. A woman was appointed the "wife" of the block of wood. The Tu'i Tonga and his wife were then said to have adopted Talaiha'apepe, thus making him "son" of the block of wood. After a time the block was declared "dead," and the block's son—Talaiha'apepe—was installed as the fourteenth Tu'i Tonga. The "dead" block was buried royally in a *langi* at 'Olunga.

The greatest of Tonga's *langi,* a four-tiered terraced tomb, was built in 'Olunga in about 1575 by the twenty-ninth Tu'i Tonga, Telea (or Uluakimata I). The structure is called the Paepae o' Telea. The huge rocks that line the edge of the terraces were quarried, cut, and brought in from the distant island of Uvea by canoe and give testimony to the monumental labor that the Tu'i Tonga, by this time, could command.

European contact occurred briefly in the seventeenth century, when the Dutch explorer Abel Tasman was entertained onshore by the thirty-first Tu'i Tonga. Tasman wrote with admiration about the landscape and the industry he saw—the beautiful, lush allotments, all cultivated, surrounded by reed fences. James Cook, the famous English explorer, was similarly impressed in the late eighteenth century. The houses were surrounded, he wrote, with perfumed flowers and set in the middle of vegetable gardens. The planting was in rows. There were numerous pigs and fowl. It is said that Cook's famous journals prompted missionaries to visit Tonga before many of its neighbors.

George Vason was a missionary turned native who lived in the 'Olunga area for four years from 1797. He became a landholder under the patronage of a local chief in a land "cultivated like a garden." "There were groves of cocoanut and plaintain trees," he wrote (1810: 128–29), "with its smooth lawns diversified by little habitations . . . [T]he land was so lush that a small plot of land could support many inhabitants." Vason was part of a growing missionary presence that set out to convert "heathen Tonga" at the beginning of the nineteenth century. Vason and other missionaries made contact with Tongan society at a particular phase in its history, a time of civil war. The sacred authority of the Tu'i Tonga was being challenged by powerful secular lines, and the titles of the highest lines were vacant and in contention.

Thirty years later, about 1830, one of the most powerful rising chiefs— the eventual titleholder of the Kanokupolu line—converted to Christianity, partly to challenge the sacred powers of the Tu'i Tonga. He was baptized as "George" in 1834. With Western arms and Wesleyan missionaries backing him, this Protestant chief became Tonga's first king, George I, the leader of a British-style constitutional monarchy. The Tu'i Tonga, still based in 'Olunga, along with the people of 'Olunga would later convert to Catholicism in dissent. George I then formally abolished the title of Tu'i Tonga, replacing it with one less politically and spiritually charged. He moved the seat of the monarchy from 'Olunga to Nuku'alofa, the current capital.

Between 1839 and 1875, the king turned some chiefs into nobles, with hereditary estates, and commoners into taxpayers. The Tongan parliament, fashioned on the British system of an upper and a lower house, was established in 1862. The Tongan constitution of 1875 prevented the appropriation of commoner labor and possessions by chiefs, at least in theory. It entitled all Tongan males age sixteen or older to register a plot of bush land and a plot for their houses which would be theirs to use and pass on, without chiefly intervention. The constitution and its provisions helped the monarch to weaken the relationship of commoners to chiefs, paving the way for national loyalty to the crown. It would be decades, however, before commoners took advantage of constitutional provisions by registering land or by voting for a commoner as a Parliamentary representative.

There have been three monarchs since George I, all in his direct line. Under George II, who ruled from 1893 to 1918, Tonga became a British protectorate, a safeguard for Great Britain's strategic interests in the Pacific, a status that primarily affected Tonga's foreign policy. For most of the twentieth century, Tonga's leadership was in the competent hands of Queen Sālote, George I's granddaughter, who promoted a policy of building the country while maintaining traditional values and activities. Under her rule, health, education, and social reform were advanced. Queen Sālote actively sought to replace foreigners in government and civil service with Tongans. Since Sālote's death in 1965, her son and successor, King Taufa'ahau Tupou IV, has led Tonga toward "modernization," focusing on economic development and the encouragement of private enterprise.

Modern Tonga is an agricultural country with an export base of bananas, coconuts, pineapples, melons, and vanilla. It has grown from a population of about twenty thousand at the turn of the century to almost one hundred thousand people. In 1970 the country became an independent nation and a member of the British Commonwealth. Tonga remains a constitutional monarchy, the last surviving Polynesian kingdom.

In the 1950s, a century after the development of the monarchy, the inhabitants of Tonga's small outer islands began moving to its larger islands, and those in the hinterlands began moving to Tonga's larger towns.[4] Work and school drew large numbers of youth into Tonga's main centers. The village of 'Olunga, although rural and no longer the capital, gained population during this time because of its main island location. By 1976, 19 percent of the village's population consisted of migrants from other areas of Tonga.[5]

In the latter half of the 1960s another process began. Three thousand years after voyagers first settled Tonga, Tongans began leaving the islands—at first to work in New Zealand, Australia, or the United States and return home, but later to live permanently overseas. By the mid-1970s, overseas migration began to escalate, burgeoning over the next two decades. By the early 1980s, despite high birthrates, Tonga had begun to lose population. By the early years of the twenty-first century, the population of Tongans living overseas will likely exceed that in Tonga. It was in the middle of this process, in 1981, that I came to the village of 'Olunga.

'Olunga in the Early 1980s

Traveling along the main road that skirts the island, a visitor could see a stone Catholic church by a lagoon. It was one of the landmarks signaling that you had reached the village of 'Olunga. 'Olunga had remained a Catholic village in a Protestant country, and its religion was one aspect of its distinctive, often rebellious character. A rural development officer once described 'Olunga to me as that "helter-skelter"–looking village that, as many townspeople from the capital agreed, harbored those "difficult" people.

Walking eastward from the church along the shore of the lagoon, you arrived at the *langi*, the terraced tombs that were visited by occasional grazing goats. There sat the Paepae o' Telea, built four centuries ago, impressive and undisturbed. Across from the low grass-covered terraces was the village craft center, which had been named the Paepae. It was oval, like traditional Tongan houses, and built in the old way, securing post to lintel by wrapping thin hand-woven rope around the beams in cross-hatched patterns. The lines of ritual and technical specialists who were once centered in 'Olunga still had descendants in the village. The village, in fact, claimed more *matapule* (chiefly attendant) titles than any other village in Tonga. The Four Houses still served the noble of the area, whose inherited title of Kaliniuvalu was instituted when the Tu'i Tonga title was abolished in the last century.

If you knew to look for them, you could have met men and women in this village "who knew things": a respected composer of Tongan dance and song, a man famous for his expertise in playing the nose flute, a woman with special knowledge of Tongan history and lore because her mother was a titled attendant to the Queen, the only woman in Tongan history to hold such a title.

The village of 'Olunga was a large settlement of approximately 1,800 in 1981. The village is located near the region identified as Mu'a on the map, lying to the east of Nuku'alofa, the capital, along the main road of the island. Until recently the portion of the road at this eastern end of the island was poorly paved, and the trip to 'Olunga from the capital was slow and rough traveling. The main road cut the village in two, the side to the north bordering the lagoon, the side to the south toward the bush.

A second coral road forming a T with the main road split the village again east and west, and continued south to the start of 'Olunga's bush land and then three kilometers farther to the ocean on the southern side of the island. Smaller roads of dirt crisscrossed the village, and 'Olunga's houses lay in somewhat ordered lines on either side of its many roads. In the rainy season the smaller roads and paths became deep with mud, making access by cart or vehicle difficult. During my stay in 'Olunga, the government paved the village paths with coral so that even the cumbersome local bus could negotiate the back roads. There were a number of public buildings in the village: a convent, a community center built by village women's groups, four small wooden tapa-making houses, a public elementary school, and a Marist high school. But most of the village consisted of households situated on partitioned "town allotments," the 2/5 acre plot of land that holds a family's dwelling house, kitchen, latrine, and bathhouse.

As in Tongan villages generally, the homes in 'Olunga were no longer predominantly thatched and "picturesque." Although in 1955, 71 percent of Tonga's population lived in traditional thatched homes, by 1984, 64 percent of the village's 264 dwellings were wooden and boxlike. There were scattered concrete block houses (11 percent) throughout the village and small pockets of thatched homes, representing only 22 percent of village dwellings.

A household often had more than one house, and the average household in 'Olunga consisted of seven to eight people. Many households maintained a smaller house for sons who had reached puberty, since by Tongan custom postpubescent brothers and sisters must "avoid" one another. In practical terms, this meant that brothers and sisters could not live in the same house or talk about a variety of topics from marriage and pregnancy to borrowing. When a brother passed a sister on the road, he cast his eyes down and away. Brother-sister "avoidance" is part of a complex set of customs that resolves the differences in power held by males and females in the same genealogical line and the awkwardness this can create, particularly among people of high rank.[6] As with many customs, compromises have been made. Wood and concrete houses with rooms separated by walls were sometimes considered enough to provide appropriate distance. In these cases, brothers and sisters might live in the same house.

Inside, few houses had furniture. Floors were covered with layers of pandanus mats that created a soft floor on which to sit. Most homes had a chair or two reserved for honored guests. In the wooden houses, photographs and pictures—of Tongan and British royalty, of Jesus, of the pope, and of relatives—decorated the painted wallboard that separated rooms. They hung almost from the ceiling and tilted downward from supporting wires toward people seated on the mat floors.

The typical home was surrounded by a fence to keep the pigs from rooting in the gardens. Within the fence were flowers and decorative plantings, but increasingly, as land shortages continued, food crops were planted close to the house.

In 1984, 54 percent of the village had electricity, although in practice this usually meant a single outlet per house for an electric lightbulb. There were a handful of telephones in the village, including one at the convent, another in a storekeeper's home, and another at the town officer's home. When it was necessary to make a phone call, a 'Olungan would use the telephone of the owner with whom the caller had the strongest kinship or friendship bond.

Since the mid-1960s, when public taps were placed at intervals throughout the village, everyone has had access to piped water. The groundwater was drawn up from the local aquifer by a village-operated pump that ran for a few hours in the morning and then again in the evening. Water cost an affordable dollar a month per household. Rainwater, preferred for drinking over pumped water, was collected by many households in cement catchment tanks from their tin roofs.

Families with cash resources paid for extra pipelines to carry water directly into their homes. They built indoor bathrooms with flush toilets and indoor kitchens with taps, where they would prepare and clean, if not cook, food. Still, more than 75 percent of village households maintained an outdoor pit-latrine toilet, shielded from view by a patched iron and wood or thatch-covered stall. Most households also had a thatched bathhouse, which held a washing tub of water, and a thatched cookhouse as well, where family meals were prepared on an open fire. Meals were eaten in the dwelling house.

Most households in the village farmed. Even though the adult males in 70 percent of village households spent the majority of their time farming, only about 16 percent of the village derived their primary cash income from the sale of crops. This may seem surprising, but it is a statement not so much about the place of agriculture in village life as it is about the place of cash. The majority of farmers in 'Olunga sold no food. In the village in the early 1980s, subsistence farming clearly remained the basis of village agriculture.

Even so, that was changing. People said that a generation ago one would have been ashamed to sell food to neighbors and fellow Tongans. By 1982, 47 percent of sample households reported selling some produce during the year. As landlessness had increased in Tonga, the number of people who regularly bought food for consumption had mushroomed, and this had created new market pressures. The Talamahu market in Nuku'alofa, first opened in 1970, sold produce for local consumption six days a week. Even the small village stores marketed produce from local farmers.

In 1982 crops and copramaking (splitting and drying coconut kernels for commercial sale) together provided the primary income source for just over a quarter of sample households. Another quarter of the village earned their primary income from wage labor. Most of these wage earners worked in town as clerks, government office workers, and teachers. Another quarter of village households earned their primary income from handicrafts. Money from overseas relatives (remittances) was a primary source of income for only 14 percent of village households, but it was the secondary cash source for more than one-fifth of the village.

Almost every household in the village had a second source of income, and the majority of households in 'Olunga had three or more different sources of cash income, including fishing, remittances, copra making, and handicrafts. Many younger men got income by working sporadically on the farms of others for a small payment.

Income statistics had become more important in the village because, in practical terms, cash held an increasingly important place in daily life. Few villagers bought the big-ticket items displayed in the capital, such as tape decks, electrical appliances, washing machines, automobiles, and refrigerators. But it had become commonplace to make a trip to the local village store, sometimes several a day, to buy a growing list of imported products—from washing detergent, soap, shampoo, and toothpaste to plates, cups, and cooking utensils to cooking oil and kerosene, cigarettes and toilet paper. Packaged snacks, candy, and ice cream were popular sellers, and villagers came on a regular basis to buy bread, rice, butter, flour, lamb flaps (a fatty low-grade cut of New Zealand lamb), and other imported items that supplemented or replaced local staples. Even though many people made their own clothes, cloth and thread still needed to be purchased at the store; shoes and notebooks and pencils were bought for school and church. Although villagers went to the bush by horseback, by horse-drawn cart, or by foot, a trip to town—to shop, to market produce, or to attend school or work—required bus fare. Certainly, all major breaks from traditional living—whether a wooden house, electricity, or a flush toilet—were under-written with cash.

Perhaps the most burdensome ongoing cash expense for a Tongan was school fees. Primary education in Tonga was government-run and free, but secondary schools—largely under the private auspices of churches—required annual fees for each student. The Tongans I observed placed a premium on education, and every family with children who qualified academically to enter high school sacrificed to divert resources to education. In 'Olunga, school fees ran approximately T$90 annually per child, about one-tenth of yearly income. It was not uncommon for a household to be paying for the education of three or four or five of its children in one year, amounting to half the household income.

Income in 'Olunga, as in Tonga as a whole, tended to be irregular throughout the year and even from year to year. A remittance check from overseas, the harvest of a crop, a hurricane, or a family funeral could suddenly change a family's fortunes. Consumer behavior tended to follow the erratic patterns of cash income. Villagers would spend what they had when they had it, a pattern that resulted in marked times of lean and plenty. A windfall from abroad could spur a spending spree on clothing, beer for friends, and imported foods. Long-standing bills at the local store and school fees might be paid off in full. One month later, though, the same family might be eating topai, a boiled coconut and flour mixture, for three weeks or more.

A Day in the Lives

For the entire month of March 1983, ten households in the village completed daily diaries for me.[7] The diaries gave detailed accounts of participants' activities and exchanges, including what they did each hour, and what they gave, received, or bought each day.

From these diaries, and my own notes during this same month, I have reconstructed what life looked like in five of the sample households on March 11, a Friday. The day was chosen randomly, and the five households were selected because they were all at the same stage of life. The adult male and female in each household (most Tongan households are nuclear families) had been married in the 1960s and now had between four and six children, several of school age. They lived in close proximity to related households. Some maintained separate dwelling areas for teenage sons. Most were farmers.

⅋ Atu awakens before Malia, but soon Malia is up and outside in the cool morning, lighting the open fire in the kitchen hearth for breakfast. Atu is dressed in his ironed white shirt and *tupenu,* the dark wraparound calf-length cloth he wears to work and meetings. He wears polished black shoes with no socks and carries the hard black briefcase that holds his work and meeting papers. He will teach at the elementary school, and then come home only briefly before he goes into town for his meetings. There will be a rugby union meeting. Then there is Atu's kava club where Tongan men drink the mildly narcotic national drink made from the root of a pepper plant. He will miss dinner at home and return to sleep around 2:45 A.M. The major household expenses this week will be for the rugby fund, Atu's kava drinking club, and the church. The family's income comes solely from Atu's salary, $T93 every two weeks. (A Tongan dollar is roughly equivalent to a U.S. dollar.)

There is an outside tap to draw water, but Malia will use the sweeter water from the tank that collects rain from their tin roof. She will finish cooking the breakfast of boiled green bananas, then feed the five children who live at home. Four will go to school. Her grown son will go to the bush, where the family has planted a small plot of food crops. She will spend more than six and a quarter hours today, as she has all week, completing her quota of beaten bark for the weekly meeting of her tapa cloth-making group.

There are fourteen women in the Clear Day tapa-making group, which will meet for fourteen weeks. Each week they will put together two cloths for one woman, chosen by lottery, until all the women have their cloths. During these fourteen weeks, there is time for little else. Each woman will beat her bark pieces into wide paper-thin white sheets and attach them to form a long roll of beaten bark. On Saturday, the members of the group will show up with their rolls of beaten bark at the falling-down tapa house, with its half-open roof and missing floorboards. Here they will spend the day joining all the pieces together into two large double-layered cloths and then dyeing them, a process called a *koka'anga.* Sitting on either side of a split coconut tree laid lengthwise in the house, the women take a burnt red dye and rub it on the white beaten bark laid over the tree. The rubbing reveals geometric relief patterns that have been nailed across the tree. A design comes through, as in rubbing a penny. This group uses a pattern that honors the local princess. Later, the owner of the cloth will highlight the pattern, outlining or emphasizing pieces of it in a black dye that she applies with a vegetable brush.

If these women are like other village tapa makers, the cloths will not stay in their possession for long. Some of the women will sell one of their cloths to get extra cash for household needs or obligations. The majority of the cloths, though, will be given as gifts, commonly at occasions such as the funeral of a close maternal relative, the wedding of a daughter or niece, the departure of a visiting relative or person of rank, a thank you for hospitality given or anticipated when making a long-distance trip, or an affirmation to a suitor who has come to court one of the household women. Gifts of tapa cloth and pandanus mats, another traditional form of wealth made by women, are part of the social fabric of Tongan life. Such gifts are both the evidence and the symbol of a family's ability to meet its obligations to others. In the giving, they confer prestige on the givers and cement social relationships among givers and receivers. A woman who cannot procure enough cloths for her obligations will buy them (at a cost of about half a year's salary apiece!).

Fefita and Mele are women from different households, but they are also in tapa-making groups. Fefita's day will look much like Malia's. Mele, though, is behind in her beating, so her sister will come over today to help her finish in time for the *koka'anga* tomorrow. They will beat bark continuously from early in the morning until 3:30 A.M., when they finally finish.

Their husbands, Manase and Fotu, are both farmers. Each man will work in his own bush land. After school some days, and on Saturdays, their sons and sometimes wives and daughters may join them. Fotu and Mele belong to one of the most successful farming families in the village. They plant their eight acres with both food and cash crops, and they have borrowed eight other acres from overseas relatives to plant more cash crops. Fotu will plant and sell pineapples and melons. With double the acreage of most people, they will make out well. This will be a lean month, though, because school fees are due for next semester, and the watermelon seed must be paid for. Mele will decide to sell one of her tapa cloths for the $T220 that will allow them to make ends meet.

Fotu works hard, but he could not grow this acreage with just the help of his family. He is the head of a men's rotating agriculture group which he has belonged to for the past twenty-three years. The members take turns working one another's plots, so there are days when Fotu will have a whole crew come and do the heavy work that a man and his wife and children could not do alone. One day Fotu will be the town officer of 'Olunga.

Manase will work less. He has planted only two acres this year, and it will be used only for household needs. Like many farmers, Manase grows bananas, yams, manioc, taro, and sweet potato to eat, and he sells a few coconuts. He will get $T16 from selling coconuts later on. A tourist will buy two pocketbooks that his wife, Fefita, had left to be sold in Paepae, bringing in another $T5.80. But this month they will be rich because their eldest son, who is working in Australia, will send them $T300. With the money, they will pay their younger children's school fees, they will give money to three of Manase's sisters, and they will hire a plow to turn the soil in their bush land.

Kalo and Kepu live just down the road. Kalo would ordinarily join the tapa group of Fefita and Malia. But not this round. She cannot afford the time, and she has no bark ready. Today she and Kepu will ride a horse-drawn cart to their bush land with their dogs. They will work all morning and cook lunch in the bush. Lunch will consist of something ready for harvesting in the bush—one of many kinds of yam, taro, manioc, green bananas, or breadfruit. The couple will *tunu* (roast their lunch on a stick over an open fire), drink coconut, and sleep for an hour or two afterwards. They will then work again until they are ready in the late afternoon to return home.

Kepu has started a small banana plantation. He pays a men's work group to hoe the land for bananas, and this year—like last—he will sell his bananas for export, making almost $T1,000. Kepu used to be a pig farmer, but just when he'd built up a good stock, the local noble would come and ask him for pigs for his feast or his outing to the beach. Kepu is one of the many men in the village who do not hold formally registered land. He works the land at the noble's pleasure, and he was afraid to refuse the noble his pigs. It was better, Kepu thought, to stop raising pigs and give the noble some bananas. Kepu will work his untenured land from Monday to Saturday this week, and Kalo will help him in the bush.

Lisi and Pita, her husband, have no bush land. This means that, except for the occasional gift of food from relatives or neighbors, they must count on buying their food. Their primary income is from Lisi's sale of cakes, a concession that she must nurture by attentive and often unpaid labor for the church or the Marist Brothers. They live in a little thatched house at the very edge of the village. It is the only electrified thatched home in the village because the school has allowed the family to run an electric line with a lightbulb into the house.

Lisi will arise two hours earlier than her husband and four children. At 5 A.M. she is already boiling the little dough cakes for the school canteen.

She will make cakes for four hours. At lunchtime, the schoolchildren will buy them from her for ten cents each.

The deep-fried cakes have become daily lunch fare for many village students. So has another nutritional nightmare and common lunch: a half loaf of white bread (brought by truck from the town bakery) into which children will pour a bottle of Slake, a highly suspect and much too brightly colored orange, green, or yellow locally bottled soda. Lisi will take a relative to the clinic in the afternoon by bus.

Pita, her husband, will spend the entire day making tikis, those shellacked wooden carved tourist items. Tomorrow he will sell his tikis to the tourists who come from the boat that docks once a month. He will pay a van $T6 to take him and his tikis to the beach where the tourists go. No public buses run on boat days. All the available buses are covered in fresh vines and flowers and are used to carry the tourists from their boat to locations around Tonga. Pita will come home with $T20.

In the evening on this Friday every one of the households will listen to Tongan radio for at least an hour. There was no television in Tonga in the early 1980s. Tongan radio, which was broadcast twice a day for a few hours, was a featured evening activity in the village. The radio station played Tongan music and offered a local and world news report. One of its most important and most listened-to features was personal messages.

"Mele F—— from Ohonua, Vava'u, has a message for Soane L—— from 'Olunga. She will be coming on the boat from Vava'u on Saturday. Meet her boat."

"From the Kautai family to Lopeti M—— and Taniela E——: We couldn't send the shipment of dried octopus on the Thursday boat. It will come on next Tuesday's boat instead."

After dinner and radio time, several residents of the sampled households will attend the Friday night movie. This week the movie will be sponsored by one of the five women's "development groups" who worked this year to build water tanks for its members. They will raise money for their group from the admission charge (fifteen to thirty-five cents, depending on age).

Movies first appeared in Tonga in the 1920s, but the first movie to be shown in 'Olunga, in the 1950s, was a well-remembered event. A local man brought in a generator to run a rented projector. He showed the movie in his home. By the 1980s, most movies were shown in the women's hall, which had electricity, and the banana shed. Each week, different village or family groups sponsored the movie and paid for the rental of the hall or shed as well as the movie, projector, and posters, which were brought in from the capital. Mostly they were American action films and Japanese karate films, but sometimes there was other fare.

On this one day in March, the people in these five households will go to the local store thirteen times to purchase items such as canned food, lamb flaps, flour, sugar, cigarettes, a school notebook, a pen, batteries, kerosene, a length of cloth, washing detergent, cloth dye, and kava root.

On Sunday of this week, eighteen plates of food will go out from these households to other households. Today, people in these households will either eat at someone else's house or feed a visitor eight times. Three of the five households will either borrow or lend something to a different household.

Villagers are devout churchgoers, and this week the majority of household members will attend Mass or a church-related function such as a choir meeting, the Legion of Mary, or a church youth group.

Three of the five households belong to "savings associations"—more specifically, to eight associations of two types. Straight savings associations worked like a bank without interest, a kind of "Christmas club" that runs for a year. Every week a woman must put in ten cents for each member of her household who is signed up as a savings group member. She might sign up herself and two children, and would thus be responsible for paying thirty cents. The group meets to collect the money and record it in a ledger. It functions as a kind of forced savings plan that creates a nest egg the family cannot dip into during the year without a loss of face.

Another kind of savings—for those, usually, with a salaried worker in the family—is permitted by rotating credit associations. In these groups, people must put in $T10 every two weeks, a very large sum indeed for people who make $T3 to $T4 per day. At each meeting one woman gets the whole pot. The order is determined by lottery on the first day. With twenty-two members, it will take eleven months for the cycle to complete itself. This is a serious commitment, and households who cannot count on cash income will be wary to join. From my sample group, only the households of Malia and Lisi, with regular cash incomes, will join this year. They will receive $T220 when it is their turn—a sizable fund of cash. The recipient of the pot makes a meal for the others, usually a big plate of taro or bananas or yams with lamb flaps, so the rotating credit association meeting is an entire social evening of collecting and dinner.

The village will have one funeral later this month that will last ten days. All households will send representatives to the funeral, many for at least part of every one of its ten days. The relatives of the deceased will make food for hundreds of people—three meals each day. All five households will receive feast food from this funeral. The village dances will be canceled during the ten days of the funeral, but there will be several other dances this month. A regular schedule of dances in the village, usually held on Friday and Saturday nights, began in the late 1960s, and every week young people and accompanying parents pay a small entrance fee to listen to Tongan bands or recorded music and dance. Sometimes there is a big dance at a nearby village, and a bus is rented to take the village's young men and women and their chaperones back and forth.

If dances or movies are not offered, village women often visit with one another for a few hours in the evening. The small groups talk about the events of the day, about the goings-on in the village, and the conversation often bubbles over raucously with laughter. Several of the men will attend their kava clubs, where they sit in circles and drink until close to dawn. They will discuss politics and sing village songs in four-part harmony and entertain one another with jokes and stories.

A Land of Scarcity?

With this brief glimpse into daily village life, you are in a better position to interpret two misleading statistics about Tonga.

First, Tonga was, and still is, one of the poorest countries in the world. 'Olungans earned more than the average Tongan, but even so, the median income of an entire household, normally between six and seven individuals in 1982, was $T800 (at the time about $760 U.S.). By world standards this would have placed 'Olungans and Tongans well below the poverty line.

But such figures fail to represent what few members of an industrial society can appreciate: that villagers in Tonga could live a comfortable and enjoyable life without a substantial cash income. Income makes much more of a difference when, as in industrial societies, one's entire existence depends on the purchasing power of money.

When the district officer of the area went on a sponsored government trip to Mexico, he was startled and appalled by what he saw. When he returned, he lamented to me, "People came up to me in the streets for help! I gave them the money from my pocket. It was terrible what I saw there." Mexicans probably earn more per capita than Tongans, but there is no significant land base to bolster those who are impoverished.

In Tonga's rural areas the subsistence economy was central to the quality of life. It was possible to grow staple food; to supplement this diet by fishing and by raising chickens and pigs; to procure building materials, flooring, bedding, cooking fuel, and many other necessities of life from the land and sea. Kin and neighbors could be relied on to subsidize those who could not procure the basics. As a result, a small stipend of cash went a long way.

This did not mean that 'Olungans lived lavishly on $T800 year, or even that villagers always had as much as they would have wanted. There were many meatless meals of manioc, bread, or topai in the village, and there were many homes in disrepair,[8] many households with no electricity or indoor plumbing, and many families who scrambled to pay school fees. But one would have been hard-pressed to find abject poverty, starvation, or homelessness in Tonga.

The second related statistic about Tonga is its landlessness. 'Olunga was a land-rich village in comparison to the rest of Tonga, but even so, land shortage was already acute in the village in 1981.[9] Only 35.5 percent of 'Olungans held registered land by 1984, and both locally and nationally, the landless were becoming a geometrically increasing segment of the total population. Such statistics conjure up familiar notions of a desperate and restless proletariat. While this outcome may indeed be in the offing, my village land study in 1983 gave some insight into why it was not yet the case.

Only about one-third of 'Olungans were landholders, but two-thirds of the adult population belonged to a household that had land. What is more, the majority of those households *without* any landholder had access to land or its produce through other relatives. Of the 33 percent of households that did not directly control a registered plot of land in 1983, 9 percent had a borrowing relationship with a landholder and used all or a portion of the landholder's plot for growing food. Another 6 percent of the landless population were the adult sons of landholding fathers who jointly worked the land with their natal family. Another 9 percent of landless households reported that they regularly received food from a landholding relative. Truly landless households—those with no regular access to land or agricultural produce—represented only 10 percent of the total sample. So, although the great majority of 'Olungans held neither registered nor unregistered land, few villagers were totally without access to land or produce. Kinship and friendship in Tonga largely mitigated the differences between village haves and have-nots.

This picture muddies explanations of migration. When thinking about why people would uproot themselves from their homes and their loved ones and travel across an ocean, the images that come to mind are of desperation, poverty, hardship, war, or political upheaval. These were not the images or the realities of life in Tonga in the early 1980s.

Migrants were leaving a place with a 99 percent literacy rate; where every family owned a home; where there was free elementary education, no foreign ownership of land, free medical care at local clinics and the national hospital, affordable clean water; where there was negligible crime and no civil or foreign war. It was a country where one could lead a peaceful life of decency and dignity. Tonga in the 1980s was no Eden, as movies and travel brochures paint the South Pacific. But neither would one expect the exodus from the village that had already begun.

2

Why Migrate?

〰︎   The official census of 1976 showed that there
were 1,993 Tongans in 'Olunga. Over the preceding twenty years, the population had climbed steadily in the village. With high birthrates, and an influx of outer island people to the main island, 'Olunga had grown at about
2 percent annually, adding 40 percent to its population between 1956 and
1976.

By the 1970s, the population growth rate in the village had already
slowed.[1] When I conducted a house-to-house census of the village in 1981,
I discovered that there were almost two hundred people fewer than in the
last census only six years before.[2] 'Olunga seemed to be losing population
for the first time in its modern history. And what was happening in 'Olunga was happening throughout Tonga.

To get a clearer sense of what was occurring and why, I tracked village
population movement for the following year (November 1981–November
1982). I limited the tracking to one geographical block of 412 people, an
area where I had many personal contacts and much daily interaction and
knew that my results would be reliable. I returned to this block exactly a
year later and recorded who had come, who had left, where they had gone,
and why.

Forty-six people, more than 10 percent of the block population, had left
the village during the year.[3] Some had married and moved to their spouse's
village. Others had relocated to Nuku'alofa or another village to be closer
to work or school. Six people had died. But of the majority of those leaving
(twenty-four of forty-six) had gone overseas. In the same year there were
ten births, and eleven people had moved into the village, two of whom were
returning overseas migrants.

With all the comings and goings taken into account, 'Olunga had a net loss of twenty-five persons in that one year, an annual population decline of 6.1 percent. Gains in population from births and in-marriages equaled losses through deaths and out-marriages. The number of villagers who had moved to another Tongan village was about the same as the number of those who had come into 'Olunga from elsewhere in Tonga.[4] The difference—and the source of population loss—was clearly overseas migration.

In this one year, twenty-four villagers in thirteen separate migration incidents had been lost to overseas migration, while two overseas migrants had returned, a net out-migration of 5.3 percent. Households had suffered deeper disruption than the 5.3 percent figure might indicate. Although less than 6 percent of the population migrated in 1982, almost one in five households lost a family member, and in almost half the cases it was the head of household.[5] There was only one case in which an entire domestic unit—mother, father, and children—migrated overseas at the same time, keeping the family intact.

"Who in your close family are overseas and which ones live here?" I asked this question of a sample group of adult villagers in the following year.[6] In all, about a quarter of villagers' significant kin network were already living overseas. And even if only one of the average of five children in each Tongan family migrates overseas in a generation, the loss of kin increases geometrically. A twenty-year-old Tongan today will have lost 38 percent of his kin group by the time he and his siblings are parents. And by the time his children, nephews, and nieces have children of their own, 51 percent of his close kin group will be living overseas. In a little more than one generation, then, if migration patterns hold, more Tongans will be living overseas than in Tonga.

Why are people leaving? Are Tongans no longer satisfied with what Tongan life has to offer? Have they become so changed and co-opted by the promises of a Western "high life" that they can no longer abide by Tongan customs and ways?

In the early days of my residence in the village, I saw Western sensibilities and values overtaking the Tongan way. It appeared to me everywhere in the images of village life as a duel between anomalous symbols of Tonga and the West, a duel I noted in my journals:

Designer jeans and tapa cloth hang together, drying on the chicken-wire clothesline.

Glossy pages of a slick Australian fashion magazine—make-up ads, winter fashions, and plates of food—have been glued together and wall-paper the inside of a thatched hut.

Kinsmen of the deceased move with difficulty in thick tattered mats drawn at the waist, extending from knee to shoulder, as they distribute funeral feast food in clear plastic bags.

(excerpts from my personal journal, 1981)

Migration, to me, seemed one of these warring forces. Migration was foreign, Western, representing a desire for things and money that opposed tradition, staying with family, living the Tongan life. Neither set of images was what it seemed. I came to see a different picture, one that changed my notion of traditional and modern, indigenous and Western, and ultimately of migration. It is this new sense of understanding that the rest of this chapter is about.

Western and Tongan Meetings

Take anything in the village that seems unquestionably Tongan—such as bark cloth, a traditional form of wealth. Then take something that is certifiably Western—such as money. If you delve very deep into the details and history of any phenomenon you are absolutely certain is either Tongan or Western, traditional or modern, you will become confused.

The wooden mallets that women used to beat mulberry bark into tapa cloth made a musical sound throughout the village. The mallets came down rhythmically on the bark strips, flattening the bark into sheets and reverberating off the wooden beam on which the strips were laid. It was an old traditional sound in the villages, a sound that the earliest visitors to Tonga noted in their writings.

The tapa cloth and the cooperative cloth-making groups that one saw in the village in the 1980s were not really traditional, though. These groups represented the third major social change in tapa making. There has been numerous technical changes as well since the nineteenth century—changes in design, in color, and in technique—of which most village women were unaware.[7]

Originally, tapa cloth was the exclusive possession of chiefs. A commoner woman might make the cloth, but she would do so under the auspices of a chiefly woman who would call the commoners into action and decide how much cloth would be made and for what purpose. Chiefly women made the relief patterns that would come through into the cloth, and these always depicted significant events and accomplishments in the life of the high chiefly ranks.

At the turn of the century, as chiefly fortunes became more dependent on the government, many chiefly people moved from their rural village abodes into the capital. Both their interests and their rights in the production of commoners began to wane, and it was in this context that the *kautaha*—a cooperative commoner group for making tapa cloth—was born.

There was only one woman in Tonga who remembered a time before the *kautaha*. When I interviewed her in 1981, she was 106, the oldest person in Tonga. It was her mother's generation that had begun the *kautaha*. During the first two decades of the twentieth century, *kautaha* groups began springing up all over Tonga with the express purpose of making cloth for their own commoner members. In the beginning, these cooperative tapa-making groups were often headed (nominally) by a chiefly woman or her designee. The groups continued to provide cloth to their chiefly patron, who built the tapa house, provided the design stamps, and donated the land to grow mulberry bark. Increasingly, though, as ties between chiefs and commoners became thinner, so did the ties between *kautaha* groups and their patrons. Commoner women took over the full functioning of the groups in most villages.

Kautaha had their own names, their own tapa houses, their own "membership seats" of about thirty women. Some of the first wooden houses constructed in the village were *kautaha* tapa-making houses, built collectively. Women grew bark together; they made dye cooperatively. They also did many other things together: they fished together, they collected seaweed from the lagoon, they traveled to other women's groups, and they hosted visitors in the village. They were lifelong members, replaced by their daughters or daughters-in-law.

Each woman could have her *kautaha* make her cloths, but she was expected to provide the bark necessary for her cloths and the labor in beating it. The beating of the bark was done in families. A senior woman might distribute her bark among younger women relatives, and they would help her beat enough bark for her tapa-making day. It could take years to grow and beat enough bark for a *koka'anga* (the occasion when the group would collectively join and dye the beaten pieces). But this was not all. There were other expenses. A woman whose clothes were being made would provide feast food—pigs and yams and other special items—for the tapa-making group as well as kava for the men who would come and cook the food. The cloth making, and the feasting and kava drinking, might go on for a few days.

Making a cloth was a significant occasion, then; it required resources and the status to command the labor of others. This was why members of *kautaha* were senior women in the family or women of rank. The ability to make and own tapa cloths was thus both a result and a symbol of prestige. A woman danced a dance of joy when her tapa cloths were complete, and a woman of that day would store her cloths publicly in the open rafters of her home.

In the 1950s and 1960s, the *kautaha* began dying out. Many houses went unrepaired until they collapsed. Women said simply that they were too lazy to rebuild them, but their "laziness" was generated by the changes occurring in society. Some of the younger women thought that tapa making went too slowly in the *kautaha*. It took too long to collect and beat enough bark for several cloths to warrant a *koka'anga*. And then there were the onerous feast expenses for food and kava for several days of clothmaking.

Within two decades, most *kautaha* had been replaced by the new tapa-making form: the "rotating" form, described in chapter 1. It consisted of ten to eighteen tapa makers who together made part of the cloth each week for one member, in turn. They made the same number of cloths for each person, usually two. Although the woman whose "day" it was might provide a special pot of stew for the group, she was under no obligation to do so. Each woman was expected to come with her own food. The midday meal ceased to be an occasion; it resembled, instead, a brown bag working lunch in the United States. Men no longer cooked for the women. There was no kava drinking or celebrating.

Production was fast. A group with fourteen members would take fourteen weeks to make twenty-eight cloths. Each member beat a quota of bark each week. If her bark was not ready in the bush, she borrowed it from relatives or bought bark in town. If an entire group did not have the resources for two full cloths, they might decide to make only one, or one cloth plus a piece. In modern Tonga, groups can make just a "piece" because gifts of tapa cloth have gotten smaller, as little as one-tenth of a full cloth (a full cloth is about seventy-five feet long). Nevertheless, no matter what the group decided, a member could not come to the *koka'anga* day without her expected quota.

In the 1930s, when a woman's cloths were finished, she would pile them in her house rafters for all visitors to see and admire. Women of the 1980s chuckled that they never could keep their cloths long enough to display them as their grandmothers did. Finished cloths were quickly given away as gifts and used at ceremonies to fulfill family obligations, or they were sold. Turning cloth into money was a common way to pay for costly items such as school fees, an airline ticket, a fence for the property, or even the bark to join the next tapa-making group. In 1983, 42 percent of women in the village reported having sold some of their tapa cloth within the previous decade.

Throughout the century, the tapa-making process changed with the shifting relationship of chiefs to commoners and the relationships of commoners to one another. What passed in the 1980s as "traditional" was thus the third social transformation of tapa making since precolonial times. Tapa making had "democratized," it had "monetized," and it had become based less on status than on financial means. In short, traditional Tongan wealth and its manufacture had come to embody some very Western characteristics. Western money, conversely, slowly became quite Tongan.

꙾ Money was introduced to Tonga by European missionaries in the nineteenth century. For Tongan commoners it was something to be used in the interaction of Tongans and Europeans. By the 1880s, Tongan commoners were using cash to pay taxes to the government and make contributions to the church. But cash was still not used in local transactions between Tongans.[8]

It took some time before Tongans began using money more locally. But when they did, money, like many seemingly Western institutions, was transformed by the system it entered. A clue to the "meaning" of money lies in its early uses. Consider these three examples. In 1909 one of the two biggest cash expenditures in Tonga was for imported foods (the other was for drapery). A village woman remembered that in about 1928, she had made a major acquisition of a Western product: a fancy English tea set. In 1932 one women's tapa-making group exchanged with a mat-making group on a different island. The leader of the mat-making *kautaha* was given a special gift: cash.

Why buy imported food in an agricultural society? Why would a commoner living in a thatched home buy an English tea set? Why should a tapa group give a cash gift to its most important hostess?

The answer was prestige. Imported food, like imported goods generally, was associated with people of status. Having and serving imported food at the turn of the century was a sign of great resources, and it signaled a higher, more prestigious and chieflike lifestyle. The tea set was likewise a show-piece that would be brought out for guests. Western goods and money thus functioned—in part—as prestige items, and this is why the *kautaha* leader (usually a woman of higher status than others) would be given money. This was not an example of budding capitalism. Money and Western commodities had significant functions as gifts, as expressions of status and symbols of prestige. And since cash was operating in the sphere of prestige, it had to follow its rules.

One could not just purchase anything because one had cash. A tea set or curtains or Western clothing was within bounds, but a wooden house might be considered too presumptuous. There were psychological limits within the prestige system, and a commoner had to be careful not to act too chiefly, which could be shameful. While people might desire a wooden house, and might actually have the money, it was another thing in the village to buy one.

An older village man recalled a discussion with his father in the 1930s. They had accumulated enough money to build a wooden house, and the son was urging his father to purchase the lumber. But the local chief with whom the family was affiliated did not yet have a wooden house. The son remembered his father's words: that he would never build a wooden house while the chief lived in a thatched home.

Community or collective houses were another story. Many of the early *kautaha* houses were among the first wooden structures in the village. The prestige of the *kautaha,* and their association with wealth making and chiefly women, made them prime candidates for a show of status. Several *kautaha* groups in Tonga, and at least one in the village, began a savings association in the 1920s so they could purchase the lumber to build a wooden tapa-making house.

The social changes embodied in the histories of tapa cloth and money were not unique to these domains. In the hundred years between the adoption of Tonga's constitution and the 1980s, many other institutions in Tongan society changed in similar ways transforming both what was traditional and what was Western. The result was what has been called a "compromise culture."[9]

In the compromise culture, traditions were not "lost" to Westernization or commoditization. What happened, more accurately, was that traditions were transformed by the new social conditions in which they existed. At the same time, capitalism and Western institutions were filtered through Tongan social relationships, and they came out looking different too. Tapa cloth became monetized and democratized. Money traditionalized, becoming part of a system of prestige and reciprocity.

The legacy of this process was apparent in the village of the 1980s. Although Tonga had become fully monetized, it did not develop the capitalism one might have envisioned. And although traditions in the village remained quite strong, many village institutions that passed for traditional were in fact radically changed from their pre-contact versions. In the village, kinship and capitalism, Tongan and Western, were thoroughly enmeshed, producing something, as we shall see in the next section, that was both and neither at the same time.

A Lesson in Village Economics

When I first moved to the village, I never understood why villagers would wait patiently at the bus top in the capital for the bus that had 'OL-UNGA written on its side. There is only one road to the eastern district of the island, and any number of buses with destinations beyond 'Olunga can stop at the village. Yet 'Olunga people waited for the 'Olunga bus.

I came to see that "bus behavior" paralleled many others. To accomplish banking business in the capital town—everything from a question to a deposit to an overseas cable—you found one of the few 'Olungans who worked at the bank to handle the exchange. Whether the business at hand was the bank worker's responsibility or not was of no consequence. If the worker had gone to lunch, you waited. It was the same with government offices, technical services, even police matters.

By the time I left the village, I found I was doing the same thing. The modern capitalist sphere was alienating, with all its forms and formalities and social distance. One was among 'Olungans on the 'Olunga bus, and this engendered a certain quality of interaction, a certain sense, if you will, of family. On the 'Olunga bus, a child without bus fare might get a pinch from the fare collector, but he would get a ride home. Snacks and food of all varieties were passed among passengers throughout the entire trip. So were crying children, until a lap that pleased them was found. If you were returning with a heavy load from town, or even if you had trouble walking, the driver from 'Olunga could be persuaded to detour to your door.

Tongan kinship, reciprocity, and prestige all played a role in the modern capitalist sphere as it existed in the village in the 1980s. The same farmer who sold baskets of coconuts in town for sale at the local market, or for export, would give away drinking coconuts in the village. He would not sell pigs or produce or services to a fellow villager, even a nonkinsman, at "market" price.

Similarly, when plans were discussed for a local poultry cooperative, they took into account village loyalties. Eggs were to be sold for a profit to nonmembers but given free to cooperative members. Nonmembers outside of 'Olunga, however, would pay eleven cents an egg; nonmember residents of 'Olunga would pay six cents.

Even wage labor took a different form in the village. In 1968 villagers and outside laborers worked together as a group to build the local convent. One woman remembered:

> When it was time to eat, the town officer spoke and then a van would go to get food from the bush and we'd all come together and cook again. The village was divided into three sections, and each cooked once per day and brought the food to the workers. They paid the workers, but in Tongan work, you don't let Tongan people do work and then go and eat someplace else and then come back. Everyone was happy and feeling warm. And they worked fast, because they saw we were happy and taking care of them and they do their work well.

In 1982 villagers offered the same hospitality to the work crew from the Tongan Electric Board who were extending electric lines farther into the village. These men were on government salary, yet households in the village took turns cooking for the crew, and bringing them drinks and cigarettes.

The difference between Western and Tongan versions of money and economic exchange deeply affected my own work. In 1982, when I wanted households to keep diaries for me, it never occurred to me to solicit help the way I ultimately did. Because I knew the diary task would be an imposition, the remedy I came up with as a Westerner was that I would "pay well" for the trouble involved.[10] Any participating household would receive the school fees for two children—a generous payment by Tongan standards at the time, which I thought would ensure that every solicited individual would participate.

From my sampling procedures, I knew which village households I wanted to participate. I decided to visit each one, tell them about the project requirements and the pay, and ask them to sign up as a participant (or refuse) at that time. Before proceeding, I went to my neighbor Malia for her advice.

The pay is excellent, Malia told me, but this is not a way to ask people to do the diaries. Describe your project, she advised, and then ask the people simply to do you this favor because it is important to you, your work, and your schooling. Just ask them, with no talk of money.

I did as she said, and every household I approached agreed immediately to participate. Following my neighbor's counsel, I then thanked the participants for their help and support and explained that, in gratitude, I wanted to give them a gift. The gift was that I wanted to pay the school fees for two of their children. The people I spoke with were moved and delighted, and thanked me for so generous a gift. We usually then ate some food together. Both parties ended up with expressions and feelings of gratitude, a sense of gift and countergift rather than the sense that participants were "employees," to be paid for services rendered by an "employer."

The example just described was not a thin disguise for the conduct of "business as usual" but an authentic departure from it. Cash and the cash economy had thoroughly penetrated the Tongan village. But they had also been reshaped historically by village values and relationships, and they emerged different animals.

To argue, though, that Western things and values simply became Tonganized in village life would be misleading. Although the capitalist mentality that "business is business" was an unfamiliar concept in 1982, village life without Western goods, money, and capitalist exchanges would have been equally unthinkable. Cash relationships had permeated even the smallest Tongan village, and commoners had become quite competitive among themselves in demonstrating their means. By the 1980s, a fine house was no longer a potential source of embarrassment for a commoner. It had become a symbol of local success and respect and, like other signs of success—an advanced degree, a truck, or a salaried job—it was totally enmeshed in the Tongan system of prestige.

In the 1980s a respectable Sunday family dinner had come to all but require canned corned beef, a prestige food, and there was not a single Tongan feast I witnessed that did not include an array of imported food items. My household income studies showed that the single biggest cash expense in the village—more than 50 percent of family income—was for food! This is an astounding fact in an agricultural society, but it is directly related to the role of imported food in the daily and ceremonial lives of Tongans. Money, buying, selling, credit, wages, and imports had become so infused in Tongan life that one could not take care of community, even traditional, obligations without them.

Even if one had never aspired to a high school certificate, to a wooden house with electricity, or to a regular diet of imported food, not having cash would severely have limited one's life within the village. Nightly events—everything from dances to movies to social occasions—demanded an entrance fee for admission. The informal circles of men who met nightly to drink kava, sing, and discuss politics anted into the collective pot to pay for their kava root. And there were endless numbers of village-sponsored events that called for contributions from the community. The water system, the kindergarten, building projects at the local school—all were supported through local donations and fund-raising events. In the 1980s community spirit and kin obligations required cash.

Titled chiefly attendants, including members of the traditional Four Houses, joined savings associations in order to accumulate a fund with which to fulfill their social and ceremonial obligations to the noble. The main source of traditional expenditure—funerals—had come to involve huge cash outlays. While the formal public arena of funerals was an enormous public exchange of tapa cloth, mats, and feast food, behind-the-scenes cash contributions were always necessary to subsidize funeral activities. Envelopes of cash, sometimes thousands of dollars, changed hands informally.

In the village, then, things were not what they appeared. Making money was just as much about fulfilling tradition as making tapa cloth was about acquiring capital to fund one's business. The local village store might have seemed to outside eyes a straightforward means for its owner to earn a living, but within the village it was a symbol of prestige, a way to cultivate patronage and obligation.

As a result, the village store operated differently from a U.S. business, even of the mom-and-pop variety. Stores in the village did not support families the way they did in true capitalist contexts. No one became wealthy from owning a village store. Government policies, which included duties on imports as well as strict price controls, made profit margins very small. Some stores even lost money through too generous credit policies. Even so, the store stayed open, if its owner could afford it. But when the store owner sponsored a dance or a village movie or a kava-drinking evening, many people would come. The store owner was a villager who had cultivated obligations and prestige. He or she would do very well financially from the sponsored event, which might appear to outsiders to be a purely social village evening.

The Changing Quality of Village Life

Kinship and capitalism, traditional and modern, Western and Tongan were thoroughly entwined rather than diametrically opposed in the village. And this is one of the reasons why villagers could not choose between them.

A woman could not make tapa cloth just for family or just for sale. A chiefly attendant needed to grow kava so he would have a plentiful supply for his obligations, but he also needed cash for his savings association so that he could supply a pig to the noble. A farmer could not grow his crops just for food, unless someone else in the household did something else to earn cash. And the farmer who used his land to grow bananas for sale also had to put aside some bananas for relatives so they could eat. To be a good Tongan, and to keep up with one's obligations to friends and family, one needed to do both. This took more resources and more time, and village life eventually became very much more complicated.

What villagers said is that their *kavenga* had increased. *Kavenga* translates roughly as "obligations" or "responsibilities." One informant pictured *kavenga* to me as a heavy sack that one must carry. The sack, almost everyone agreed, was getting heavier. How did people do everything? It was quite clear from the details of their lives that people accomplished "everything" by lengthening their days and intensifying their labor.

If you asked Tongan men at a kava circle about Tongan life versus Western life, where these questions regularly come up, they began with a familiar refrain: "Over there it's work, work, work. But here we can sleep, and if we don't work, we still eat. We can stay up all night drinking kava, and tomorrow we can stay home from the bush and sleep all day if we want."

The talk, in 1982, no longer matched the daily realities. The diaries the 'Olungans kept painted a different picture, one that was not all visiting, leisure, and sleep. An adult villager raising a family spent an average of 6.7 hours each day doing work.[11] Another 0.8 hour was spent working in the service of the community, kin network, or church. An additional 1.93 hours a day was "obligated time," devoted to community, church, and work-related meetings, funeral attendance, and other obligatory social functions. Taken together, work and obligations consumed an average of 9.45 hours daily, or 66.2 hours each week, hardly a life of leisure.

In fact, whenever the talk at kava circles got serious and moved beyond the surface, the Tongan kava drinkers often spoke about these changes. The older men, those with adult children of their own, remembered a time when life was noticeably slower, when there was more opportunity for visiting and sleeping and feasting. Ethnographic descriptions and interviews with 'Olungans converged unmistakably on the memory of a less hectic, more leisurely life. This was not merely nostalgia for lost youth. Forms of work organization confirmed the accuracy of these impressions.

The women's tapa-making groups that "rotated" were a significantly more intensive form than their predecessors, the *kautaha*. They produced much more cloth in a given period of time, and this was one of the reasons why women began them in the first place. Women produced for themselves *and* for sale, and they needed to do all of it in less time so they could make handicrafts to pay for school fees.

One year during my residence in the village, when the rotating tapa cloth group was well into its fourteen-week cycle, a funeral was held. It was a ten-day funeral, as were most commoner funerals in the village. One of the conventions surrounding funerals is that villagers can make no unnecessary noise during the funeral period. Tapa beating stopped for ten days. When the funeral was over, the beating began again, and women tried frantically to make up for lost time. Then another person died, stopping the beating again. The women were upset that they would not get through their cycle in the appropriate time. This one and that one needed her cloth. Members insisted that the group had to end on time so they could start something else. The women began sneaking deep into the bush to do their beating. Skirting funeral customs so they could come up with the traditional wealth for funerals seemed ironic. But with the new pace of life in the village, custom interfered with custom.

The same intensification of labor had occurred within men's work groups. Men's cooperative agricultural groups (called *tou ngoue,* or "agriculture in rounds") typically organized their labor by the day, working one member's plot as a group in turn each day. It was in the late 1940s that work groups began apportioning their time by blocks rather than days, a cooperative work form called *lau houa,* literally "counting hours." Villagers can remember the appearance, for the first time, of watches in the village because they needed them to track the time spent in cooperative work on member's bush land. In 'Olunga in the 1980s, all groups "counted hours."

Since the 1940s, the extent as well as intensity of working time had increased. The first counting-hours groups worked two plots a day (or one plot in a half-day). Since their inception, the number of rounds in a day had increased to at least four, and as many as six. There have been parallel increases in the number of working days in a week and the number of working weeks in the year.

The changing pace of Tongan rural life thus meant that villagers needed to work harder and harder to keep up. There were, as people in the village said, more *kavenga* to meet. There were greater economic and social pressures in the village, and these changed the quality and substance of life for most Tongans.

So, consider the situation of a Tongan village couple. Ofa is a member of the tapa-making group that had to stop working for a series of funerals, and Tevita, her husband, is a farmer. One of the funerals involved a relative on her husband's side, and Ofa and Tevita gave a small pig, some yams, and some money they had earned from making copra.

Ofa is making two tapa cloths. She is trying to put aside cloths so she will have an appropriate wealth store for the wedding of her daughter, who was then twenty-three. Should her daughter marry, Ofa would have important responsibilities, and all the village would look to see how well she performed them.

But she and her husband also needed to pay for the school fees of four children. The copra money was meant for the school fees, but there was none left now. There would be money from the pineapples that her husband and eldest son tended in the bush, but not until late December. Ofa spent most of the first six months of the year making pocketbooks for sale at the Paepae crafts center, but only one sold this month, and that did not bring in enough money. The cruise boat comes only once a month.

She might have sold a tapa cloth to pay for school fees, but because of the funerals, she will not have her cloth until next year now. Maybe . . .

Maybe their eldest son, who has finished school, could go and work with his father's brother's son, who does gardening in California. Maybe just for a little while. Their eldest son might have his own reasons for wanting to go—the excitement of living overseas, or escape from daily obligations to relatives. Perhaps you can understand why the young man's parents, even though they would cry to see their son leave, might begin to talk about migration—how leaving the village might become the best way to fulfill a Tongan life.

America as a Tongan Concept

Migration of Tongans to the United States, Australia, and New Zealand would never have happened without the huge profits that colonial powers extracted from their colonies and the income differentials this created around the world. The promise of Western opulence penetrated Tonga, as it did almost every nonindustrial country, through magazines and movies, music tapes and action videos, and world news and commercial products. At the same time, the means to migrate were made more easily available through the expansion of international airline routes. These global factors, together with land shortages and limited earning opportunity in Tonga, spurred large-scale migration to industrial nations.

To understand Tongan migration, though, one has to understand more than these things that apply to any one of many migrating countries. The character of migration, while a product of global capitalism, was also a particular outgrowth of Tongan history.

༃ We all sat on mats on the floor of the banana shed watching the B movie brought in from Nuku'alofa. The shed was wall-to-wall people. Patrons were draped over one another, sitting on the pandanus mats that they had brought with them. Two women wedged me in from either side; there was a child in my lap, and someone behind me had put her knees up for me to lean on. We were watching a soap opera tale that was American-made even though it probably had never played on an American movie screen. I remember little of it, except that it was set in an opulent context and was about a man's dealing with the assault (and rape?) of his fiancée.

The conversation around me focused on things the filmmaker probably did not have in mind. "Look at that light!" someone called out, commenting about the chandelier in the scene. "What kind of food is that?" someone asked a companion, as a man and woman on the screen engaged in a lengthy dialogue over dinner. The film was in English, with no Tongan subtitles. Many people talked during the movie, asking constant questions: "What is he doing now?" "Who is that girl?" A woman nearby could not follow the story and asked a woman on my mat what was happening in the film. The woman on my mat responded, "The brother of that girl is angry and he is going to kill that other man." This was not what I thought the movie was about (and I speak English very well). In many ways the American movie had become something else, something Tongan. This was a little bit true of "going to America" too.

By 1981, Western influence had bored into the fabric of the village. It was right there in the banana shed, in the American media occupation of the village. But in other ways Tongan history and culture had shaped how Western things appeared in the village and what they meant. In an important sense, America was a Tongan concept.

"Foreign" and "overseas" have long had meaning to Tongan commoners. Traders, missionaries, and colonials could enter the Tongan chiefdom only through its existing authorities, its chiefs. Strong associations, both social and symbolic, developed between things and persons foreign and those chiefly.

Historically speaking, the first Tongans to go overseas were chiefly people. George I, Tonga's first king, traveled to Australia in 1853. Since this time an overseas visit, an overseas education, and overseas products have been prerogatives and symbols of the Tongan nobility. In 1929, for instance, the only car in Tonga owned by a Tongan belonged to the queen. The other 198 cars in Tonga were owned by Europeans.[12] Wood houses were built for chiefs and government offices and Europeans. The street that ran through the capital and led to the royal residence was ceremoniously lined with imported English pines. The Street of Pines, as it is called, was one of the patterns that regularly appeared on tapa cloth, where "chiefly" motifs appear. In the 1930s you might also have seen a tapa cloth that was specially designed to mark the year that the present king left to pursue his degrees in arts and the law from the University of Sydney. The King, like his mother and many other members of the chiefly class, were educated overseas.

Overseas people resident in Tonga have long inhabited positions of church and government authority, and rubbed elbows primarily with Tongan people of rank. Those foreigners whose business was with commoners generally interacted with them in positions of authority—as priests and ministers, government agents, teachers, and store owners in town.

To many Tongan commoners, then, European places, people, and things had a veneer of prestige. This explains why some of the oldest tapa-making groups in the 'Olunga area, begun during the second decade of the twentieth century, were called "America," "Russia," "Britain," and "Germany." Village women ostensibly wanted their tapa groups to have important names, so they selected the names of the foreign powers involved in World War I. (They dropped the name "Germany" after the war.) It is interesting that these names were chosen by commoner women at a time when the Tongan nobility was fighting British colonial influence and attempting to divest the nation of foreigners.

The World War II years were the first time that many Tongans had met ordinary Americans. Both the United States and, later, New Zealand sent troops to Tonga in anticipation of a Japanese invasion in the area. Anyone who was alive during that time remembers the war, and the "white people" (at least one regiment of whom were African-American). It was a scary but exciting time, as most people described it—more scary for the older people, more exciting for the young.[13]

The Tongan government ordered all villagers into the bush for their own safety (both from the war and from the occupying soldiers). Tonga, though, did not turn out to be a threatened area. It was never attacked, but the visiting soldiers were stationed there for several months, so there was considerable time and opportunity for Tongans to get to know Americans. 'Olungans, who felt they were paid exorbitantly by the Americans for fresh fruit and food, for doing laundry or getting coconuts, were generally more curious than afraid.

An older man remembers: "They were friendly! They ate with us and they wanted to stay in our houses. They were generous; they gave us food and chocolate and money."

One woman in the village, then a child, recounts: "There was a house that the soldiers came to often in the evening and they would hold a dance. I remember going with the other little kids and standing outside to see the soldiers—the white people. That's what I remember. Seeing lots of soldiers. But the dance was in a little wooden house."

Another man, then a boy who watched the soldiers, remembers a soldier who gave him a candy bar.

"Do you know William from Ohio?" one village woman asks me forty years after she and the soldier had an affair. To this day she thinks of those years with affection. She was one of several women who had amorous relationships with American soldiers. Her first child was "William's" daughter, of whom she is very proud. She has since had ten others. "I do not know what happened to him," she told me. "Maybe he was killed. Because I think he would have written. He was crazy about me."

Americans made a lasting and favorable impression on villagers in 'Olunga and in Tonga, particularly on its young people. Villagers did the soldiers' laundry. Younger men and women left the bush to meet the soldiers. 'Olungans loved that Americans came and ate with them in their houses, that these soldiers brought them special food and money. Their legacy was a sense of benevolence and awe. Americans were good and generous people. And they were rich.

One of the first commoners to leave 'Olunga for overseas—Fa—went to Fiji in the early 1950s. "In those days," one of Fa's contemporaries tells me, "it was a big thing to leave. Anyone who went overseas came back 'high.' When Fa came back to the village, the people talked to him, but he could not talk back to them."

"What do you mean?" I asked.

"People said he could no longer speak Tongan," the man explained. "After three months in Fiji, Fa told the people that he had forgotten how to speak Tongan. And I thought about this, and I said to the people . . . 'If he can't speak Tongan, then tell me the language he can speak' [because he couldn't really speak English either]. Then people realized. He was just trying to be big—to be bigger than Tonga."

"Even today," the man continued, "those who go overseas are big. Many say that those who go to America are biggest. America is 'high.'"

That, in the beginning years of Tongan migration, was the promise of America to Tongan migrants.

Leaving the Village

The complexities and pressures of village life in the 1980s went beyond simple dichotomies of Western/Tongan, indigenous/foreign, as I have tried to show. Leaving the village—migration—worked the same way. Migration was not about rejecting a traditional way of life, or leaving Tonga and family behind, or replacing Tongan values with American values.

Viewing migration in these ways, you would have overlooked the possibility that going to America, the ultimate act of Westernization, was Tongan. Migration was not a rejection of Tongan traditional ways because, as you have seen, a "traditional" way of life was no longer really possible. Tongan life was changing, whether one left or stayed. In fact, under the social and economic conditions of Tonga since the late 1960s, a strong sense of tradition and family obligations might well have led a Tongan overseas. It was in American and New Zealand and Australia where one might have the best chance of securing a good Tongan life for oneself and one's family back home, where one might find the means to become "bigger" and rise in importance within the kin network, and where one might become a patron with the means to help one's extended kin.

If there was an "ideal version" of overseas migration in Tonga through-out the 1970s and early 1980s, it was that a family member would move overseas to work for a few years. During this time he or she would manage to send precious dollars home to Tonga on a regular basis and put aside a sizable savings as well. After three to five years or so, the family member would return home with a cash nest egg—overseas savings large enough to build a home in Tonga. The family would then work their land to provide daily food, construct a cement house with fitted glass windows, and live out their days happily in Tonga.

There was a slightly different scenario in regard to the youth of the com-munity. A child might do well in school, earning a university certificate to study abroad. He or she would then go to an overseas university to learn engineering or accounting or medicine and later return home to Tonga to a steady income and a good job in the government. His or her parents would be proud and well cared for.

In the early 1980s, when I first observed emigration from the village, more than half the people who left fit these categories. The emigrants were family emissaries, cutting a path to mobility. Single children and husbands leaving to find work were making sacrifices for the future of the family, a family that often saw a rosier future in Tonga.

After more than a decade of migration, those who had left for overseas had begun to fulfill their promise, both nationally and locally. Beginning in the mid-1970s, remittance dollars—the money sent home from relatives overseas—grew in national importance, eventually exceeding all receipts from exports.[14] In 'Olunga remittances had, by 1983, become a major in-come supplement for local families. One in seven households depended on overseas money for their primary income, and the majority of families re-ceived some small windfall during the year from relatives abroad.

The consequences of having a relative overseas were often conspicuous in daily life in the early 1980s. New store-bought outfits, a household ap-pliance, or frequent trips to the village shop were local signs that a letter or package had come from overseas. A house in the village with a sink or bath-tub, sometimes sitting uninstalled on the property, was an indication that a husband working overseas would soon be returning.

Remittance money fueled the purchase of imports—everything from canned Australian corned beef to New Zealand lamb flaps to American cig-arettes. But it also supported school fees, donations to the church, and Ton-gan events and ceremonies. For many villagers, such as Ofa and Tevita, remittances provided the little bit extra that they needed to meet their obligations, releasing them from yet another income-generating task. In this way, money sent from overseas preserved the subsistence agricultural economy that undergirded the Tongan way of life.

Airport departure scenes in Tonga poignantly reflected the mixed emotions surrounding the migration process. They were bittersweet. Relatives and friends would live and sleep en masse with a departing villager in the days before the trip and accompany him or her, literally by the truckload, to the airport. The singing, excitement, and tremendous support of the community was coupled always with deep sobs and fears of not meeting again. Parents of departing children told me that they thanked God their child had an opportunity to go abroad, but these same parents could not bring themselves to go to the airport on their child's departure day. Parting moments crystallized Tongans' highest hopes and greatest losses—a kinsman who might fulfill the Tongan family dream while at the same time ceasing to be a tangible part of the family's daily life.

After they left the airport, family members would return home and pin photos of their migrant relative to their clothing.

II

A R R I V A L S

༄༅ The stream of Tongan emigrants began in the 1950s as a trickle. They were temporary migrants, sent by the church or family for education overseas.[1] They were single men looking for the high wages of unskilled overseas work. Their primary destination was New Zealand, the closest industrial nation at 1,300 miles away.

Leaving Tonga was the culmination of many forces both inside and outside Tonga, as you saw in the last chapter. Conditions throughout the twentieth century had produced rising commoner expectations for mobility. By the 1950s, the first generation of educated commoners had begun to take their place in government, and many farming households were producing copra or crops for sale overseas. Over the next twenty years, however, a dwindling land base and limited jobs would prevent many commoners from realizing their climbing aspirations.

By the 1960s, the stage was set for migration. Overseas wages could provide a bridge between commoner aspirations and opportunity, and it was under these conditions that labor needs in industrial countries easily triggered movement out of Tonga.

The Mormon Church in Tonga was instrumental in the early migration of Tongans to the United States. The church funded the migration of hundreds of Tongans to Mormon centers in Hawai'i and Salt Lake City. Without a village context for viewing migration, one might interpret Tongan migration to the United States as a religious phenomenon, motivated by a commitment to the American-based Morman Church. It is more accurate to say that the Tongan commitment to the church was motivated by the opportunity it provided for overseas migration. The fact that the Mormon Church facilitated the migration of Tongans to the United States was one of the major reasons why Mormonism was the fastest growing religion in Tonga during the 1960s.[2]

By the 1970s, the Tongan government had become actively involved in enabling Tongans to work temporarily overseas. Migration solved a growing problem of land, jobs, and population for the Tongan government. The population of Tonga had continued to climb throughout the 1960s against a backdrop of land scarcity. Despite government efforts at increasing employment in the public sector, and various schemes to develop local industry, there were not nearly enough jobs to absorb those who sought work. A 1972 government report determined that only 5 percent of school leavers (Tonga's high school graduates) would find paid employment.[3] With government encouragement and the demonstrated promise of remittances, migration out of Tonga during the 1970s (primarily to New Zealand and Australia) became substantial, and significant at the national level.

It was during this time that United States immigration laws changed dramatically. Before 1965, immigration law was based on country quotas that heavily favored European nations and discriminated against the Asia-Pacific triangle. Two changes were initiated, beginning with the Immigration Act of 1965, that repositioned the United States as a destination for Tongan migrants. First, the national origins quota system limiting the number of visas granted to each country was abolished.[4] Visas would be granted on a first come, first served basis within a preference system that encouraged the uniting of families. Second, included in the new laws was a visa preference category (called the Fifth Preference) for the uniting of siblings. This came to be the most frequently used category of immigration applications, and it allowed early Tongan migrants to bring over their sizable sibling networks. Asian and Pacific Islander immigration increased sixfold by the late 1970s.[5]

By 1980, more than 5,000 Tongans had made their way to the United States, and the next decade was to see these numbers swell as each stream of migrants brought over the next. By 1990, the United States had become the preferred destination of Tongan emigrants. An estimated 25,000 Tongans (both Tongan-born and American-born) were living in the United States in 1995, equal to more than one-quarter of the entire population of Tonga.[6]

〃 The next three chapters describe the histories, thoughts, experiences and words of Tongan migrants to the United States. The people you will meet are all part of one extended family whose home was originally in 'Olunga.

They migrated from Tonga to the United States at different times, from 1963 to 1990. You will encounter these migrants, and their relatives who did not migrate, throughout the book. The reference chart of names and relationships on page 55 is a convenient guide for remembering who is who.

Chapter 3 begins in 1963 with Seini, the third-born child of a family of twelve, who was the first of her siblings, and among the first few hundred Tongans, to come to America.[7] From 1965 on, she and her Mormon husband began bringing over their extended families. Chapter 3 focuses on the first sister she brought over, Eseta, and her husband-to-be, Manu, who settled together in northern California and brought up two American children. It is through Eseta and Manu's family that you will see Tongan life in America.

In the years after Eseta and Manu migrated, emigration from Tonga to the United States burgeoned. More than 17,000 Tongans were legally in the United States by 1990, and California had become home to almost half of them.[8] San Mateo County, Eseta and Manu's place of residence, had become a small center of Tongan community in the United States, home to 2,600 Tongans by the early 1990s.[9]

Chapter 4 follows one family of these new migrants, Eseta's sister Malia and her family, as they moved from 'Olunga in 1990 to San Mateo, to live for their first year with Eseta. Chapter 5 describes the life memories of a young woman in this Tongan family, the only one of four sisters who decided to migrate. She talks about her childhood and her decision to leave. You will see her life five years after her migration as she has "Americanized" and plans on staying permanently in the United States. (The story of her older sister, who came on a visit but decided to stay in Tonga, is the focus of chapter 9.)

The final chapter in Part II describes an arrival in a different direction: the anthropologist's arrival in Tonga. Chapter 6 recounts significant incidents that occurred over a fifteen-year period, beginning with the author's formal fieldwork and extending to the new dimensions of experience that unfolded as Tongans continued to migrate to the United States.

More than most other chapters in the book, the chapters in this section (and chapter 9 as well) rely heavily on the words and remembered histories of family members. Stories that were told in English are reproduced nearly verbatim, with a minimum of editing of content or grammar. The interviews conducted in Tongan, or those recorded with notes and without a tape recorder, are my translations. I have tried to remain faithful to the tone and text of what was said. Where you hear people recounting their own life stories, I include my own questions so the reader will understand better the context in which the story was told.

Other chapters in this book are written to make particular points and to defend particular arguments. These chapters, which draw on people's narratives of their lives, are written differently because there is always more to people's lives than the points I might wish to make with their stories. There is certainly much to learn in these chapters, from the diverse reasons why people came to this country to the striking social distance between Tongan migrants and the dominant society to the generational gap between migrants and their children. However, the life histories in these chapters, while focused by questions and edited somewhat, take their own dips and turns. I offer them to you as material worth reading in its own right.

The Family Migration: Who's Who

SELA AND AISAKE
1926 — married, and gave birth to 12 children, 3 of whom are the subjects of the next two chapters

SEINI
1962 — became the first to migrate after she married SIMI, a Mormon.

SEINI brought over her sister, ESETA.

ESETA
1968 — migrated to the U.S., and then married MANU. They raised two American daughters

From 1970 to 1990, ESETA and MANU were host to scores of relatives including MALIA and the family

MALIA
1990 — and her husband ATU migrated. They had had 9 children, 5 of whom died. One child and a grandchild migrated with them

Sara & Alyssa returned to Tonga in 1994 for a visit

Sara

Alyssa

Vei, has applied for a visa

FINAU married Samlu

Losana

Tomasi

These two sisters are the subjects of chapters 5 and 9

PALU (EMMA)
1990 — came to America

Lio drowned

His son, Lio Jr. was adopted by Malia and Atu and migrated with them.

Vili committed suicide

Latu married Feleti, and has 3 children

Aleta

Liu

Malia Jr.

3

Coming to America

Eseta wanted to go to America because of her sister Seini.[1] Seini was the first in the family to leave for overseas. A nurse in Tonga, she worked at the island's only hospital. One year Seini tended to an older patient whose son came to visit his father regularly. That is how she happened to meet her husband, Simi, a teacher and a Morman from a different village. When they married in 1958, Seini converted to Mormonism. The Mormon Church was already funding Tongan congregants to come to the United States, and in 1963, when the church offered Seini and Simi the opportunity to go to Hawai'i, they took it.

They arrived in Oahu. Simi, the teacher, worked in a warehouse. Seini, the nurse, worked as a nurse's aide in a convalescent home. They soon moved to California, and Seini and Simi began bringing over family. First, they arranged the trips of Simi's father and brothers and their children. Next, Seini wrote to her sister Eseta to come. Eseta recalled:

> I stayed home—I was the only unmarried one—and I took care of my parents. My sister Seini would send us money to help, when my father was still alive. She wrote me to come there. She told me, "Oh, you have to come here and work to have your family. It's better here." So I decided I must go. So I forget everything else: friends, making tapa cloth. I decided I would go to America.
>
> I did have a "best friend" [boyfriend] though. He left first and went to Samoa and waited there for me. We were supposed to get married in Samoa, and then come over to the U.S. And when I went to Samoa to meet him, right on the plane, I changed my mind.

Eseta knew that if she married her fiancé, they would stay in American Samoa. Getting to the United States would still be far off. She recalls think-

ing on the plane trip from Tonga, "Please don't let me stay in Samoa." The
groom, his father, and his family were waiting in Samoa for her to arrive,
but her own family, knowing her feelings, telephoned her relatives in
Samoa. By the time she got there, her relatives had already talked to the boy's
family and had arranged for Eseta's plane ticket to the United States. The
family's reasons for interfering with the marriage were different from Eseta's; the boy was not from the same church as Eseta and they disapproved.
The family, of course, did not say so directly. They talked about the need to
wait awhile before getting married, about how Eseta should take a trip to
the United States and then come back.

So when Eseta landed in Samoa, a relative met her at the airport. The
marriage was off, and she was scheduled on a departing flight to the United States.

Were you happy with that?

Oh, yes. I went to see my boyfriend and I told him, "You stay here. I'll be
back. In five years."

Did you ever want to just go back to Tonga?

No. Except the first week I came—staying with my sister. I didn't work
yet. Then I felt homesick. I said I wanted to go back. And then the very first
time I worked—it was too early for me to wake up. "It's still night!" I said to
myself. My first job I had to be at work at 7 A.M. So I had to get up at 5:30 A.M.
It was dark. But after this, I was never homesick.

When I first came, I sewed for money. Then I got work in a hotel. I sewed
eight hours a day, and then weekends I was a maid. When I got my first pay-
check, I gave some to my sister, and every week I do the shopping for the
whole family. So I bought food. And I worked for my green card.

I never spent much, though. Food was cheap. A whole bag of potatoes
was twenty-nine cents. A whole chicken was twenty-nine cents. Eggs were
nineteen cents for a package. After a few years, everything jumped up. Those
were hard times, though. I didn't have a car. I walked everywhere. My broth-
er-in-law sometimes dropped me at work in the morning, and then he'd go
to work and I walked home. It was two miles.

In those days, I spent nothing. I spent only a little on food, and saved every
dollar to buy a used car for myself. In a few months I had a car already. I
asked a friend to teach me to drive, a Tongan girlfriend. We went to open
parking lots, and she taught me. She showed me everything. Then I moved
to a place of my own.

Eseta and Manu

Growing up, Eseta and Manu had seen a lot of each other at Viliami's store and roller rink in the village of 'Olunga. Manu had worked there for seven years before going to New Zealand. A roller skating rink was an unusual thing to have in a Tongan village. Built by Viliami, a Swiss national who settled in the village after World War I, it became a centerpiece of village life which villagers today remember fondly as part of their growing up.

Eseta loved to skate. For Eseta, who was shy and did not socialize easily, going to the skating rink was a passion she pursued with enthusiasm. Eseta's mother remembered that she would steal away to the rink every moment that she could. It was here that Eseta met Manu, but, as she says, "We were just friends. Not one who I thought of to marry."

Manu had not intended to marry Eseta, either. After many years of thinking about going overseas, Manu finally went to New Zealand in 1966 to work, when he was already thirty-nine years old. Manu had been interested in New Zealand ever since he was fifteen, when he befriended a New Zealand soldier who was part of the island's occupying force during World War II. New Zealand suited Manu, as he told the story at age sixty-five:

> I loved New Zealand. Up until today, I like New Zealand better than the United States. Because I like New Zealand air. Some people they say it's too cold, but it wasn't cold to me. Only on the mountain do you see white—but in the town, no frost, no snow. I loved New Zealand. But I hear now it's the same everywhere. It changed from before.

After fifteen months working in New Zealand, Manu returned to Tonga in 1967 with the intention of marrying a girl from the village and returning with his new wife to New Zealand and settling there. But then his plans changed suddenly.

> I was supposed to go and marry this girl on Wednesday. But on Monday I told her, "Don't let your family know. If they know, they'll object." On Monday, she decides to talk to her family. The family says no!
>
> So after that, I was really mad—so I wrote a letter to Eseta. And I told her I wanted to marry her. I had been at the kava circles where Eseta made kava many times. I know her and she know me. I told the guy who wanted to marry her, "In my mind, you can't find anybody like Eseta. That's why I think you should go marry her." And he left to marry her. But when I got to Samoa,

I saw that he had married with someone else—someone in my family, not her.

So then I thought I want her for my wife. I write this to her (not her father). I want her to come back and go to New Zealand because I have a job there. But she says, "No, you come up here because America is better than New Zealand." But I don't believe that. That's why I write a letter again, and I say I like New Zealand and the company hired me. But she said, "You come up here because I already have a green card." And she will file for me to stay. She win! So I said I'll be out.

And so this is what I did. I came up and stayed with an adopted son of my father's sister—a man named Siaosi. He was the only family I have here because at that time, there was not much Tongan people here. Very few. I think maybe I am the first man from my village to come up to here. From ['Olunga]. I think maybe I am the first ['Olunga] person to come to the United States. And I stay here, like I said, I come up and stay with Siaosi. And I fly up in the thirteenth of October 1969. We do our marriage on the first day of November.

Eseta told her own version of their marriage:

Maybe I got a letter a month or two before. I wondered how he got my address. I asked him, and he said he wrote a friend and asked him. I told him [Manu] the same thing—"wait in Tonga five years, then I'll be back." I got plenty of letters from the guy in Samoa, and said the same thing. In that time, whoever come first, I will marry with him. Finally, Manu came first. We get married in November, and maybe after two months or so, the other boy came. And he was angry too because I had a ring from him. And his family was here and my sister—they talk about it . . . .

So, it was Manu who makes a surprise for me. My relatives phoned me at night to come after dinner and look at this letter. They told me it said someone is coming from Tonga. So after I ate, I went over to see this letter from Tonga. I could drive then. So I drove over by myself and went into the house and there he was.

Manu continued the story, describing their life in America:

On the thirteenth day after I came to America, on the first of November 1969, Eseta and I got married. After the marriage, the first night, I slept with Eseta in a hotel—at that time they call it The Lebanon. But we cannot afford to stay there. The next day is a Sunday, and I move from there to a motel and I stay with her in the motel for maybe two or one and a half weeks. They charge in that time $40 per week. That's why I move—I can't stay there. It costs too much. And I move again to another motel, close to where I live now. I stay there a little longer.

At that time, I do a visa for Eseta's brother and his wife. When they all were ready to come, I go with Eseta and look for an apartment—so they can stay with us. We get an apartment with three bedrooms.

My first work was as a dishwasher at night. I took a job at the Hotel Lebanon, where I spent my first married night. I start at 10 P.M. and go to 6 in the morning washing dishes. I took a second job in December, working in the airport working for National Airlines. I empty or load the plane. So, I have two jobs in that time—night and day.

Eseta worked in sewing—all the supplies for hospital, like hospital gowns. At that time, the workers tried to belong to a union, and the company did not want the union. The company went under. I think maybe what happened is that the owners sold the company, and the new owners, they did not want a union.

Eseta, who had been listening, entered the conversation, picking up her own story:

Then I got a job in a laundry, but I saw there were holes in some of the linens that came to the laundry. So I asked them if they wanted me to sew it. And then I would take the work home. I saw that there was a linen store next door to the washing business. And I started taking things home to mend. In a little while they started giving me stuff—twenty-five cents per hole. I'd come home with a full basket and mend one after the other [tablecloths, sheets, and so on] at home, and then take it back to work.

Manu continued:

This was how we afforded our apartment and brought over Eseta's sister. Eseta made good money in that time. But when I go to work at two jobs, I started at $2 per hour. Both jobs were $2 per hour. But it was cheaper—everything—at that time. Like food and something.

A fish—a head of a fish—they throw away. Like a chicken bone or a beef bone, they did not sell it. But you know, the Tongan people they eat everything. That's why when I want something like that—I have to lie. "Can I have a bone like that for my cat or dog?" And they give me a box for free. I don't have to pay for that. And it will take care of my family for a week. And when I want a fish, I go to the bay. I wait for people who go fishing. When they finish, they clean up the fish and they throw away the head. That's when I ask, "Can I have the head of the fish that you throw away?" And they give

me however much I want! And a beautiful head! That's the way I build mine
and Eseta's family.

Nobody help me and Eseta. From that day I married until today, nobody
help and I did not need any help. I can take care of my family.

As they described it together, Eseta and Manu barely saw each other during their early life in California. Once the first baby (Sara) came, they had
to stagger their working hours so that neither of Manu's two jobs was at the
same time as Eseta's job. By the time Manu's second shift ended, it would
almost be time for Eseta to be at work.

Every weekday evening Eseta would leave the house with the baby and
a prepared meal for two. She would drive to the same place every night, a
mile marker beside the freeway between two exits. Manu would be waiting
there. And there, every day, is where they ate dinner together. Then Manu
would drive Eseta to work and take the baby home in the car.

It is not uncommon to see Tongan men caring for babies; indeed, most
boys take care of younger siblings. But in Tonga there are other people to
help—other children and adults, neighbors and kin—in close proximity. A
first baby in a strange land and among strangers was another story for Manu.
He laughed out loud as he remembered those early years:

> Eseta would be at work, and the baby would start to cry and cry. I didn't
> know what was wrong, and I think maybe this baby is sick, and I'd run with
> it to the emergency room of the hospital. Every time the baby start to cry too
> much, I go again to the emergency room with her. It was funny.

Bringing Over Relatives

Some twenty-five thousand Tongans are concentrated in small pockets
of the United States: in the San Francisco Bay area, on the outskirts of Los
Angeles, in Hawai'i (northern Oahu, Mau'i), and around Salt Lake City.

There is a reason for these concentrations. The first Tongans began migrating to the United States, as Seini and Simi did, in the 1960s. Like other
voluntary migrants to this country, their very first order of business was to
bring over family. Other Tongans migrated along the paths set up by their relatives—what is called chain migration—settling in the same communities.
When U.S. immigration laws changed in 1965 to allow Fifth Preference sponsorship, Tongans began sponsoring the visas of their brothers and sisters.

Eseta and Manu took full advantage of the new, more family-oriented
laws. Between 1970 and 1990, Manu and Eseta were instrumental in bring-

ing more than thirty members of their extended families to the United States. Typically, they would apply for a visa and sponsor the relatives by promising to be responsible for their debts. Tongan migrants took whatever jobs they could get, often in gardening, elder care, and janitorial or maid service work. When a job opened in their company, they brought in another Tongan to fill it.

New migrants typically stayed a year or two with Eseta and Manu, then found a place of their own. All of those who came helped to fund the trips of others who wanted to come. Nobody repaid the money to the person who had given it. Everyone saved money for the next arrival. That is how Eseta's siblings and their spouses and children came to America. Sister brought brother, brother brought sister, siblings brought their spouses' relatives, and together they brought over their mother, Sela.

When Sela came to America, it was with much prodding from Eseta and her other two children in America. Sela was widowed in 1965, but she still had many children and relatives in Tonga. Coming to America was not an easy decision. This is how Sela remembered her trip:

> I lived in Tonga. I was afraid to come and fly. It was my first flight, and I told my children I didn't want to fly. But Eseta said come, and I came by myself. My children in Tonga took me to the airport in a truck. But I was afraid to go in the little door of the airplane. I didn't want to climb up the stairs. I asked the white woman on the plane to help me climb the stairs and hold my arm. I don't know if she was a nurse or what. I was afraid of falling. Funny, no?
>
> I was surprised after I climbed the stairs and saw it was all full inside with people and things. The woman held me and told me to sit in one of the little chairs. She stayed near me and held me, though. And then the plane went up. I was afraid of falling from the sky. We changed planes. I don't know where. Maybe Hawai'i. And when we left the plane, that woman came back and held onto my arm, and we got off that plane and then we got on another plane. And then Eseta was at the airport to get me.

During the next ten years Sela was to see all her children come to the United States. Eseta and Manu provided the channel through which most of their siblings arrived, organizing the support and usually providing the residence. The most recent migrants arrived in 1990; and part of that group were still living with Eseta and Manu in 1995.

To bring over their relatives, Eseta and Manu had to become U.S. citizens. The decision to do so was not without financial risk and much thought, as Manu explained:

There is a law in Tonga that was proposed that if you go and be a citizen in the other country, then you lose everything. That's why—I talked many times with Eseta—and Eseta, too, she did not want to lose her house on the island. I wanted to be a citizen to bring over my family. But I did not want to lose my home.

One day I was at work and I was thinking, I love my family, and at that time I called to my lawyer and said, "I want an appointment." He said, "What do you want an appointment for?" I said, "I want to be a citizen." He said, "OK, anytime you want to come, just come." I call on Monday, and say, "OK, on Wednesday I'll be up at 4 P.M." And when I come back home and I talk to Eseta and I say, "I know you do not want us to lose our home, but in my mind now, it's better for me to lose my home"—I want my family to come. And Eseta says, "OK." I say, "I think maybe this is better. Lose the house, but help the family. That's what I've been thinking about." And she says, "OK, go do it." So Wednesday I go to file for my citizenship. When I get the citizenship, I hear that in Tonga they take a letter to the king [about losing your house if you become an absentee] to sign into law, and the King said no, he don't want to sign that. Because the people who are going out of Tonga, those people they help Tonga. In that time I talked to Eseta and said that day they take my home, I don't want to send one cent anymore to Tonga.

Most overseas Tongans—I would go so far as to say all overseas Tongans—still have relatives in Tonga. The relatives who don't migrate and the relatives who do maintain strong connections on a number of levels. Within families, the relationship takes the form of remittances—both cash and manufactured goods such as clothing, furniture, and appliances—sent from the United States to Tonga.

Eseta sends things to her eldest sister, still resident in Tonga, and occasionally gives money to other relatives in need of school fees for their children's education. Malia, Eseta's sister who more recently migrated, still has three children in Tonga. She regularly sends clothing for her grandchildren, and has made numerous purchases—a sofa, a wooden cabinet, flooring, a television set—for her children. She pays for the contributions that her children will make to the church and the seminary fees of her youngest daughter's husband.

Besides supporting individuals, Tongans overseas support Tonga; they send money for various projects and public occasions—usually, but not always, at the village level. A fund drive petitioning overseas Tongans in 1985 built the outdoor auditorium for the Catholic high school that sits on 'Olunga's village property. Although the school is regional and church-affiliated, as are most high schools in Tonga, there is a local loyalty that draws the contributions of overseas migrants originally from the village.

In 1992 the Water Board of 'Olunga wrote to ex-villagers in the United States asking for help with the village water system. Piped water is provided through a village-owned pump that draws water from an aquifer into a community tower. Each household pays a flat monthly bill (in 1984 it was only $1 per month), but it does not come close to covering the cost of providing water to the village twenty-four hours a day. What happens is that a pipe ruptures, or the pump breaks down, and there is no bank reserve from past revenues to get it fixed. It is then that the village will appeal to former residents overseas, many with homes or land in the village. Villagers in the San Francisco area sent $5,000 to purchase a new pump.

The flow of resources that go from Tongan-Americans to their relatives in Tonga remained enormous in the 1990s. Overseas Tongans might repair the local island church, or contribute to the centennial celebration of their high school, or pay for the school fees of a relative who has passed her exams for the next grade level.

As you will see in the next section, support is a two-way street. Tongan island relatives tend the village lands and houses of migrants.[2] Tongan villagers send Tongan kava and wealth items to their U.S. family members and often receive the hundreds of U.S.-born children sent back home. "Returned" children may be those born out of wedlock—a much greater problem in the United States than in Tonga—who are sent to a grandparent or aunt or uncle for care. Others have discipline problems and so are being purposely sent to a stricter community and school environment.

A Tongan-American Household in the 1990s

Eseta and Manu's household is a window through which you can look at Tongan life in the United States in the 1990s. As such, you must see their household in context. An outsider might describe them as an ambitious working-class couple in a multiethnic California suburb, struggling to gain a foothold in the middle class. Theirs is not the story of Mormon Tongans who were segregated into predominantly Tongan "wards" in Utah, a state that is 93 percent white. Nor is it the story of Tongans in poor urban Los Angeles and Salt Lake City, where Polynesian gangs have already made their first appearance.

In 1995 Eseta and Manu owned their own home in a modest neighborhood in the expensive Bay area suburbs. Their household income was close to the steep median income of San Mateo, though it took four contributing wage earners to accomplish this. Compared to other Tongan migrants in

America, Eseta and Manu have done well, owing in part to their personal energy, hard work, and talent, and in part to the timing of their migration.

Generally speaking, Tongans who migrated earliest to the United States have the most to show materially. U.S. Census data for 1990 showed, for instance, that only 29 percent of Tongans who had migrated after 1980 owned their own homes. Of the Tongans who migrated between 1965 and 1979, however, 40 percent owned homes, and of those who migrated before 1965, 66.6 percent owned their own homes.[3] The same was true of income. Those migrating before 1965 had a 71 percent higher per capita income than those who migrated after 1980.[4]

Still, the majority of Tongans in the United States migrated after 1980, and many Tongans in 1990 were on the brink of poverty. Twenty-one percent of Tongan families (double the national average and three times that of white Americans) were poor; 58.5 percent of all Tongans lived within 200 percent of the poverty level.[5]

♔ Like most American households, Eseta and Manu's household consisted of a number of individuals, each engaged in very different daily routines. What distinguished their household, as it did many other migrant households, was that it contained more people at more varied life stages. The median size of a household in San Mateo was almost three people.[6] In Eseta and Manu's household there were seven people from age seven to eighty-two. They lived with their daughters, Sara and Alyssa; with Eseta's mother, Sela; and with Eseta's sister Malia and her grandchild Lio Jr.

Their household was not atypical for Tongan-Americans. More than one-quarter of all Tongan households in California had seven or more people (with an average of between five and six), and the majority had two or more wage earners.[7] To allow the lives of everyone to work out required a high degree of mutual coordination within and among households.

Two-thirds of the working population of San Mateo were in managerial, professional, and sales positions.[8] Few Tongans occupied similar positions. Only 8.5 percent of Tongans in the United States worked at managerial or professional jobs. One-third were laborers and farm workers; another quarter were in service and support occupations.[9] Relatively few Tongans (less than 12 percent) were in business for themselves.

In 1994 Eseta, who had learned computer skills, worked as a data entry clerk in a steady municipal government job. For extra money, and to allow a Tongan friend a day off, Eseta also provided home care one night a week to an elderly woman. Manu had a day job as a janitor, from which he returned at 5 P.M.

Their elder daughter, Sara, was then in community college working toward an associate degree in marketing; she held a part-time job in a department store. Alyssa, who planned on attending college as well, was still in
high school. Manu and Eseta, like many Tongan parents, were keenly interested in the education and advancement of their children. Unlike most
Tongans in the United States, however, both their children would graduate
from college. Of Tongans living in the United States over twenty-five years
of age, only 6 percent have earned bachelor's degrees or better, and another 5
percent have completed two-year associate or technical degrees.[10] Because
of large school loans, side jobs, and parental insistence, Sara and Alyssa
would avoid the path taken by one-third of all Tongan youth, who begin
college but drop out to work before completing their degree. Both would
earn their bachelors' degrees from a private Catholic college near home.

Eseta's younger sister Malia, whom you will meet again in the next chapter, also lived in the house every Friday and Saturday. She worked at a convalescent home a half-hour away, where she would spend the week, returning
every weekend to live with Eseta's family. Malia's grandson Lio Jr. stayed at Eseta's and attended the local elementary school during the day. Arrangements
were made for someone to be at home when the boy returned from school.

Sela, Eseta's eight-four-year-old mother, remained in the house during the
day. She knitted and sewed, wrote letters home to Tonga, read the Bible,
watched TV, and went for neighborhood walks. Some days Sela stayed there
alone, providing company for Lio when he returned from school. "Sometimes, if she's not well," Malia explained, "she goes to our eldest sister's house
for a week, or one of her girls comes here. She goes around from house to
house like that." Eseta and Malia's eldest sister, Neti, lived nearby. Besides
looking after Sela if she was ill, Neti sometimes filled in for Malia on her days
off or on vacation. The family had two cars, and with the number of household members and the level of activity, it required careful coordination to get
everyone where he or she was going and home again at the appropriate time.

Being Tongan-American

In most ways, Eseta and Manu's house in the San Francisco suburbs was
very much like any other nicely kept home in the neighborhood. Outside,
a short white picket fence enclosed a tiny lawn, where flowers had been
carefully planted. Inside, the house bore little resemblance to the stark, mat-
covered interiors of Tongan homes in the 1980s, where the one chair was
reserved for important guests. This was clearly an American home, with its

couches and coffee table, easy chairs, dining room table, and a piano for their daughters to practice their music lessons. The teenagers' rooms in the house were filled with wall posters and prom pictures and personal photos.

There were, however, faint signs of another cultural reality. To accommodate the many relatives who have stayed for months, even years, at a time, Eseta and Manu have had to transform the physical arrangement of the house and the use of its space. The garage had been converted to a bedroom and laundry area that housed a second refrigerator as well. Extra walls partitioned one room into two, creating a spare bedroom. The back porch had been enclosed to become an additional living area, functioning as storage or sleeping space for more people. Malia, with three daughters still in Tonga, had stacked several boxes of clothes against the porch wall—marked "boys," "girls," "infant"—for eventual shipping to Tonga.

To most Americans it would seem curious that the doorway between the kitchen and the dining room—the one that the builder had obviously created for convenience—was closed off. The dining room table, large enough to seat twelve, extended from wall to wall, past the door opening. To bring food from the kitchen to the eating area, one needed to exit the kitchen from the opposite end, walk down a hall, and turn right into the dining room.

To a Tongan, though, this arrangement is familiar. Cooking is low in status, while eating is high, and the two must be properly separated. Typically in Tonga, food preparation and cooking are confined to a separate structure, outside the living space. Even when the kitchen is inside the "house," as it often is in the 1990s, efforts are made to distance the kitchen from the living and even eating areas.

Earlier in the century, Tongans displayed their wealth—bark cloth and pandanus mats—on the rafters of their thatched homes. In contemporary Tonga, this wealth doubles as a mattress, or if the family has a store-bought bed, it is laid flat between the bed frame and the mattress. In Eseta's California house, there was a door that opened into an inner room, a space that might be used as a laundry and ironing area. This room, though, served as a wealth storage room, a place where piles of bark cloth and mats and other items of Tongan wealth could be kept. The room was testimony to the continuing celebration in the United States of events that require an outlay of pandanus mats and bark cloth, and of the importance of Tongan community and tradition in everyday life.

The aspects of Tongan culture evident in Eseta and Manu's home—the importance of extended family, the persistence of customary sensibilities, the salience of traditional values and the presence of community—were evident elsewhere in Tongan social life. The Tongan community in California, however, was not readily apparent. There certainly were other Tongans in the general vicinity, but the northern California suburbs, where prices are prohibitive and neighborhoods are already established, are not easily turned into a Tongan enclave. For the most part, a Tongan-American's neighbor or schoolmate or fellow worker was not another Tongan.

Eseta and Manu's immediate neighborhood was racially and ethnically mixed. Their zip code area, like the entire state, was 30 percent nonwhite, mostly Filipino, Japanese, Chinese, and African-American, and 20 percent foreign-born.[11] The schools that Tongan children attended were similarly mixed; often only a small percentage of Tongans attended school together. A neighbor on one side of Eseta and Manu's house was Euro-American, replacing an Iranian immigrant family which had left. El Salvadorans lived on the other side, and their boy was a close friend of Lio Jr's. Eseta bought fruit from the "Chinese ladies"; Malia worked for an eastern European immigrant; Mexican vendors sold migrants their Tongan food; "friends" mentioned at work included Americans of European, Filipino, Central American, and Japanese descent.

The people who turned up casually in family narratives of daily life reflected the ethnic mixture of the region, but it was rare that a non-Tongan walked into their home. Despite being geographically scattered, Tongan-Americans—including many native to this country—generally socialized with other Tongans. As one Tongan-American observed:

> There are people from all over Tonga here: Tongatapu, Vava'u, Ha'apai. There is a mix of people from different places in Tonga. It's good, the mix. Tongans get married to Tongans from other places. Tongan boys like to mix with Tongan girls from other places. Very few Tongans marry *palangis* [Caucasians or Euro-Americans]. Like *palangis*, they want to marry other *palangis*. The kids hang out with their friends. If their friends are *palangi*, then they invite them. But most kids have Tongan friends.

The "kids" that the speaker referred to sometimes objected to this characterization. Those of Alyssa's girlfriends who were not relatives included an African-American and a Puerto Rican woman; Sara's closest friends were Euro-American. But it was still the case that, especially as the girls got older, the circle of people with whom they spent their social time became more Tongan. Alyssa explained that she had simply had "more in common" with Tongans since high school—such as belonging to the same church youth group. Sara was often so busy between work and family obligations that she had little time for her friends. She dated both Tongan and Euro-American boys, but the pressures from her own family to marry a Tongan and the "coolness" she occasionally encountered from the parents of her white boyfriends made doing so an act of will and courage. As a result, even among the first American-born generation, a preponderance of time was spent with other Tongans.

On our trips throughout various California neighborhoods, Tongans could point out to me where other Tongans (and half-Tongans) lived. Sara and Alyssa drove me to an exclusive Bay area neighborhood where rental property commanded $10,000 per month in 1996. They pointed out the gated property leased by the government of Tonga for the royal princess, where sometimes Tongans could be seen sweeping the driveway, wearing the traditional mats of respect around their waists. There was, in northern California, a Tongan world within a world.

Church activity was one center of Tongan life. Most Tongans attended Sunday services in the church of their choice, typically Protestant (Wesleyan), Mormon, or Catholic. Where the population of Tongans in a church was large, there were designated services attended primarily by Tongans. The Catholic Church has a Tongan service once per month, rotating among four communities which attended Mass together on that day. When I went to this joint service in 1996, the Tongan-American Mass—which had four Tongan choirs and was conducted in the Tongan language—followed the Mexican-American Mass. In all churches, though, there were special events, clergy visits, speakers, and fund-raisers that drew Tongans alone. More than a thousand Tongans, many in traditional garb, attended the service and sermon given by a bishop from Tonga. There were Tongan choirs, Tongan church youth groups, and Tongan women's groups that functioned very much as these same groups did in Tonga.

There were also church-associated "Tongan" dances. For example, a women's church group might sponsor a dance at a hotel and invite the Tongan youth groups to attend. The proceeds of the dance would go to supporting a Tongan choir group. Although tickets are distributed through the auspices of the church to the membership at large, it is overwhelmingly Tongans who buy the tickets. Hundreds of Tongans show up for the dances, and Tongans who migrated from different villages and islands get to meet one another and socialize. As a recent migrant observed with surprise, "The place was filled with Tongans. . . . There were very few palangis. People came in American clothes, but it's not that different from Tonga."

While every Sunday involves church activities with other Tongans, almost every Saturday is a Tongan social event, the preferred time to celebrate marriages and birthdays or to hold a Tongan dance. There is no dearth of traditional ceremonies—mostly Tongan life-cycle events—in the United

States. As most Tongan-Americans will tell you, there are probably more "traditional" Tongan events in America per capita than in Tonga, and a greater display of traditional wealth in any one of them. Tongan-Americans regularly boast about the outlay of food and traditional wealth that occurs in the United States as opposed to Tonga: "They do lots more here. Like a king does in Tonga. A commoner funeral in the U.S. will be like a king in Tonga," one man explains.

Although the speaker exaggerates, there is no doubt that Tongan tradition in the United States is more elaborate and embellished than parallel commoner events in Tonga. Tongan-Americans use their U.S. wealth to signal their generosity and status in a Tongan sense. They hold elaborate feasts, they invite many people, they display and give many items of traditional wealth. As some Tongans point out, events can take on a competitive flair, with different families attempting to outdo others. The result is that commoner wedding in the United States can come to resemble a chiefly wedding in Tonga in terms of the numbers in attendance, the lavishness of the food, and the display of mats and tapa cloth.

In Tonga, first birthdays and twenty-first birthdays (for women) are occasions for special celebration. In the United States, the number of birthday events has proliferated. Tongan-Americans hold a big celebration for a girl's sixteenth birthday, following the U.S. "sweet sixteen" custom. As one woman complains, "Older women now do birthday parties. Women who are fifty and sixty. I think it's silly! There are celebrations all the time."

Throughout the week there are other Tongan social events. Older Tongan men typically form kava-drinking clubs, where they discuss service projects and political issues. Manu's kava club met on Friday. It was this group that sent $5,000 to 'Olunga to buy a new water pump. Next year the club will send three of its members to Tonga to see what the villagers have done with the money. The Water Board sent back kava root for the club.

There was choir practice on Tuesdays, youth group meeting on Fridays, and formal get-togethers for the frequent visits of Tongan clergy and nobility. In the summer of 1996, when I was in San Mateo, Tongans were busily preparing for the visit of the King of Tonga to the area. It was the talk of the weekend, even of the year—what each church would do; who would perform at the dances; what the relatives, and relatives of relatives, of the royal family were preparing. The King would see, people said, a turnout and a display of goods that was beyond all he had seen before. There is substantial money expended at these events, including donations to the clergy and monetary gifts to the nobility. As Manu put it: "We do everything here the same as in the islands. Only here, it's more and it's better."

In addition to time and cash, most Tongan events involve the appropriate disposition of traditional Tongan wealth. The mats and tapa cloth necessary for staging and attending Tongan events are made only in Tonga, and Tongan-Americans must acquire new wealth to meet their obligations in the United States. Sometimes island relatives send traditional wealth, just as Tongan-Americans send remittances. But increasingly, Americans buy their wealth. In addition to shipping costs, purchasing a full tapa cloth at a Tongan market can run as high as $800. In the lavish world of Tongan-American giving, an appropriate display at a single birthday party can involve ten mats and two tapa cloths, an expense running into the thousands of dollars.

To get their wealth, Tongan-American women also conduct exchanges with Tongan islanders. A California group that needs woven mats might arrange an exchange with a group of Tongan islanders who want household furniture, appliances, or cash. One or two women from the United States, or relatives of group members resident in Tonga, might make the trip to the village with which the overseas group will exchange. Eseta conducted such exchanges in 1992 and then again in 1994, spending $2,500 plus a stove and other items between the two exchanges for a dozen or so woven mats. An active network of wealth exchange now exists between the Tongan islands and Tongan communities in the United States, New Zealand, and Australia designed to supply overseas Tongans with the traditional wealth necessary to fulfill the obligations they incur.[12]

If one converted all the time, food, and traditional wealth necessary for U.S. funerals, weddings, birthdays, dances, and fund-raisers into U.S. currency, the outlay would be massive—easily thousands of dollars for every large occasion and constant small outlays for every dance, fund-raiser, and kava club meeting.

Eseta's sister Malia, a new migrant, talked about her own obligations since coming to the United States:

My day off, I go to a Tongan event almost every single Saturday. There are very few Saturdays when something isn't going on. Sometimes, I say to myself, "Why do you have a day off? You just waste what you earned by working all week!" If I stayed and worked, I wouldn't spend all that money on the celebrations. Because there'll be a tau'olunga [dance] at the event and I'll have to go and put money on the dancer. You lose a lot on your day off!

Some weeks, they'll do a funeral and I'll go to L.A. because the family is busy working and I'm free on Saturday so they tell me to fly to the funeral and represent the family. So I'll do that and come home too late to get to Sunday work on time. Some other week, they'll do a funeral in Seattle. Then I'll fly there. And then I'll give up a day of work again and come back late. I take three days off in a week if there's a funeral. If it's another kind of event, then, no. I only miss work for funerals. You *must* do Tongan things. Even if it means not having a day off some weeks so I can go to the funeral other weeks.

Why do this? a fifth-generation American might ask. The outlay is the other side of the help and support that a Tongan-American can draw on in a country of relative strangers. Who would a Tongan-American turn to if he needed a place to stay, a job, money for a medical bill, or a contribution for a daughter's wedding? The answer: other Tongans, including relatives, people from the same village in the old country, or Tongans living nearby in the United States. Many Tongans get their first job through another Tongan, not necessarily a direct relative. Tongans help one another. Even a total stranger, if he or she were Tongan, might buy your tapa cloth to fund your airplane ticket home to the islands.

Mutual aid, a function of being and acting Tongan, supports people's lives and well-being in the United States. One of the more interesting mutual aid arrangements among Tongan-Americans is a version of the rotating credit associations that have been active in Tonga throughout this century. In the village, the most aggressive savers would contribute $5 every two weeks. In one year the twenty-five women members would receive the biweekly pot of $125 one time each, their turn chosen by lottery. For a woman who could earn perhaps $2 per day at a village corner store, $125 was a sizable fund of cash to have in her control for household purposes.

The twenty-six participants in the Tongan women's rotating credit association in California put in $250 every two weeks. They are not all relatives or neighbors or even close friends. As in Tonga, a lottery determines the order of receipt of the pot. The day that I attended, Malia's daughter Palu received the pot. It was $6,500, enough to buy the used car she wanted. As the money recipient for the day, Palu prepared food for the other participants—individual meals apportioned in twenty-six Styrofoam take-out containers. After the meal, one woman conducted a raffle ($1 per ticket) for a large family-size pack of ramen noodles and other snacks. Another woman passed an envelope of money to a third woman. It was a funeral donation collected from the group meant to help the woman with the expenses surrounding the death of a close relative. These women did not all know one another in Tonga, but in the United States they are part of a mutual help network.

The deep involvement of Tongan-Americans with one another in the United States and even with Tongans half a world away, contrasts with the polite distance that many Tongan-born migrants keep from members and institutions of the larger dominant U.S. society. Tongan-Americans are very cordial with other U.S. residents. Most Americans, they would say, are fine as neighbors, yet many Tongans would prefer that their children not marry a non-Tongan.

The boundaries are clear as Manu speaks about his views on marriage:

> I already explained to my daughters two things. The first thing is to marry with your own people. Don't marry with the other people. The second is the church. It is right for them to marry Catholic.

Do you care if he's Tongan-American or a Tongan from the islands?

No, any Tongan. Because it's easy. Easy for family to stay with same people, easy with the same language—I understand everything, and his family would also. But if a marriage takes place with another kind of people, they can't talk good with the family, they can't understand what language we use.

Although Manu frames his preference for Tongan marriages in terms of language and communication, his feelings may well run deeper than this. The Tongan-American boy whom his elder daughter was seeing socially, with Manu's approval, did not speak Tongan, and he was not Catholic. The issues seem to be about other things as well. A Tongan boy will understand why his daughters should keep in close contact with their parents, why his daughters should take care of their parents in their old age, why they should bring up "Tongan" grandchildren.

"I can tell you this," Manu said to me in a subsequent conversation when his daughters were both present. "If you marry *muli* [a foreigner or outsider], you will be divorced. And if you do not divorce, then you will end up separating from your family."

Manu cited a number of stories about tragic marriages with non-Tongans that had occurred throughout the extended family: one nephew who married a *palangi* woman and has no contact with the family; a niece who married a black man, and everything in their house was broken; the most successful boy in a branch of the family who lived with a *palangi* partner in San Francisco and died of complications from AIDS; another sister's son who married a *palangi* woman who left and divorced him. These unhappy endings are more the rule than the exception, according to Manu.

His own children, who rolled their eyes in the background as he proceeded with his monologue, cited numerous counterexamples within the family, but the successful cases of Tongan marriages to both Euro- and

African-American spouses did not change Manu's overall impression. Manu's feelings were typical of his generation.[13]

The circumstances surrounding Manu's retirement from his job offer a sense of the cordial distance—the estrangement, really—from the larger culture with which his life in the United States is entwined. Manu worked as a day janitor in a medium-sized corporation for eleven years. When I visited Manu's home in 1993, he had just had his annual company physical, and doctor's report indicated that he should stop working. Take sick leave until the end of the month, they told him, and then retire. It was something about his breath, he said. Manu had stopped going to work, as the company had recommended.

"What is it?" I asked. He did not remember the name of the sickness, just that he should stop working now.

"Do you want to know what illness you have?" I asked him.

"Yes," he said. "You find out; I'm not sure what that doctor told me."

I called his company personnel office. "Are you a relative?" they asked nervously.

"No, I'm a family friend. He doesn't know what illness he has that is causing him to retire."

"We cannot release any information to you—"

"Hold on," I interrupted, realizing that this conversation would go nowhere, "I'm putting Mr. ——— on the phone."

"I don't know what is my sickness," he said into the phone. The personnel office finally referred us to the doctor who made the diagnosis. Several phone calls and explanations later, a kindly nurse retrieved Manu's records and told me, "Mr. ——— has emphysema. We have recommended that he stop working now."

I was in the house when Manu received a follow-up call from work. "Thank you," I heard him say, "but please just forget it." There was more talk at the other end. "That's very nice, but please don't mind about that." As he spoke, he had a social smile on his face, and an embarrassed expression slowly turned flustered as the conversation continued. Office workers at the building where Manu had been a janitor for more than a decade had called him. Wouldn't he come in for a last day so they could give him a cake and a little party? They'd already planned it. Manu declined a second time, anxious now to get off the phone.

Manu never walked into that building again. The following year, in January, Manu requested a lump-sum payment of his pension money, which went toward building his new house in Tonga.

4

One Family's Story

〰 The story of the family's migration begins in about 1925 with Sela, whom you met in the last chapter when she was in her eighties. Here she is sixteen, the eldest daughter in a family of nine children, the most prestigious but most controlled position in the household. As a teenager, Sela would spend her evenings with other young unmarried women, covering their bodies in sweetly perfumed coconut oil and laughing and talking. Like many eldest daughters, who become symbols of their family's status, Sela had never learned to cook or sew her clothes or do other Tongan work. It was all done for her. Her special status was, perhaps, what led to the events of her sixteenth year: Sela's betrothal to an older man who would care for her well, as her family had done. Many years later Sela described this time:

> When I was sixteen, I was still little. A boy came—a friend of mine—and talked to my father and said he wanted me, to take care of me. My father said to me, "Do you like this man?" You know, the man was much older than me. But I said yes. My father wanted me to have someone I could rely on, trust. This man was skilled, mature. He was forty-something or maybe fifty. People said to me, "He is old and you are still young." But my father said to me, "Do what you want. If you want to marry him then do, or if not, don't, but he is *fakapotopoto* [sensible, wise, shrewd]. He works. There are many women who want him. He came with a pig." He said he loved me a lot. And I told my relatives I would marry him.
>
> I remember a time when a car came. There were not many cars then. And a car came for us, and we went to town. And there were tapa cloths and mats to cover the car. And we rode like that into town, with the car covered. . . . He took me to his house. The area was beautiful. I went visiting, went to church. I stayed there and was content.

Sela had twelve children by Aisake. And Aisake proved to be, as her own father had predicted, a devoted husband and skilled, forward-looking father. Aisake grew Tongan tobacco for sale, and put all of his sons and his daughters through school. He also sold bananas and plaintains to local stores, and for extra cash he dried the inner kernel of the coconut for copra. As one daughter recounted, "My father tried to get us all educated. My father was the only one in his family that had every one of his children go to school."

It was Aisake and Sela's third child, Seini, who was the first in the extended family to migrate. By 1980, Sela and all her children except two, each now with children of their own, were living in the United States. Only Sela's second daughter, Finau, and her seventh child, Malia, remained in Tonga. What follows is Malia's story, and that of her family.

꩜ Malia had been very close to her elder sister, Seini, the nurse who began the story of migration in chapter 3. Seini had been frail since childhood. When she gave birth to her first child in 1958, she became quite ill and was hospitalized. Malia literally moved into the hospital—an informal privilege for a nurse's sister—and looked after Seini and her baby during her sister's convalescence. Malia lived in the hospital for two full months. When Seini gave birth again the following year, she became ill once more. Seini and her husband went to the hospital, and Malia took the newborn home with her to the village for five months. It was quite a time, Malia recalled: "I had the baby all day, and I made kava for the men all night."[1]

It was during Seini's first hospital stay that Malia met Atu. Atu was studying at the Teacher's College. He had broken his hand during a rugby game and came to the hospital. "There's a boy from 'Olunga in the hospital," people said to Malia. "You should go see him." Although Malia didn't really know the boy well, she visited him. They were married two years later.

Malia's mother was not happy about the marriage. When Atu asked Malia's father for her hand in marriage, Aisake asked Malia, "Do you want to marry this man?" And when Malia said yes, a loud cry went up from Sela.

"She didn't want me to marry outside of my church," Malia told me. In Tongan style, Sela took her protest to the street. "I will go and die," Sela said, and she ran outside and walked up and down the village paths crying aloud.

Malia's father attempted a compromise. Aisake knew that Atu was scheduled to leave for a northern Tongan island to take his first teaching post. He told Atu, "You go to this island and teach for a year. Then you come back and get married."

Atu knew this was a stalling tactic. If he did so, he might come back to find Malia married. Atu and Malia eloped to town with conspiring relatives. The noble family of the village, sympathetic to the marriage, helped smooth the way by bringing the couple home to the village and visiting Malia's mother to try to reconcile her to the match. Two days after they were married, Atu and Malia left on a boat for the remote island of Niuatoputapu.

Malia described these days as the happiest in her life. The outer islanders were wonderful to her and Atu. Malia remembered that almost every night someone brought them fish or cooked for them. She and Atu had much time together in these sweet and relaxed days early in their marriage, when few responsibilities bear on a young couple. Within a year, Malia became pregnant, and when she was almost ready to deliver, they returned to Atu's parents' house to have the baby. It was her sister Eseta who came to help Malia after she delivered the baby. Eseta worked during the day as a teacher. She brought home milk and food for Malia's household, and helped with the baby when she returned from work.

It was at about this time that Seini, her husband, and their two children got their papers to go to America. Was the family upset to see Seini leave the country? I asked Malia. "Yes, they were," she answered. "My family and Seini's husband's family, we cried a lot." But, she added, "We were happy too. Seini and Simi were free to do what they wanted and to develop themselves. We were happy to get help from overseas," Malia explained, "but mostly, they could help to bring other people over."

By the time Seini wrote to her sister Eseta to come to America, Malia and Atu were already making their life in 'Olunga. They lived there with Atu's parents, whom Malia loved and cared for until their deaths. By 1968, when Eseta left for America, Malia was already pregnant with her fifth child.

Malia and Atu had nine children together. Three of them died before the age of five. When I met Malia and Atu in Tonga in 1981, they lived with their four girls and two boys. Atu's siblings and their children lived nearby. Malia was one of only two of her twelve siblings who still remained in Tonga.

Eastward Bound

Malia and Atu had thought enough about migration to put in a visa application in 1981. I was already living in Tonga—was in fact their next-door neighbor—and they asked me to fill out the forms. Atu was able to read and write in English, but I was an American, and the forms were American. It seemed advisable to everyone in the family that I be the one to fill them out.

When I initially asked why they wanted to migrate, their reasons for leaving sounded neither singular nor immediate, and were different each time they discussed the matter: opportunities for the kids to go to school, maybe a well-paying job, or a chance for Malia to be with her mother. They never seemed to talk much about migrating or to plan for it. The move always sounded temporary—a place to go for a few years before returning home—and something in the distant future, when the visa would one day come through. In the meantime, the family focused on their life in Tonga. In 1982 Malia joined a women's development group; they earned money to buy materials for each member's new kitchen, which the group built in turn. Malia's new bamboo kitchen had an open-fire cooking area and a family-sized table with benches. In 1986 Atu's pension and their son Lio's salary were enough to procure a bank loan for $5,000, a formidable amount by Tongan standards, to renovate their house.

Atu had started to build the new house in the 1970s while they lived in a thatched home. He constructed a new wooden and cement block house with a cement floor. The thatched kitchen and the bathhouse and outhouse remained. The new house had windows with glass louvers. Inside, wallboard had been erected, dividing the house into rooms and separating the living and entertaining area from the sleeping area. But Atu was unable to finish the house because the children were then all in school, and their school fees had to be paid. This was the priority.

More than ten years later, when school expenses had abated, Atu and Malia were finally ready to finish their house. They repainted it, built a front sitting porch, and refurbished the old cement blocks. They replaced old wallboard, framed the windows, and put up new walls, separating an indoor kitchen (for food preparation only) from a living room, and creating three small bedrooms with doors. Their greatest pride was the plumbing. Piped water was run into the house, and there was a kitchen sink, an indoor bathroom (where a sink and shower were installed), and a separate area with a flush toilet.

꒘ There is no American embassy in Tonga, so in order to apply for a U.S. visa, you must submit papers to Fiji. There your name goes on a list of those who want a permanent visa to the United States, based on your country of origin and the category of relative who will sponsor you. When your name finally gets to the top of the list, you are notified. It took nine years for the family's U.S. visa to come through.

The visa application had been entered for the whole family, but by the time they received word nine years later that they would be allowed to migrate, the family situation had changed. Two of Malia's children were over twenty-one and could no longer be included on the family's visa. Besides, the eldest son, who often displayed aberrant behavior, had stayed in Australia after his visa had expired and had been deported.[2] He could not get another visa and so would have to stay in Tonga and look after the house.

The eldest daughter, Finau, had been an excellent student throughout her school career. She completed the highest grade .evel in the Tongan school system with honors, and went on to receive her teaching certification. She, too, was over twenty-one now, but she also had a strong commitment to her teaching career in Tonga. By 1990 she had completed her certification and was a salaried teacher in her first placement on another Tongan island. Finau would not leave for America with the family, opting to stay and teach.

Vei, the next-eldest girl, probably would have left for America too if it hadn't been for the tragic death of Lio. Lio was the sweet and steady stalwart of the family. At the time of his death, he was working six days a week in town in order to help pay off the bank loan for the family's house. When he came home at night, he would sit quietly in the corner of the family room, as brothers are supposed to do. Lio and his elder brother officially lived in the kitchen—the family's version of the separate house where older boys are supposed to sleep. But often, Lio would fall asleep in the main house, on the family room floor. The girls did not mind because Lio, as they often described him, was kind and respectful. From time to time, when Lio came home after drinking beer or home brew with his friends, no one judged him harshly. He deserved his playtime. He worked hard for his family every day but Sunday. He was always responsible, and even when he occasionally got drunk on his one day off, he was never mean or loud or disrespectful.

On Sundays there was church in the morning, after which the men of the family prepared the best food the family could muster in an underground stone-pit oven (*umu*). Everyone ate until they were stuffed. The family sent plates of food to other households and received plates of food delivered by a neighbor or relative's child. Then everyone slept or wandered at leisure, to visit and relax. One Sunday, right after the big midday meal, Lio and his friends went to the sea for a swim. They drank beer along the way and were probably inebriated by the time they got to the water.

His friends told the family that Lio was there one instant and gone the next. They were all swimming together, and the sea was not rough. All of a sudden, one young man said, they looked around and he was not there. He had slipped beneath the surface of the water and quietly drowned.

Lio had fathered a son by a woman in the village. Although the couple had not married, both sides of the child's family maintained their obligations to the baby and their relationships to each other as in-laws, as is the Tongan custom. When Lio died, his family asked to raise Lio's son. The baby came to live with Atu and Malia and his father's brother and sisters. So it was Lio Jr., renamed after his father, who came to America and Vei who stayed and worked in Tonga as, it would turn out, the lone member of her household.

Latu, Vei's younger sister, would never come to the United States, although the family had always thought she would. Even today Latu and her husband, Feleti, giggle with embarrassment when they talk about the time of the migration because it was also the time of their marriage. Malia had tried to stop it. She recalled:

The boy asked me for permission to marry Latu. He talked to me first and then to Atu. Atu asked Latu, "What do you want?" And she answered, "I'll do what you want." And Atu said, "Fine, I'll do what I want." He first thanked the boy for coming to him and wanting to marry Latu. Then he said, "I want Latu to come to America and finish her school before marrying. And when she gets her green card, we'll come back and you can marry. Then, with her green card you can both come to the States if you like." And Latu and the boy said OK. "He yessed me, but in his heart, the answer was no." The boy left, then he came back and talked with Latu. Perhaps they were talking about eloping. Because right after, they snuck into town and got married.

"But isn't that just what you did, Malia?" I asked her later. "No," she laughed, "not exactly the same. If I could have gone to America, I would have gone." She continued, "So afterwards I said to Latu, 'OK, you marry and you'll live here. Look at your passport and your visa and your ticket.'" She paused dramatically in the telling. "Leave all of them. I will go to America. You," she repeated with uncharacteristic sarcasm, "will go to *Podunk*."[3]

On August 23, 1990, four members of the family—Atu, Malia, their daughter Palu, and Lio Jr., the two-year-old child of their drowned son— left for America. Their remaining son and two of their daughters stayed in the family house, while their eldest daughter, Finau, lived by herself as a

teacher on another island. Within three weeks of the family's departure for
the United States, their last living son, firstborn of Malia and Atu, hanged
himself in the village, leaving a note saying that he wanted to be closer to
God. His letter was so beautiful and eloquent that it was printed in the Tongan national newspaper.

Malia and Atu dealt with the tragedy among relatives they had not seen
in more than twenty years. Having just spent all their resources to get to the
United States, they had no money left to return for the funeral. Finau, aid-
ed by the extended family in Tonga, carried out the ten-day funeral in the
village, taking out a loan against her teacher's salary so she could pay for the
mats and tapa cloth that would be needed for a proper ceremony.

In the United States, Malia and Atu and Palu and Lio Jr. did as many of
their relatives had done before. They moved into the home of Malia's sister
and her husband, Eseta and Manu, where Malia's mother also lived. In 1990
this was considered the best house in the entire extended family. The house
and its inhabitants had been shuffled around to accommodate the four new
family members. Atu and Malia moved into the converted garage. Palu slept
with Grandma, then eventually moved into Malia's room with her. The back
porch became an extra storage area.

Atu chuckled as he described his first days in the United States:

We came from the airport, and it was all so busy. There were buildings and
noises on the street and cars moving, but then when I looked I could see no
people. Where are the people? I thought it was funny—the people were all
inside things.

Palu remembered too:

I was looking at these vehicles everywhere and thinking this is like the people walking around in Nuku'alofa.

Malia's first reaction to America was about her kin:

I was very very happy to be able to see my mother and my family. When I
saw my mother, I cried lots. My mother cried too. It was our tears of joy.

For Palu, the most startling thing about America was the different social
customs she immediately encountered.

On the first Sunday, I went to church and I was surprised—there was a lot of Tongans but it was not like in Tonga on Sunday, where the shops all closed down and there is no noise. We went driving and I saw all those people around the street and the stores and everything. It's all the same *every* day. And we went to a church meeting, and we decided that we're going to have some entertainment for one of the nuns coming from Tonga and it was on a Sunday and we were all supposed to dance, but I didn't dance because I thought this is weird, dancing on Sunday. I'm not going to do that. But then time goes on and I get used to it.

There's another thing I get used to. In the month after I came, it was my twenty-first birthday. Sara, my American cousin, gave me an outfit. It was a skirt, but not a skirt like in Tonga. The skirt came up to here [Palu cringed as she pointed to a spot on her thigh midway between her knee and hip]. And I couldn't even wear it. I just put it on so Sara could take a picture, and after I take it off and give it back to her and I told her, "I can't wear it." But now I'm used to it, and I like it. I like it a lot.

Little Lio took to TV like a fish to water. He watched it incessantly, with the result that he quickly became fluent in English. The family laughed at how rapidly he lost his Tongan ways. After the unreliable plumbing and many outhouse visits required in Tonga, Lio Jr. would use only the bathroom in Eseta's house because it was the only bathroom clean and bright enough to suit his new American tastes.

By the time I visited Atu and Malia in their California home in September 1991, there was an air of tension in the house. Eseta and Manu had helped many relatives, but the expectation was that the new arrivals had come to work and that they would find jobs. Malia was working as a hotel maid. Palu had found a relatively high-paying job in the mailroom of a mutual fund company. The family had tried to line up a job for Atu, but nothing had, as yet, worked out. It was hard for Manu to understand this, and it raised old issues between the two of them that dated back to their childhood.

Like Manu, Atu was a Tongan commoner, but a commoner who, within the limited mobility of the times, had aimed his sights high ever since he was a boy. School was the key. When Atu spoke of his childhood to his own children, he talked about his desire to go to school. It was hard for his parents to come up with the money, so he had worked selling coconuts and making copra to earn his school fees. He went to school in Nuku'alofa, the capital, and was, he said, the only one from the village at the town school. The town folk were wealthier and from higher-status families, and they looked down on him. They all wore shoes, and could afford to buy their books and uniforms. Every weekend they went home. Atu had to stay at school because his family had no car or truck or other transportation. "Never mind," Atu would say, "I am going to make something of myself."

When a classmate from the city accused Atu of copying answers off his exam, Atu once told his daughter, Atu had picked him up and thrown him out the open first-floor window. Palu remembered her father saying that the city boys never bothered the country boy again. Atu eventually passed his teacher's exams. He remained a respected teacher in the Tongan schools, retiring at age fifty. He then became the national president of the Tongan Credit Union; he was also an important figure in the Tongan Rugby Union and served on many regional and national service committees.

Atu's life in Tonga helps to explain why, at age fifty-five, he could not bring himself to take a job sweeping floors for a living, despite the fact that wages in California were so high that he would earn more as a janitor in the United States than as a teacher in Tonga. To other Tongans, including Manu, this was a high-and-mighty attitude that had no place among commoners, and certainly not among newcomers to this country.

In September 1991, just a year after their arrival, Malia and Atu moved out. Malia took a new job as a live-in aide in a convalescent home. The job provided room and board for Atu, herself, and Palu. Lio remained with Eseta so that he could continue to go to his elementary school. Atu, still without work, helped Malia to care for and bathe the male convalescents at the home. But, as was consistent for Atu throughout his life, he became involved in Tongan public service activities—raising money for the water pump in the village, presiding at Tongan cultural events, attending kava-drinking evenings—and in keeping an eye on the house and the children back in Tonga. On July 27, 1993, Atu unexpectedly died of a massive heart attack on the Hawai'ian island of Mau'i, where he had traveled to help direct the Tongan choir.

㊂ Malia spoke of her life in the United States:

America surprised me. I always thought that Americans were all *palangi*. But when I got here, I saw there were all different kinds: Spanish, Iranian, Filipino. When I first came, I went to the market to get Tongan food—there are special markets to get Tongan food—and the people they were yelling, "Ha'u heni" [come over here]. "Ufi ma'ama'a!" [Cheap yams!]. "Ko e fiha eni?" [How much is this?], I asked. And they say a price. And I say, "That's very good," because food here is cheap. And I ask them what village they come from. And then I see they cannot answer because they are not Tongan. They were Spanish! But they learned the little words they needed to know so they can sell to Tongans. It surprised me very much.

My life has changed here. I stopped doing Tongan work, and what I do now is foreign work. Here I do sewing, crocheting, and I go and work at taking care of the old people. In Tonga I sewed clothes sometimes for money and did Tongan work [such as making tapa cloth] and sold it. But here I work in the hotel. I was a maid. I worked eight hours and had to clean sixteen rooms in that time. Sometimes there were fourteen rooms only. I made six dollars and fifty cents an hour. I got coffee time, and lunch and sick time.

How was it to work there at the hotel?

It was OK. I spoke a little English, which was better than a lot of the people, who only spoke Spanish. It was easier for the Tongan workers. There were six Tongan workers there. Our boss was a *palangi* guy named Richard. There were three Tongans who knew the work and could supervise. Two of them trained me for two days. On the third day I started alone. I could do the work because it's the kind of thing if you see it, you can do it—how to do the bathrooms and the bed. The supervisors check our work. Sometimes I would forget the little soap, and they would have to remind me. There were lots of tiny little things—soap, shampoo, how many towels, things like that. There were cups and coffee and many things.

Four years after her migration, Malia still lived in the convalescent home where she worked during the week. Palu had moved into her own apartment. Because her husband of thirty years had died, Malia returned to Eseta's house on weekends to live with her family and care for Lio Jr.

Lio Jr.'s residence at Eseta's during the week was easier in the beginning, when he was still very young, but it had gotten more difficult over time. As Lio grew older and became a consummate bike rider, he had taken to skipping dinner and riding his bike late into the evening with his friends. Sela, now in her late eighties, could no longer chase after Lio when he came home from school. Everyone in the family worked, and even when Eseta returned home in the late afternoon, Lio carefully avoided her watchful eye. One weeknight, when Eseta admonished Lio for coming home past dark, he retorted that if Eseta yelled at him or tried to hit him, he'd call the police. Eseta laughed, shaking her head, when she told me this. "He must have heard this from one of his *palangi* friends," she said. But to many Tongan parents, the inability to discipline their children as they see fit is not so funny.

Malia maintained a close and warm relationship with her grandson. Besides using her salary for living, she regularly put aside money for life insurance to cover Lio's school expenses, should something happen to her. She also bought clothing, furniture, and other items for her children overseas, and sent money when they wrote asking for help. When she was able, she also put money aside in the bank.

In 1995, this is how Malia described her typical day:

I'm awake at 6 A.M. I get ready and change and begin getting the old people for their morning wash-up. There's five of them. After they wash their faces, brush their teeth, they come into the living room and they watch TV and wait for me to make breakfast. After breakfast, they watch TV again. After serving breakfast, I go into their rooms and clean up, make their beds, and vacuum. Then I wash the dishes in the kitchen and clean up there. After that, I go and do their laundry. After the laundry, then I sit down with the old people and watch TV. During that time is when I do a little work for me, like knitting. Then I do that until I have to get ready for their lunch. At 11:30, I stand up and go and make lunch. After lunch, I do the dishes and clean up the kitchen again, and after that I relax. They swallow their pills at breakfast. I sit down and watch TV or listen to the radio or some music. Some days I bring the old ones outside, if it's a nice day. They walk outside. About 3 everyone comes back inside and watches TV. Maybe some people want to go and lie down then on their beds. Then about 4:30 I get up and do the dinner cooking because every day I serve dinner at 5. Everyday there's breakfast at 8, lunch at 12, and dinner at 5. After dinner, I wash the dishes, clean the kitchen, and get the wash from the line outside. If it's sunny, I put their wash outside on the line to dry. After dinner the old ones watch TV and talk. They listen to music. At 6:30 or so, they go and sleep. They sleep through the night. While they sleep every night, I do my sewing and then I sleep around 12 or 1.

What is your thinking, now that you have been in America? What do you want people to know who read this book?

There's a lot of Tongan people in America, and the families are friendly with each other. But they live far away. Something happens, like a funeral, and the family and the children can't go to it. My thinking is that in coming to America, I want to return to Tonga. I will work as long as I can still work to save money, but then it's better to go back to Tonga.

What do you see in the American lifestyle that's different from Tonga?

I see there is lots of work. Your body is a prisoner to the work—to the time. You work every day. When you relax, you still think about when you have to work because it's very important, because that's how you get the money that allows your family to live. The good thing is that it's not so wearing on your body, like working in Tonga. You work a lot in Tonga, and your body feels weak. You have to rest, to sleep. A lot of times, you don't have good things to eat. America is different in this way. You work a lot, and you get paid a lot, and you can buy good food—all different kinds of food—and get clothes and other things.

People come overseas to get money. That's the number one reason. To get a life that is higher, more developed than what they had. You can get so many things here.

Atu—he wasn't happy here—he wanted to go back to Tonga. I thought we will go back. Tonga is better for us, maybe. There, you can lay in the house, and you don't have to pay for everything. A little work pays for things you want. If you don't work here, you don't have money for food.

Would you like to see your other daughters come to America?

Well, I'd like them to see this, and then choose. But I'm glad that they're there because when I go back to Tonga, they will be there. That's my thinking. I'm not like other people who think that people should throw away their work in Tonga and come here, except if it's like Palu who tries very hard here. Maybe this life is right for her, is suited to her. Maybe Vei would be happy here. If not, then its OK to go back.

In the next chapter, you will meet Palu, the daughter who Malia believes is suited to America.

5

Palu, the One Who Left

～～ Of the six children of Malia and Atu who sur-
vived childhood, Palu was the fifth born. She was quiet and dutiful as a
child, often too shy even to come visiting next door. Unlike her three sisters, Palu did not meet and entertain young men in the traditional *faikava*
(kava-drinking evenings) in her home.

Oh, I never serve kava to the men in my home. Only the three of my sisters
did. I didn't really like it. I didn't like if there's a lot of people. I don't like to
get people's attention; that's the main thing I didn't like. The boys are sitting
around and they're all looking at me. I don't like them to all look at me. I
was really shy!

Her mother describes her as the daughter who "tries hard"—that is, she's
got perseverance—"but she's quiet." "Her thoughts," Malia says, "are silent."

Family members ask things of her, and she doesn't tell me so I won't know.
She just gives it. She thinks that if she tells me, I'll tell her to stop, but I won't.
I smile at her thinking. She tried hard to help her family. Here, when a family thing happens, she wants to go to it. She goes and wants to help. I see
that she works hard to be able to help her family. And she likes to go to these
things.

Palu's earliest memory was the story accompanying the pictures she had
drawn over and over again in childhood. She and a friend are climbing up
a neighbor's tree to steal some ripe fruit. The man who owns the tree comes

out of his house and sees them. He begins to yell and chases them. They scurry from the tree, falling halfway down, and begin to run as they hit the ground. "We were so scared!" Palu remembered, as the neighbor chased them through the village. The two children ran and hid in a ditch that runs through part of the village. The picture on the next page is one of these drawings which Palu had given me when she was a child.

My formal interviews with Palu all date from her adulthood, after she had migrated to the United States. They span a period of two and a half years from 1991 to 1994. The latter ones were conducted in English.

A year after the last interview, Palu came again and read what I had written, based on her recorded words. There were points in her reading when Palu spontaneously laughed. "This is good!" she exclaimed. There were some pages that she responded to with dead seriousness, others with restrained disapproval. "What's the matter?" I asked. There were different issues. In one place she had contradicted a family member and did not like the prospect that her relative might see the account. In another place the opinion she had held a year earlier was, in her mind, no longer entirely true. In yet another place she wanted to edit out material that might be offensive. She had a number of initial requests: Could she take out the sentences that started and stopped and started over again? Could she change words that were not proper English? It bothered her that her early memories were not in order: Could we rearrange the incidents she discussed in chronological order so they read more like a story?

We talked together about the purpose of the book: why it might be important to include some "difficult" material; why memories did not need to be in chronological order if she hadn't originally thought of them that way; how we might better protect some people or mask their identity; what needed to be added to her earlier comments to satisfy her about their accuracy; what absolutely had to come out; what else was so important that it had to be there.

What follows here is Palu's edited version of this material, based on her changes and additions and our conversation together.

One thing I remember is when we went to school, and we're supposed to wear shoes, right? but we can still walk to school without shoes if we don't have them. One day, my parents just bought the shoes for Finau, my older sister, and they didn't buy any for me, so I was sad. I was sad, and I walked to school with no shoes. I was so embarrassed.

I would have liked it if I could walk in *some* shoes even if it was just when

STEALING COCONUTS. This childhood drawing by Palu was an assignment for school, a present that Palu gave me when she was ten years old. As part of Tongan schools' emphasis on developing English-language skills, children begin early integrating English words into their school assignments.

In this assignment Palu fulfills her charge to represent a nicely tended house, with a hand-swept lawn, planted flowers, and fenced areas to keep in household animals. It was part of a children's awareness campaign, "Keep Tonga Clean and Beautiful," the translation of the caption that appears at the bottom of the drawing. At the same time, it depicts a salient childhood memory, one that Palu associated with excitement, fear, and laughter. It was a scene, in altered versions, that surfaced in many of Palu's childhood drawings and then again in her narratives of childhood.

On the right two children, depicted in different stages of their adventure, decide to steal coconuts because they are thirsty. One climbs the coconut tree, entreating a second child, waiting at the bottom, "Don't make a noise," while the drinking coconuts are thrown down.

Householders spot the children. One woman yells to her sister, "Hey! sister, look up. [S]he steal our coconuts." "Let's chase them," returns the sister. A man, who has picked up a stick, threatens, "HA!HA! I'll come and hit you!"

At the top of the coconut tree, the child tossing down coconuts realizes that they have been discovered and slips while trying to make a quick getaway down the tree.

we went into the city. All the schools go to Nuku'alofa—you know, marching in a big ceremony. All the children wear the same shoe, the same kind of shoe, like sandals. This one year, my school goes to join the marching in the city. From my school, all the students with the shoes goes in the same group. And the students with no shoes walk in the back! And I was one of the ones who walked in the back. I didn't want to go that day, but I went. That's one thing I remember.

I remember my grandmother. Atu's mother. I wish she was still alive. She was great! She told us the stories of long time ago—histories. One thing I remember, there was one *eiki* [noble or chief] who died and she was singing for her. The song was sad, and it was about this *eiki*. And one day, we were listening to the radio and her song came on the radio and we heard my grandmother singing and I was surprised. She used to sleep with the queen, with Queen Salote. Do you known when everybody began braiding their hair in a circle on their heads? She was the first one to braid the Queen's hair like that. One thing I did a lot in Tonga was sewing and braiding hair, too. I know how to do that by just watching my grandmother braid and Malia sew every day.

When my sister Latu was little, I liked to sew her dresses and take care of her hair. Later, when my aunt's daughter died, we had to cut our hair short. I cut Latu's hair and styled it. I didn't do anything with my hair that time, but I start learning by doing her hair.

Oh, OK, this is another thing. I was older. One day, I still had my job in the credit union, and I was sewing. And I sewed and ironed and laid out my clothes for the next day for work. And this one morning Finau woke up and she saw my clothes on the bed. I went to take a shower and my clothes were ready and I came back to put my clothes on and she was wearing them. I started to cry. And Atu came—[Palu starts to cry here. She can't finish talking. When she recovers, she continues.] And then he came and told me to let her wear my clothes. Because it's OK, because she was the oldest and she can take anything, but it wasn't right with me . . . that's one thing I won't forget. When he left, I was yelling at her. I told her, it's MY clothes. I have to go to work in MY clothes. I have to wear my clothes. It wasn't right with me.

I asked Finau about her life, and she said she felt like she worked very hard and had to do everything. Do you think that's true?

"I don't think so," she answered laughing.

Who did most of the work, do you think?

The youngest ones. 'Cause Finau went to school and she studied and slept
a lot. And Latu had to do her laundry. Vei and Finau were always saying,
"Run to the neighbor and get this, do this, do that!" And I was always mad
because they didn't really do anything and they always tell Latu to do this,
do that, wash their clothes. . . . and go to the neighbor and borrow their
irons and the tubs. And it wasn't right for me. I got in many fights with my
sister Vei at that time standing up for my little sister. When I earned some
money, I would give some to Latu to go to the movies. One day, when they
told Latu to go do this and go do that, I said, "Why don't you just *ask* her?"
And they just stood and didn't say anything.

When Palu read this passage again in 1995, she wanted to change it. It
wasn't accurate, she explained, only something she said at a time when she
was angry with her sister. While it was true that the younger kids did the
bulk of the fetching and grunt work in the household, her eldest sister, Finau, *did* work very hard in the family—not so much at housework as in other ways. Palu saw Finau, as the eldest, trying to lead her siblings, to set an
example for them in her personal life. She tried very hard at school, con-
sciously attempting to pave the way for her sisters and to make her parents
proud. She was, as Palu described her, their pathfinder, and the responsibility for doing well and being strong fell heavily on Finau's shoulders.

When we were little, Atu put a paper on the wall with our names and what
we had to do. But since Atu build the new house, then I was the one who
did that. Like sweeping outside, and cleaning the house inside, and who's
doing the dishes, who's cleaning the bedrooms and the bathrooms and the
toilet. And who's doing the laundry. And I rotate the jobs! [She laughs.] Finau wouldn't do it. But then I tell her, "If you won't do this, I won't do this.
If you won't do that today, the next day I won't do it." And then, she did it.
And on Sunday, all of us work together, and do whatever we have to do on
Sunday.

Tell me more about your sisters.

We did get along. Really. We slept in the same room. There was one big bed
and one small, and one sleep in the small and two sleep in the big. We like
it. It was fun. But Finau used to sleep in her own room because she studied,
and she used to stay up late and study. But sometimes one of us would go
and sleep with her. The other room was Lio's, my brother. He slept in the
house because we really like him. Vili was already in Australia.

The happiest times I remember were at night when everybody was there. Malia would play the guitar and we'd all sing. All the girls, and Lio, and Atu and Malia, and we'd just listen to the guitar and sing. I loved that.

What about school?

I didn't like going to school because of the teachers. Because they hit the students. When we go over our homework in class, they beat us in any part of the body if we don't have the right answer. [She laughs.] That's the thing I hated.

I stopped going to school because one of my weakest subjects was mathematics and my math teacher was a priest and he likes to ask me a lot of questions. And I didn't know anything. [She laughs.] It was the first day of school. The first year in high school. I failed my math exam. And then I came back the next year. And the first day, the teacher started asking me a lot of questions about math, and I didn't know the answers. The next day I say, "OK, I'm not going to school tomorrow." And I didn't.

Then I got my job—my first job—in the credit union. It was typing and answering the phone and taking notes in the meetings. I was seventeen. But before that, when I was still in school, on the school holidays, that's what I did.

Did your father help you to get that job?

Yeah. Because he was there, at the credit union.

How much did you make?

Five dollars a day. That was good. Some people only made $4.

I didn't like that first job. The only thing I was right to do was typing because my typing was good, but the rest of it—like taking notes in the meeting, the board of director's meeting—I didn't want to do it. Atu told me if I stay and try, he'd give me $20. So I stayed. [She laughs.] And then they also had a training where they train some people from the clubs in all the different villages, and I didn't want to stay then either. So Atu told me, "OK, you stay and be the secretary to the managing director and you serve the food to the trainees and there's an allowance of $30." That was big money! And I say, "OK, I'll stay." And that's how the job started. But I didn't really like the job.

After the credit union job, Atu's cousin from the next village—she was running this sewing business in Maufanga—and she came and asked Atu and Malia for me. She want me to come with her to run the business. I didn't want to go because I was embarrassed.[1] There was no other people my age there, but only me and four other old women. But I went there. The place was comfortable. We sewed, and we cooked together for lunch. I like it there. And then after a year, or almost a year, I get the job in the government, in the education office. Our neighbor Mele helped 'cause she already worked there. Mele and her secretary came all the way to the sewing business to tell me the position is open and she want me there. And I have to take it. And that one is my last job. I really like it there. I was there two years.

And then you came to the U.S.?

Yes.

Tell me about your decision to go to the U.S.

I wanted to go there. I knew I wanted to come to the U.S. The people I work with in Tonga, they ask me, "Why do you want to go?" because they knew my sisters didn't want to come. And I told them, "I want to go."

Why?

Well, one thing was English. I studied English when I was still in school, but I couldn't really say anything in English. So when I came to America, I wanted to learn English and I wanted to learn more about life. And when I came here, I can see my world is bigger.

Palu's first job was part-time work in a mail room. She made $10 an hour, an incredible sixteen times her salary in Tonga. Within two years she had a used car, her own apartment, and a non-Tongan boyfriend—the latter two of which caused consternation within the family. The cultural shock Palu described earlier gave way quickly to a sense of growing identification as an "American." Her account of her life in 1995 follows. Palu's sister who remained in Tonga discusses her choice to stay in chapter 9.

The Americanization of Emma

In the United States, Palu changed her name to Emma, a version of her Tongan first name. She prefers to be called by her American name. By 1995, a resident for five years, she has been promoted in the company where she works to a full-timer, but she makes the same hourly wage she did when she began working there four years before. Emma is now in a permanent relationship with an African-American man, Greg, with whom she lives. When Emma read this chapter, she wanted to talk more about her relationship with Greg, which, two years earlier, was just budding.

Emma met Greg at work. Young women in Tonga meet men in chaperoned situations; their "dates" are either in the home or at village dances, where many parents are in attendance. It is only recently that some village girls might go into town to a "club," but even these excursions are made in large groups. So when Greg asked Palu out, she literally did not know how to behave. She was very quiet throughout the evening, and Greg, sensing that she wasn't enjoying herself, took her home early. He went to kiss her at her doorstep, and Emma balked. It scared her, and he backed off and said good night.

When he called her to go out again, she said no. Greg remembered, "She did not have a good experience with her last boyfriend, and she told me that she didn't want to go out with anyone anymore. 'But I didn't have a good experience with my last girlfriend, either,'" Greg had countered. "'Some guys are nice, you know, and when they are with a girl who is nice, they treat her right.' I asked her whether she'd give me the opportunity to show her that all men are not dogs. 'OK,' she told me. That was all she said. Real simple. We went out, and I asked her out again two days later. She said yes, but then stood me up again."

"Why did you stand him up?" I asked Emma now as Greg looked on curiously. Emma explained that she had said yes to Greg because she really wanted to see him again. But then, as their date approached, she became so nervous and uncomfortable about being alone with a man that she could not show up. He was the first man to give her roses, the first one to come to her door. She just didn't know what to do or say, and her discomfort caused her to balk at the last minute.

Greg persisted because he could see beyond the silence and the insult of being stood up: "I was shy, too, as a teenager. I thought if someone had the patience that she would be wonderful—a diamond in the rough." One night he talked seriously about himself to her, revealing his pain over the recent loss of his mother. She talked too, this time about the loss of her father. "This was the first time I was able to talk about this with anyone," Emma said. This was the bond that began their relationship.

By 1995 they had been living together for two years. There were still issues between them that Greg and Emma perceived as "cultural." Emma still did not understand about men and women "being friends," and she got upset if Greg saw a female friend for lunch or coffee who was not his relative. Greg did not understand why Emma wouldn't "talk more" when something bothered her, rather than walking away or leaving the house. They were working through these things, they said, and had begun to talk about the prospect of a longer life together, their dreams of a better future, and a family.

Emma and Greg had met each other's family and felt "accepted" by them. Their social life consisted of shared friends, mostly from work, who were predominantly non-Tongan. Emma's life as a single woman—first in an apartment of her own, later in a live-in relationship—has been an ongoing source of comment and tension in her family and among the local Tongan community. By the mid-1990s, Emma nevertheless saw her time in America as the happiest in her life.

"When I talked to you about coming to America before," Emma said to me, "I talked about wanting to learn English. Now, when I think about it, I want to say more than that." This is what she wanted to add:

I think in Tonga I had too much Tongan culture. That is why I wanted to come here. Like when you have to go to church because, if you don't, other people are going to talk about you. When I came to America, I didn't really know what was there—just that there is something there that's very important for me to know there about rights and justice. I learned a lot here.

What kinds of things did you learn here?

Like to speak up, to speak for yourself. How to learn to be a positive person. To be strong.

Weren't you strong in Tonga?

No. I felt I have no rights there—responsibilities, but no rights; in everything I have to do, the decision is made by the father. I didn't have anything to say. Remember I told you about that time when Finau took my clothes and Atu say it's OK, and I was yelling it is MY clothes? Now, I come here, I get what I want and I live by myself and I feel more responsible and I feel like I have something to do. Like my job. I go from part-time to full-time, and they transfer me to another area. And my relationship. I was in a bad relationship, and now I have another boyfriend and it is good. He is teaching me a lot of things—how to speak for yourself, how to stand up and put myself up there. And I feel strong now, and in doing my job I am more active.

I feel like I am growing up. I can deal now with the Tongan people, who gossip and say things about you, something bad about you, I can shut their mouth now. [She laughs.]

How do you do that?

Well, there was this girl in my neighborhood—she is Tongan—named Luci. One day I was in the supermarket, and I met another girl who knows both of us. She said to me, "Ah, Luci was telling me that you are going out with Greg." When I finished shopping, I went up straight to Luci's house. She answered the door and I talked to her in English. And I was looking straight at her. "Excuse me, excuse me, Luci, did you tell T—— something about me?" And then she was looking around, "No!" she answered. She was talking to me in Tongan. She's been here for twelve years, and I went there and I was talking to her in English and she was trying to talk to me in Tongan.

But, me, I kept talking in English because it's easier for me to talk in English that way. Whenever I say something straight in the face and strong, I can't speak in Tongan, only in English. So I said again in English, "What did you tell her? I want to know because it was something about me." And she was saying, "No, it was nothing!"

This girl and I used to go out together and have fun and laugh, and she was surprised because I went up straight to her like that. And then she told me, "No, we were just talking about other stuff. We were talking about you that you live by yourself," and then I said, "Is there a problem with that?" and then she say, "No." And then I asked her, "Is my business important to you?" And she say, "No." And then I say, "Then shut up." [She laughs with both embarrassment and pride as she tells me this.] "If I hear something like this again, I'll come back."

What do you think caused those changes for you?

[She pauses.] Growing up in Tonga, we have nothing to say, and I have the feeling I am always dumb there, and I'm always down on myself. I start to learn to never put yourself down, right? And feel good about yourself. Not like before—I felt that I was less than everybody else. Now, I feel good about myself! I started to know those things.

How did you come to know these things?

I read a book. The title is *Think Big.* And I read a lot of things. I get transferred at work, too, and I get more responsibility, and the people I work with are older, more mature people (not just kids). I learn a lot of things from my boyfriend, Greg, too, like to be responsible, to take care of yourself, to stay out of debts. And how to solve problems. And to take care of your priorities. I learn much about those things. In America. How to live in America.

So tell me what you know about how to live in America.

My example was, I was a really nice person. I care about other people, not only myself. I care about other people, not only my family but my friends, and I end up in a time that I knew my friends were just taking advantage of me because I was too nice. I don't care about other people if they want to take advantage. . . .

I have a friend right now—not Tongan—she used to borrow a lot of money from me. Last year she borrowed $500, and it takes a year and a few months to pay it back. She only pay because I asked her. "I need my money for this. I need my money for that," I say. And right now she have trouble with money again; she is really broke, and she always asked me if she can borrow $200, and I told her I can't. I tell her, "I wish I can help you but I can't." And she asked me, "Why? How come you change now?" And I tell her I have to take care of my priorities before I take care of other people. And I'm happy for that.

We used to be close. Whenever I buy some food, I buy food for her too, and we eat together, but now I don't care. Now I have to save my money.

Later on, Emma clarified her remarks:

I don't really mean I don't care. She was my mother's age, and so I treated her like a mother and felt that I had to buy her lunch every time I buy my own lunch. Every day I bought my lunch I bought her lunch too because I felt that I had to. Now, I still eat lunch with her, maybe every two weeks. Only now I buy her lunch one time and she buys me lunch another time. It's more equal.

What about your sisters?

I would send some money if they ask, but they haven't written to me for a long time. They only ask Malia, and then Malia ask me. And I tell her, "OK, I give you half and you give half." I'm living by myself. I have bills to pay. [She laughs.]

Do you think when you have kids you're going to bring them up in the Tongan way?

In the Tongan way? Yes, I would do that. . . . I would tell them about the Tongan way, like helping one another. But maybe not everything would be Tongan.

When my brother Vili was little, he was spoiled, and when he grew up they couldn't do anything about how he acted. That's what they started to do with Lio Jr. when they adopt him, when they're still in Tonga, and I hated it. I remember a time when he was two years old and I was playing cards and he was crying for the playing cards, and I didn't give it to him. And Atu took away the cards from me and gave them straight to Lio. "He's just a baby!" Atu scolded. And I started to hate the way they raise him. All of them—Atu and Malia and Finau and Latu, too—they all do whatever he likes. I was happy when we came here and little Lio was separate from my three sisters. And I was thinking I can change him.

Is it just your family that is this way with children, or is it more a Tongan thing?

More Tongan. That's why I can see the difference here in the babies here, and they can walk before one year old. But at home, at two or two and a half and they can start walking.

So when you have kids, you're going to bring them up a little differently?

Yes. I'm going to bring them up different.

You know what little Lio did? He was using bad words. When Finau was here, she told him to go get something for her and he didn't want to and he says, "Fuck you." And I grabbed him, and I slap him. ["Now," she reflected in 1995, "I've learned never to hit him again because I felt so bad that I slapped him."]

Where did he learn to say that?

He watch TV a lot. Lio watches TV all the time. When we all still live together at Eseta's, I tell him at 9 o'clock the TV goes off. Lio was crying and crying because he wants to watch more. But I say no. He hated me, when Atu was still alive. But now, sometimes he call me and say, "How come you never see me? I want toys. I want to go to the store. I want a Slurpee~!" Last week I brought him to Greg's house for dinner, and he said bad words to me there. And I ask him, "Where did you learn that?" And he say, "From my friends." And then I told him, "You're not supposed to say that to me. And you know why?" He told me no. And he start crying. And I told him, "You're not supposed to tell it to me because I'm your auntie and because I love you, OK?" And he was crying and crying. And Greg told me, "Oh, you're gonna be a good mother."

It was while Emma was reviewing the material at my house that she got to a point in this narrative where she was talking about an important family memory. She called me over. "Remember when I told you about the most important thing I never forget?" she asked me. I must have looked puzzled because she continued, "About one day in Tonga when we had dinner, and after dinner all of us, all the family was at home, and we were all there and singing? Malia was playing her guitar and all of us were there together and singing?" "Yeah," I answered. "I remember that."

That's what I miss a lot. Because everyone go their own ways. I come here, and Finau went to Eua, and Latu get married and she go, and my brothers and Atu die, and we all . . . But I always have in my mind that we are split but we are one in our hearts. I miss that a lot. Sometimes, I sit back and I always remember that, why we're getting split, and I cry.

Why do you think that happens?

I don't know. I always think of that, why that happened. And my answer is, I don't know, it was just something that happened. Something that had to be, had to happen.

6

An Anthropologist
over Time

〰 This chapter exists nowhere in my field notes, or even my letters home to friends and relatives (which almost everyone saved, for some reason). Most of what is in this chapter is not on tape because it is about things that I did not think were anthropology.

I do see this chapter in the pictures I took. My early photographs are quite striking, really: 35 mm cameras with lenses I learned to use and f-stops I experimented with. There are nice shots of the village. The photographs of people are portraits. I am not a photographer, but some photos are good: a close-up of a woman intently beating bark, the beaten bark draped around her seated figure; a man driving home in his horse-drawn cart from the bush; an old woman looking pensively into the distance in profile. Many shots to get the few. Keep taking photos so that the subject gets comfortable and looks natural.

My later photos look terrible. They are taken with a sure-shot automatic camera. One lens fits all. Sometimes I took them, sometimes I handed the camera off to a neighbor so we could get everyone in. We are huddled together, posing, smiling. "Smile bigger," the person taking the shot says. "One, two, three." "Take another one," someone yells—the baby was crying in the first one. Everyone tries to pose in exactly the same position as before. These photos are a different genre. They look like my family album.

1981

I chose to do fieldwork in Tonga for reasons that were partly professional and partly personal, but in retrospect, none of my reasons had to do with issues of concern to Tongans. I was interested in "gender," and Tonga has a fascinating gender system and an active network of women's traditional and development groups. I also wanted to go to a place that would fulfill my personal vision of what anthropology was, and Tonga, a horticultural Polynesian society with a minimum of industrial development, fit the bill. I had read extensively about Tonga, of course. By the time I left, I had memorized some nouns and verbs from the Tongan dictionary, but I did not speak even rudimentary Tongan.

When I first arrived, I sought advice from overseas volunteer workers I met in the town. "Don't lend things out," they told me, "you'll never get them back." "Go to church every Sunday. Don't tell anyone you are Jewish." There were a number of Jewish Peace Corps workers in Tonga, but apparently the conventional wisdom was to skirt this topic. Tonga had been heavily missionized in the nineteenth century, and Tongans apparently still held strong prejudices: that Jews had horns, that Jews killed Christ, that Jews keep everything for themselves.

"What do you tell people you are?" I asked one Jewish Peace Corps volunteer who had lived and taught in Tonga for more than a year.

"I tell them I'm something they don't have here. Sometimes I say I'm Unitarian."

I took some advice but not all. I always lent things out, but I never, ever told anyone that I was Jewish. For the entire time I was in Tonga, I attended the Catholic church even though I told people I was "something close to Catholic that they didn't have here." When pressed for a church name, I became, like my fellow Jews, Unitarian.

I initially stayed in a guest house in the capital town. The guest house was owned by a wonderful couple who helped to acclimate Peace Corps volunteers to Tongan life and who helped me in these early weeks. In the second month of my town stay, I went out each day on one of the buses that travel either east and west along the primary road to the rural villages of the island. I would sit on the bus looking out the window at potential residence sites, glancing down from time to time at my index card with Tongan phrases written out: "Is there a vacant house in the village that I could rent?" "I came to study Tongan customs." When I saw a village that seemed to fit my negative criteria—not too little, not too close to the capital, not too far inland—I got off the bus and walked around, hoping to find someone of whom I could ask my questions.

On one of my trips to the eastern end of the island, I met a woman named Losa. She greeted tourists at the Paepae regional handicraft center, where tourist buses sometimes stopped, and she could speak English beautifully. I was happy to be able to talk at length with a villager. There was a vacant house, she said, in the adjacent village. A Peace Corps woman used to live in it, but she had left the village. A Tongan teacher in the village owned the house, and maybe she would rent it to me. She told me where to find the teacher, and the house. It was small and wooden and simple—a concrete slab floor with a woven mat—but clean and nice. The main wall had been hand-painted with little yellow and pink and blue dots to resemble wallpaper. The house had electricity in the form of one light bulb, and, best of all, it had an indoor toilet. I thought it was perfect.

The day I moved in, several neighbors came by with food. I tried to project a general demeanor of openness and friendliness without befriending anyone in particular. In these early months of fieldwork, before I knew the ins and outs of the village factions or village kinship, I did not want to associate myself exclusively with any one person or family. So I smiled at everyone and kept my door open, even when curious children came and stared at me, literally for hours, as I went about my daily business. I offered any food I had to anyone who came by. I accepted with thanks all gifts, and I tried to eat everything that people offered.

On the very first night I was in the village, I attended a meeting of a women's savings group just three houses away. They made food for the meeting—yams and a huge plate of fatty lamb flaps. After a day of politely eating whatever food was given me, I ate again, following the principle that people generally like people who like to eat their food. (At least I do.) In the middle of the meeting, I began to feel incredibly nauseated. I could not explain my discomfort in Tongan to the woman chairing the meeting, so I just signaled that I was going to go outside. I literally bolted out the door, reaching the bushes outside just in time to be violently ill. As I retched in the bushes, I felt someone put her hands on my shoulder. It was Malia.

Malia and her husband, Atu, were one set of my neighbors; their house bordered mine on the west side. Atu spoke some English, and his eldest daughter spoke English fairly well, but this wasn't the reason why I ultimately came to rely on them for help and advice. I never really remembered speaking any English in the village. I just liked the people next door. They were kind and thoughtful—not only to me but to others—and as time went on, my relationship with my neighbors to the west developed more than my relationships with other neighbors.

Malia and Atu had already dealt with *palangis* next door, some encounters more positive than others. Generally, though, they were pleased with the idea of having a *palangi* neighbor, and so were their children. Finau, the eldest, remembered:

> We had some other English people before, but we didn't get on well. Except one man. And it's a very big thing to have some *palangi* come in to stay near you or at your house. Even at school—with us staying next door to the house with the *palangi* people—people say, and at school they say, "Oh, no wonder those children are so good at English. 'Cause there are *palangi* people next door all the time."

The younger girls like the idea of a foreign neighbor. "Whoa, a *palangi*!" Palu remembered thinking. "I was excited when you came, but I was shy to come over." Vei told me that her first thought was that she could get a lot more candy from the store if a *palangi* woman moved in.

Associating with the family next door was helpful to me. Atu was a respected teacher; Malia was skilled in tapa making and active in women's groups. Both were well liked in the village. The youngest child, Latu, helped me with language. At age seven, she was infinitely patient, going over and over familiar objects. She would come to my house and point to things. "What is this?" she would ask as she pointed to her nose. "Nose," I would say to my seven-year-old teacher, and she would point to something else. I didn't feel embarrassed when I got things wrong. She would say the correct word and point again. Finau often came over with food, sometimes staying and eating with me. Palu and Vei made themselves less visible but often accompanied me on trips through the village, when propriety demanded an escort.

Malia took me to women's meetings in the village. She advised me on aspects of etiquette and answered my many naive questions. When I saw tracks of half-eaten yams leading from my little wooden cupboard to the back door, I motioned for Malia to come take a look. "A rat?" I asked, after looking the word up in my Tongan dictionary. She laughed. "A people rat," she said. She managed to explain to me that one of the neighborhood kids must have seen that I had leftover food and come and taken some. It was the beginning of my education about different attitudes toward borrowing and possessions and sharing which my life experience in the United States could have never prepared me to understand.

Malia's advice was always good. It was Malia who discouraged me, a year into my fieldwork, from setting up a fee-for-service relationship with the diary families described in chapter 2. It was her advice and her example that allowed me to transform my relationship with villagers from a colder employer-employee relationship to a warmer context of mutual favors.

Atu helped in other ways. He always made sure that no drunken boys or late-night suitors graced my steps, and I suspect that he performed a number of backstage functions that helped facilitate my research in the village. He told me stories of his mother, who had been a titled attendant to the former queen, and he discussed the issues of the day with me.

I became friendly with this household, enough to become identified with it. "Where's your *palangi*?" people would say to Malia or Atu, looking for me.

1982

Less than a year after I had moved into the village, I discovered a lump in my breast. I was advised to leave Tonga and have a biopsy. I decided to go back to Philadelphia for the medical procedure but continue renting my house, hoping to return when the tests and any ensuing treatment were complete. Malia was a great comfort to me during the stressful period before I could get on a plane back to the United States and discover that the lump was benign.

While back in the States, I talked frequently of Tonga. One evening I was at a dinner party with friends and friends of friends, including several people I had not met before. One woman, a nurse whom I will call Linda, asked me one question after another about my experiences living in a Tongan village. She seemed genuinely interested. "Oh, I'd love to do something like that!" she finally exclaimed. "Well, you can," I said. "Just go." She had a two-week vacation coming up the following month. I told her that if she got a plane ticket to Tonga, she could live in my house. "I won't be there until a little later," I told her, "but I'll give you a letter to take to the family next door, and they'll make sure you're OK."

When I saw that the woman fully intended to go through with this, I met her again and gave her a crash course in village etiquette and basic propriety. Smile, be friendly. Give people food when they come to the house, and try to eat what they offer. Don't wear shorts or bathing suits or low-cut blouses. Always walk in the village with someone else, especially at night.

I frankly don't remember whether I told her specifically not to have sex with men in the village. I guess I figured that if she couldn't wear shorts, she'd realize that she shouldn't sleep with anyone. But during her two weeks there, she met a Tongan man who was single and attractive and interested, and they had an affair. By U.S. standards at the time, I suppose this was not unreasonable. But for Tonga, and certainly for my standards about how I wanted to conduct my relationships in the village, this was outrageous. Malia and Atu, who took care of her and cooked meals for her, wrote me a letter to tell me what had happened. They felt responsible for what they thought was their fault. Their letter was painfully apologetic: Would I ever forgive them for not properly taking care of my good friend?

In later years I was to find that their chagrin ran deeper than the woman's affair. "She came to us," Malia told me, "but she didn't want to be there." Atu had gone out every night with a flashlight to check around her house and to see that no drunken boys or mischief makers were about. Apparently she felt that he was peeping or preparing to enter her house. "What are you doing there?" she asked him one night. Linda went and told an English-speaking Tongan woman in the village that she was scared and believed Atu was up to no good. The Tongan woman told Malia what Linda had said. Atu and Malia were terribly upset that she had misperceived their motives. Her lack of trust was what hurt them, being that she was my good friend.

"She was not really my friend—just an acquaintance, someone I met once," I've told Malia over the years. But whenever I hear myself explaining this to Malia, it highlights a question that I have asked myself many times since. How could I have sent a complete stranger to them? Would I have sent someone I didn't know well to stay with my family in New York? It is a hard realization that my loyalty to an American middle-class white professional took precedence over my personal relationship with a Tongan island family. I just didn't think.

1983

I am not a good enough writer to recount the growth of my relationship with the family. Finau described it this way:

I remember, you came into the home next door, and the other neighbors, they all looked at you—and everyone was bringing food and good stuff, the four faces of your houses—so we just took it easy. Because with Atu as a schoolteacher, and all of us in school, we knew you would just take your pick. You didn't go into one place and take all these people, and what they say, what they do, whatever they give—you were very smart! You were very smart picking what people would do, what kind of people would fit you. And the years went by, and you turned out to be our eldest daughter, our eldest girl in the family.

I don't know the point at which my relationship to the family changed from one of convenience to one of preference, when they changed from informants to friends, but it did. More and more, we cooked together and ate together. The children came to my house often, and I lived between the two houses. The family dog started thinking he belonged to me and began allowing the family chickens and pigs to roam on my property. By the last year of my fieldwork, I simply acted as the eldest daughter of the family might. Atu began referring to me this way. My "eldest daughter" identity was strange. I was only nine years younger than Malia, and we really were just good friends. I did not think of her maternally. My "sisters," were almost all young enough to be my daughters. Atu and I were twelve years apart. We had become close friends too, but there was not Tongan category of "friendship" between an unmarried woman and a married man.

My single marital status, the fact that people knew I was "in school," and the lack of an alternative framework, I think, are what led to the designation of "eldest daughter." In time, our "family" relationship came to be recognized by wider networks of people. Men I did not know would ask their friend Atu whether I would make kava for them on a certain evening. Atu would come to me and ask if I wanted to do it, sometimes saying that it would mean a lot to him if I did. People who wanted to borrow something no longer came to me at all. They would ask Malia and Atu, and, if my "parents" thought it was important, they would discuss the request with me. When a daughter of Atu's sister died in the village, I wore a big mat for a month, as did the rest of the "low side" of the family.[1] At the funeral, we cut our hair and worked in the kitchen (both signs of obligation and deference to one's "higher" family). The female head of the family cut only a little of my hair, while she butchered the hair of the others, but still she cut it and thanked me for doing my family obligation. I actually began to *feel* "low" and respectful when I spoke to Atu's sisters and their children.

My deepening relationships were somewhat less "convenient" to the anthropologist. They involved me in many more obligations, financially and socially, than I had planned on. At the same time, they offered me a sense of belonging and insight that I would otherwise never have had.

1984

When I left Tonga in 1984, this was, to my understanding, the end of my fieldwork. I was prepared to return home to write my dissertation on women and social change in the Tongan village, and to give up my rental house in the village. Malia and I had a close friendship by this point, and as my departure approached, we talked about future plans. Perhaps Finau would continue school in the United States—maybe even live with me when I got settled. Perhaps when the family migrated . . . There was talk of our continuing involvement in the States.

It was then, in these weeks before I left Tonga, that the lie I had told about my religion really bothered me. I am not a religious Jew, by any means, but I do identify myself as Jewish; my historical and cultural background as a grandchild of immigrant Jews is important to me. With one's "church" being so salient a designation in Tonga, I did not feel comfortable extending the lie that I was "something else" that they did not have here.

One day I sat down with Malia on the mat floor of her main room. "There's something I want to tell you," I said.

She looked at me attentively. "You know how I go to Catholic church here and I say I'm something close to that, but I'm really something else? Well, I'm Jewish. I want you to know I'm Jewish."

She looked at the floor, and after a long pause, she said, "But you're not selfish."

The comment surprised me. "I know," I said when I collected myself. "But neither are most other Jews," I added, not willing to be viewed as some exception that would prove the rule. "There are selfish people and not-selfish people, like anybody else."

There was silence.

"I want to know something," I said to Malia. "Am I the only Jew you know?"

"Yes," she answered.

"Then why do you think that way?"

"Because it's what I've heard," she answered. "The people say that about people who are selfish—it's 'the Jewish way.' I think Jews are like that because that's what I've heard. I don't know from my own experience that this is right."

I remember launching into a speech about stereotypes, replete with analogies about how when Tongans went to New Zealand, people thought they were lazy but they really weren't. It was hard for me to hear her beliefs.

They were so far from my experience—of both my own giving and loving Jewish family and of "the Jewish way" I knew that was so strongly committed to social philanthropy.

Malia listened patiently to my monologue and then told me, "That's fine. It doesn't matter." I felt relieved. But then she said, "I just think we shouldn't tell anyone else in the village." And that's how we left it in 1984.

Atu and I discussed my "studies" in the final days of my residence in the village. Atu took education very seriously, and he was concerned about how my university would know that I had learned Tongan customs and satisfactorily completed my work as an anthropologist. He thought it was important that I leave with formal documentation of my studies and progress in Tonga. "I will write a letter to your university," he told me, "that tells the headman that you have done very well in your studies here and learned the Tongan ways." I told him that he did not need to do that.

Despite my protestations, on the day I was to leave, Atu handed me a sealed letter that I was not to open until I was in the United States. It was in English. On the front was written:

Sender—Atu Lio and family and the people of 'Olunga
To: the President and lecturers of the University

I read it on the plane, and it made my cry. It began:

I myself and family and all the people of 'Olunga say appreciate and enormous congratulation on your kindness and helpfuls to people of 'Olunga, some families and some societies [cooperatives] too. The people of my village learn a lot on the searching that you've taken while you were here, and we feel much sorry on the farewell that we've taken today. I have two sons and five daughters. Cathy is one of my five daughters, she loves and helps our family very much.

Atu went on to certify as a teacher that I had successfully learned my studies about the Tongan customs, that I could speak the Tongan language, and that I should indeed "pass my examination for the doctor."

I was very grateful that Atu should want to write such a letter, but I knew that he did not understand how the U.S. graduate school system worked. No one, especially the president of an urban university, was waiting for such an endorsement. There was no official or unofficial place at all for Atu's kind and overcomplimentary letter in the bureaucracy of getting a degree.

Protocol did demand that I get written permission from the Tongan government before conducting my research. I could not begin my research without passing the doctoral exams that demonstrated my familiarity with the scholarly literature on Polynesia. There was a certain unwritten code about the length of fieldwork which I knew I had met. All that was left, officially speaking, was to write up an acceptable dissertation, something that would take me three years to do.

I never gave the letter to my university president or even to my committee chair. In retrospect, I regret that I did not lend it more importance in my final defense, for it is the document of which I am most proud.

1987

When I finished my dissertation (some ten years after I had started doctoral work), I was happy and grateful. But one of the great epiphanies from seeing my two-volume, five hundred—page dissertation finished was that it would make little actual difference in the lives of people in my village. The dissertation had been, first and foremost, for me. I decided to return to Tonga and put my dissertation on the shelves of the Ministry of Education, where it, officially, was to go. Then, I wanted to thank the village in some tangible way, through little things I could do with the savings of a graduate student.

I had three goals in mind: getting the tapa-making house rebuilt, starting a rotating credit fund for the development groups, and getting the family land officially registered.

Concerning issues of land, the handwriting was, as far as I was concerned, already on the wall. The land shortage was getting worse and worse as the Tongan population grew and as the noble class tried to maintain its economic and political clout. Nobles would not so easily allow commoners to register land, thereby giving up their control over the people living on the land. Land was one of the only sources of leverage left through which nobles could procure labor, pigs, money, and other favors. The time to secure one's rights in land by registering was now, I thought, or the opportunity will pass.

When I returned to Tonga for two months in 1987, I lived with Atu and Malia. It was then that I met Vili, Atu and Malia's eldest son, who had been living illegally in Australia throughout the 1980s. He had finally been deported from Australia and now lived at the house.

There was clearly something wrong with him. He was extremely articulate, in both Tongan and English, but he was scary on many levels. He saw sin everywhere, and most of his day was spent reading the Bible and writing accusatory letters to notables throughout Tonga—priests and religious leaders, nobles, parliament. In the evening he liked the family to pray, in prayers led by him, and we accommodated him by letting him say grace at the family's evening meal. Often he would not eat, though, and instead would stand and whistle and smile while the rest of the family ate. He was sometimes violent, bursting into sudden rages, and at other times was vulnerable and attentive. I think the medical establishment in our culture would have diagnosed Vili as schizophrenic.[2]

Lio, Atu and Malia's second son, traveled into town Monday through Saturday to work at the Commodities Board. His small salary was a necessary part of the payments made each month on the loan for the family's new house.

Atu had written me about the house. He didn't tell me everything—not about the indoor toilet and indoor bathhouse—until I got there. The house was wonderful, but it cost the full resources of the family. The land and the house, I knew, would officially go to Vili, as the eldest male. Under such circumstances, though, the eldest would conventionally share resources with his younger brother and help him to build his own house. Vili was not conventional, however. I began to worry about what would happen to Lio if Vili controlled all the family's property. And I did something that overstepped my bounds as an anthropologist.

I initiated a talk with Lio about securing separate land rights for himself, and I urged Atu to register his land. In a private talk, Lio told me that he wanted to have a separate piece of land to build his own house but he could not say so. It would be disrespectful to raise the topic, he felt. Better for me to do it, he said; better for the eldest daughter.

So one night I sat down and talked with Atu. The conversation (which of course I did not record) went something like this.

CATHY: Why not register your land?

ATU: The noble is my friend. I know him since we are children. He helped me to get married.

CATHY: I remember, but times are changing. And what if his sons don't feel the same way to your sons? Do you know that the noble's son or grandson is going to allow your son or grandson to stay on the land? Their land is getting less, too. Every generation, the noble will have more people in his family to give land to. Do it now.

I had come with money for Atu that I knew he would offer to the noble as a gesture of "good will." I gave it to him then for the land registration. Then I broached a second topic.

> CATHY: Can't you divide the town plot in two so that Lio could have some land to build his own house?
>
> ATU: Vili will take care of Lio. He is the eldest. He knows how Lio helped build the house.
>
> CATHY: But how can you know he will follow Tongan custom? You see how he acts! He follows what's inside his own head.

I am sure that Atu and Malia had talked about this before, as well as after, our conversation. But action followed quickly. Atu's relationship with the noble family of the area was a good one, and when he approached them about registering the land, his request was honored. Atu's land was formally registered, and plans were made for the future division of the land into two plots.

Nineteen eighty-seven was a happy time for all of us. Atu and I planted a coconut together on the family's lot. It was a meaningful event to both of us, and we took photographs of us digging the hole and planting the tree to commemorate the occasion. "In five years," he said, "this tree will bear nuts, and that is when you will come back again."

We would never all meet again in Tonga. It was later that same year that Lio drowned. A letter he had sent to me arrived after word of his death. And by 1992, the year I was to return to Tonga, Atu and Malia were already in the States.

1990–91

Nineteen ninety marks the year of the family's migration, the year, too, when Vili hanged himself in the village. Vili's death was more tragic than sad for me personally. I was relieved that we were all spared having to deal with his increasingly aberrant behavior; my sisters, too, were relieved and shared these feelings with me. The tragedy was that he was Malia and Atu's eldest son—a family that had already lost four of its children.

I have always wondered whether there was more to Vili's death than his illness, or more to his illness than some predisposition for psychological disorder. Was it really a coincidence that Vili first began to appear "crazy" after he returned from overseas? Was it also coincidental that Vili hanged himself "to be closer to God" only weeks after the migration of the family?

Vili had been one of many young men who ventured overseas, who adopted the slang and dress of an Australian, who delighted in his command of this metropolitan code-switching. After his deportation, when he came back to the village and slept in the kitchen, he then became one of many other young men—many bright young Tongan men—who had to know that their future prospects were bleak. If they had no education, they would be the men who stayed in the bush. If they had no land, they would be the men who worked for other men. Vili never talked about this, but I wonder, nonetheless, whether he would have killed himself if he hadn't been to Australia, if his own prospects in Tonga had been brighter, or if Australia or the United States as an alternative concept of life did not exist. There are lingering questions for me about the colonization of the spirit and its role in Vili's illness and death—the answers to which I will never really know. I realize, too, that I was part of that colonization.

꿍 The migration of the family to the United States in 1990 was, in many ways, more eye-opening and dislocating for me than for the migrants. In the first months of their migration, I felt a certain childlike excitement to see the wonders of American technology and abundance through their eyes. What did you think of elevators? (I was so scared of that little room!) And freeways? (During traffic jams, the red lights one way and the white the other were beautiful!) And supermarkets? (You can get *any* food in America, and it's so cheap!) This soon gave way to other feelings.

It bothered me that Malia was a hotel chambermaid. My bright and talented friend, having to worry herself with the little soaps and supervisors checking to see that all the sample bottles of shampoo were accounted for. Fourteen rooms to clean every day. She was well over fifty. She should not have been laboring so at this age. It bothered me.

At Malia's next job I would see her work again for long hours and little pay. The nursing home would promise to pay her overtime rates for the two months she worked without a day off, and then would renege after she had done the work. She had no thoughts of taking them to court, as I did. Malia just quit, saying that she would not work for people who lied to her. First-generation immigrants always have it toughest, I told myself. Their children and grandchildren will have an easier time. But I'm no longer so sure about these things.[3]

Palu was thrown into a whole new world as a young single woman in the United States. Within a year of her arrival, she was living on her own and dating men. She called me often for "older sister"—type advice, mostly about relationships. He said this, and she did that, and now they're not speaking. What should she do? This is not my strong suit. I realized, though, that many of the hardest problems for Palu were the result of cultural differences. Palu would often get angry about something and never tell the young man involved what she was angry about. Incidents would pile up, and she would explode and walk out. The young man would be baffled. "What's the matter? Why don't you talk to me? I'm not putting up with this craziness" or something of the kind would be said. And Palu would call me.

I gave her middle-class American advice. Sit down and talk and tell him what's bothering you. Say something when you first realize you're upset. You don't have to blow up to tell him something that he did bothers you. Sometimes we'd do mock talks on the phone. At times I'd realize, to my dismay as an anthropologist, that I was helping Palu/Emma to unlearn her own culture. Other times I just considered myself her "informant."

In 1991, the year after Atu and Malia's arrival, there were problems with Immigration. Something about the green cards. They should have come by now, but they hadn't. And if they didn't come soon, there would be real problems. Malia would lose her job, Lio Jr.'s schooling would be in jeopardy, and they all feared deportation.

I knew nothing about green cards and Immigration. I never needed to know. But in 1991 the family called me for help. Why hadn't their green cards come yet? They had phoned government agencies, and even made a trip to their local Immigration office, but had gotten nowhere. "I don't know," I told Malia and Atu, "but I'll try to find out."

I learned a lot about my country in the process. Immigration was not in my phone book. I had to call Directory Assistance to get the Arizona number for Immigration—a toll call. A machine answers in English and Spanish. Press 1 to . . . press 2 to . . . There are nine choices. I press 4, to speak with an agent.

Then there are new machine questions. Are you this, are you that? More buttons to press. It takes several minutes and much button pressing to get to the point where they are ringing through to a person—but the lines are busy. How do people do this, I wonder, when they have real problems? Especially people who do not speak the language. "Stay on the line," says the voice, "and your phone call will be answered in the order that it is received." I wait and wait. What if you were doing this on your lunch hour? I think.

You'd never get through. After thirty-five minutes or so, there is some click-ing on the line. Finally, I think. And then there is a dial tone. I have been cut off.

I was too frustrated to repeat the procedure right then, so I waited until the next day. I went through the same long process; this time I was not cut off, but instead, after an hour no one had answered my toll call. I tried only one more time. When the agent did not answer and I was put on hold once again, I hung up, furious, never able, in hours of trying, to talk to a real person.

"The hell with this!" I said out loud to myself. (Of course, only people who are not immigrants and who are skilled speakers with social power can even think of saying "The hell with this.")

I picked up the phone again and called my U.S. Senator. "I'm a con-stituent of Senator DeConcini, as well as a contributor to his party. I'd like to speak to a Senator's aide about an immigration problem. This is Dr. Cathy Small in Flagstaff." (I made sure I got the "Doctor" in.) "Please have some-one call me back."

They did. Right away. I explained the problem: legal immigrants who have filed all papers have not received their green cards. The problem was handled within twenty-four hours. The senator's staff in Arizona called the staff of a senator in California, and they called the appropriate California immigration office. My senator's office phoned me the next day. "Yes, we think we have this remedied. Dan —————— of the Arizona immigration of-fice will explain everything. Here's his direct line; he's expecting your call." He was there when I called, and he picked up the phone: "Sorry for all the problems. Their papers *were* all in order—seems their photographs for the green cards were passport size, not regulation size for green cards. It's just one of the minor stupid bureaucratic things," he sympathized. "All they need to do is bring new pictures of the right size to their local office."

They got their green cards a few days later. They were thrilled and grate-ful. I had a new anger in me for my own country.

1992

It is a long story why Finau decided to have her first child in Flagstaff with me, and I would betray family confidences to go into the details. Suf-fice it to say that, with little advance notice, Atu and Malia and Finau de-cided that Finau would arrive from Tonga in January 1992 and stay with me until her child was born. Malia would join us after the baby was born, and we would spend the first month together. I had an obstetrician friend who would deliver the baby for no fee.

Finau said she wasn't sure exactly how many months pregnant she was when she arrived. She had been with me only three weeks when she delivered. After the birth, Malia came to live with us. It was a remarkable couple of months. I threw my first baby shower. It was my honor to name the baby.

When Finau was ready to return to Tonga (via San Francisco to visit Atu), I drove Finau, Malia, and the baby to Phoenix to the home of Tongan relatives who wanted to see them before they left for the airport. We spent a nice day with them. I knew only one of the group from Tonga, and they all had many questions to ask about me. "What religion is she?" someone said, directing the question to Malia. Before I could answer for myself, Malia jumped in: "She's Pentecostal."

I looked at Malia and she looked away. I waited to say my piece until we were outside and saying good-bye. "I'm not doing this any more, Malia. I'm not going to say I'm not Jewish."

1993

Atu's death hit me hard. I already had a plane ticket to San Francisco to spend a week with Malia, Palu (now Emma), and the larger extended family. I knew that Atu would be away in Hawai'i, and I would stay with Malia in her room at the convalescent home. Emma called. I thought she was phoning about my upcoming trip. I started talking about it—how excited I would be to see her, what we would do. "Cathy," she interrupted, "Cathy, I have bad news." I was silent. "It's Atu," she said. I already knew from her voice that he was dead. I went to California anyway. Malia had already left for the funeral. I stayed with her sister, Eseta, and mourned among Tongans.

1994–95

You will read more in the next chapter about the village in 1995 and our trip back to Tonga. When Malia told me that she would return to Tonga in December 1994, I decided to go too. It had been seven years since I'd seen the village. Finau had had another child. Little Latu, who had taught me my Tongan words, now had three children. I knew neither of their husbands.

I was teaching, and could not leave until mid-December. Malia and Lio had flown in earlier in the month, so I would fly in alone. It takes two days to fly to Tonga. From the West Coast, you travel from L.A. or San Francisco to Hawai'i, then to Samoa or Fiji, and take a local flight into Tonga. As you travel west, the time zones move backwards, so that it gets progressively earlier and earlier. You seem always to be eating breakfasts and seeing sunrises. Then, as you cross the international date line, time surges twenty-four hours ahead. You lose a day. The long travel time and the changing time zones were so disorienting that by the time I arrived in Fiji, one hour away from Tonga, I was exhausted.

As I waited at the Fiji airport for the shuttle to Tonga to board, I saw a familiar face. "Tisiola!" I shouted, hoping that this grayer, heavier, older version of the woman I knew was, in fact, a friend I had first met thirteen years earlier.

The Tongan woman turned and looked at me, and her face registered a combination of puzzlement and mild alarm. Was it that *palangi* woman who had called her name? I kept my eyes on her, waiting for some recognition. And then it came. Her mouth and eyes opened wide at the same time. "Kefi," she called back, "is that you?" We embraced and waited together for the Tongan shuttle, questioning each other about where we had been, and discussing the latest news from the village.

The chance meeting released my adrenaline. Despite my exhaustion, I was so excited getting on the plane I could hardly stand it. The hour trip seemed almost as long as all the plane travel before. As we flew toward Tonga, I was nervously aware of my own nostalgia. The village was not only an object of study for me; it had come to hold an important place in my own life. Would I be disappointed to see it changed? What about friends who had migrated or died? Would the house feel tragic to me, knowing as I did that Atu and Lio should have been there with us? I tried to talk myself into an "anthropological" mindset on the way over. To me this meant that I would try not to judge as good or bad the changes I knew I would see. This proved a difficult task.

Back on the steps of the family porch in Tonga. A young man in his early twenties comes by. He is reeling drunk as he spots me sitting and talking with Malia. Despite the fact that I am twenty years his senior, the boy is undaunted about climbing over the fence and starting a flirtatious conversation. It is a familiar scene from my early fieldwork—staving off the unwanted attentions of young men, particularly when their courage is boosted by home brew or beer.[4]

"How . . . you . . . like Tonga?" he slurs in English.

"I like Tonga very much," I answer in Tongan, annoyed at the prospect of this conversation.

"Oh, you can speak some Tongan," he says, still in English, continuing this conversation. "You like this little village? You wanna—"

"Can I ask you something?" I interrupt. He looks at me.

"Who is your mother?" I ask him.

"My mother?" he responds, startled by the question. "My mother is named Latai." He is no longer speaking in English.

"Oh, Latai! How is she?"

"You know my mother?" he asks with wide eyes.

"Yes, your mother is a good friend of mine. She will be happy to know you stopped to talk to me."

He stands motionless and speechless. I can see the wheels turning.

"Did you once live in that house?" He points next door.

"Yes," I say, pleased that he remembers. "And I knew you when you were just a little boy," I say, though I'm not actually sure that I do remember him. With each continuing exchange, he becomes more and more reserved.

He rises to his feet carefully, trying to control the effects of the alcohol. He smiles and nods good-bye. "Send my love to your mother," I say. "Tell her I will come over soon to see her." He disappears over the fence. I feel a great sense of accomplishment.

᠅ Meeting new husbands and children was the highlight of my trip back to the village. As with other aspects of my trip, though, I see that I struggled with my identity, an identity formed out of my web of relationships with others.

Latu's husband, Feleti, was gentle and caring. But I had no history with him. He was formal around me. When he spoke to his children, he did what people did in the very first months of my fieldwork. "Stop crying in front of the *palangi*," he'd say to the children. "Don't make noise or the *palangi* will be mad." It's a thing some Tongans do—quiet their kids in reference to some person of high authority, in my case a white foreigner. I found, though, that it offended me. I talked to Feleti. "I have a favor to ask you," I said to him. "Please don't call me 'the *palangi*.' I want the kids to know my name because I'm family." The light came on immediately in his eyes. Two days later, when I was taking some photos of the kids to bring back with me, he directed the children, "Look at the *pala*—— Look at Cathy."

Old friends came by to see Malia, among them the ex-district officer who was a childhood friend of Atu. I had known him for years, too, and we had a warm relationship. I also knew that he was an important guest in the house, one whose opinions were highly valued. Malia and our guest and I were talking and laughing together after we had finished a meal, when the subject turned to the upcoming centennial for the Catholic church in the village. Quite suddenly he asked me, "What church are you?"

Malia looked at me and said nothing. I don't care, I thought to myself, I'm telling him. But when the answer came out of my mouth, it was a funny compromise. "I'm half Catholic," I heard myself saying, "and half Jewish."

"Which is the Jewish half?" he asked.

"My father," I responded.

"Are you teasing me?" he asked, incredulous.

"No."

The New Year: 1995

Just before midnight on December 31, 1994, I broke out a bottle of rum that I had bought at the duty-free airport shop. I poured my rum into a co-conut. Everyone else wanted their rum in Coca-Cola which we had purchased for the occasion.

With glasses raised, we drank to the family's being together in the new year. We drank to those not with us in body—Atu and Lio and Vili, and Palu, now Emma, in the United States. I shook with the emotion of the occasion, even before Malia announced that she wanted to say something. Malia is not a speech maker, so I knew that what she was about to say must matter greatly.

Lio had died; Atu had died; and what did the family have? she asked rhetorically. I felt my eyes welling up with tears. She continued: "We have lost so many, and when I look around I feel that people look at me with pity—as if my family were *faka'ofa* [sad, pathetic]. But here today, I feel good. I know other people in the village look at our house that isn't so nice with grounds that no longer look so good, and they say, 'I wonder why a *palangi* is staying there.' This day—even though our house is not so good and we have lost so much—those people are looking at the house with a *palangi* from America and they're thinking that this family must be 'well off.' I am happy today."

I did not expect what Malia said. Honestly, I didn't quite understand it in an emotional sense. It was about Tongan pride: my presence created a stronger "face" for the family in the village, a greater outward look of prosperity. It was deeply felt, I know, but to my American ears Polynesian status one-upmanship does not resonate with the things I normally feel deeply about. Yet I could see how strongly Malia felt, how much it meant to her, and it made me cry anyhow.

I knew, when she had finished, that I should say something. The family was waiting for some words. I stood and began where she had left off. "How could I ever stay anyplace else?" Then I moved on to more familiar ground, for me. I spoke about how I had come here to study and work and get a degree, but something else had happened too. They had all become like my family, and I felt that I was with my family and that I was in my home, and I would never stay anyplace but in my family home. My talk was about finding community, belonging, and love, things that are heartfelt for Americans. My own tears were flowing heavily by the time I'd finished.

When I looked up, everyone was, in Tongan style, looking away so as not to embarrass me by noting my emotion. But tears were streaming from their eyes.

There are some things that we will never quite understand about each other. Malia cried for Polynesian reasons I will never entirely comprehend, and I cried for reasons that, if you were born in the United States, you will probably understand better than the people who were present. It struck me then that no one there really grasped why I was crying.

We all shed tears simply to see the others cry, each for his or her own reasons. This is what was most poignant to me: that compassion, after all, was the great translator.

III

R E T U R N S

෴   Part II, "Arrivals," recounted the changes that occurred in the lives of Tongan migrants who came to the United States. It also showed how Tongan migration prompted many changes in my own life (as an anthropologist and an American): the integration of "informants" into my personal life; a heightened sensitivity to the inequities of my own country; and a new confusion about how to deal with Tongans in terms of my own cultural and religious background.

The United States has changed, too, as thousands of Tongans and 20 million other migrants have settled within its borders. Sixty percent of all Tongans who have come to the United States have become new citizens within ten years of their immigration.[1] Migrants make up a sizable proportion of America's neighborhoods and electorate. In 1990 they were one in every twelve Americans, one in every five in California, the state to which most Tongans have migrated.

While the effect of migration on this country is beyond the scope of this book, two examples, both directly involving Tongans, capture the essence of the American response to our changing population in the late twentieth century.

In Arizona the textbooks used in the public schools contain something that one would not have seen even a generation ago: a small section devoted to Tonga and to its long-ruling monarch, Queen Sālote.[2] "Why do you think Queen Sālote is not better known?" reads the study question posed to students at the end of the segment. The answer, as it appears in the teacher's version, is: "The students should recognize that a small country and its ruler do not usually receive much publicity."

Cultural sensitivity, though, is not always the response to pluralism. The United States has reacted to the mass influx of third world migrants with an increased attention to cultural diversity and at the same time an increased intolerance and distrust. A Euro-American woman living outside Salt Lake City confided to me that Tongans are not welcome in her neighborhood. "They kill animals for their feasts right on their property. Do you know that we've got to send our own children inside when they start digging those pits [the underground ovens for cooking feast food] because we know it means they're going to slaughter some animal? There is an unwritten agreement among people I know to never sell an animal to a Tongan."

Either through personal encounters or through politically charged issues such as English-only legislation, the fact that migration is changing the American landscape is apparent to most Americans. What is less apparent are the changes occurring in the home countries of the millions of emigrants. Some of the most startling transformations in the world are taking place in the villages left behind.

In the next four chapters, we return to the same Tongan village that we left in chapter 2, back in the early 1980s. You will see Tongan island life and relationships again in the mid-1990s, a generation after the first wave of migrants left Tonga. Since you last witnessed daily life in the village, migration from Tonga has quickened its pace. Those once thought of as "temporarily" overseas now seem to be permanent residents of other countries, and their return is unlikely. Family migration has become more common than individual migration. By 1990, the number of Tongans living overseas was estimated to be equal to about 40 percent of the island population.[3]

The 1980s, particularly the latter years of the decade, were a time of major social change in Tonga. This was not due to any sudden change in leadership or policy. Leadership had continued in an unbroken line since Tupou (George) I, the first Tongan king, and it had been guided by the same constitution. King Taufaʻahau Tupou IV, son of Queen Salote (Tupou III), who ruled from 1918 to 1965, pressed for economic development in Tonga as he had since he became premier in 1949. The five-year national development plans of 1980–85 and 1985–90, which guided government policy, were similar in content to previous policies, stressing commercial agriculture, improved public health, technical education, and the development of jobs through the expansion of government services and small export industries.

Yet, some of the most important changes of the decade were unplanned, a culmination of economic and social forces that had originated earlier in the century. Tonga was feeling the effects of two decades of overseas migration. Over the past fifteen to twenty years, despite planning aimed at the local economy, it was remittance dollars that had come to buoy the Tongan national economy, providing money for imports and private investment. During the 1980s, both Tonga's household and national coffers had come to depend on remittances. Migrants' dollars made possible more elevated local lifestyles, resulting in increased imports and spiraling inflation. And the bounty that migrants returned to their relatives in Tonga spurred even more migration.

Political changes occurred as well. After a century of social reform, commoner education, and rising individual enterprise, Tonga had a literate and aspiring population with limited options for improving their futures.[4] Some Tongans migrated as a result, but the same forces that were leading many overseas led others who stayed to question why there wasn't more opportunity in Tonga. During my residence in the village, from 1981 to 1984, the economic squeeze on Tongan commoners was expressed in private grumbling and informal kava circle talk. By 1990, these same sentiments had turned political.

The government under Tonga's constitutional monarchy, while an elected two-house system, left considerable power in the hands of the Tongan aristocracy.[5] A new democracy movement associated with a growing middle class found expression in 1986, when Tonga's tax system was changed radically. Company income tax was reduced, while a new retail sales tax was imposed on consumers. Companies and government agencies benefited, while poor people, farmers, and heavy consumers, including the rising middle class, lost.[6]

In the next election, six of Tonga's nine seats in the lower (People's) house of parliament went to new educated candidates who were willing to criticize government policy openly, sending a new message about the readiness of the Tongan electorate for greater fairness and participation in the governing process.[7] The pro-democracy movement has continued to center on a small cadre of commoner-elected, overseas-educated representatives to the Tongan parliament who are questioning the processes of government and the allocation of public funds. Using a number of public forums for publicizing nongovernment views,[8] pro-democracy thinkers have initiated public inquiries into issues such as the fees that Tongan officials charged the government for attending extra public meetings, the cost to the government of the princess's residence in California, the government's selling of Tongan citizenship to foreigners (at $10,000 per passport), and the appropriate destination of revenues received from the rental of Tongan satellite space.

The 1990s saw rising popular support for the pro-democracy point of view, particularly among educated middle-class commoners. Migration, while it has thinned the ranks of the discontented, has contributed to the democracy movement by financially bolstering the middle class and by introducing large numbers of Tongans to foreign democratic systems. Family members resident overseas, returned migrants, and overseas-educated Tongans are among the growing numbers that have direct experience with these alternative systems.

In returning to a Tongan village in the next section, you will witness many other changes in daily life and relationships which often escape the notice of national-level observers and statistics. Each of the next four chapters highlights a different facet of the non-migrating side of the migration process, as we look at the changes that have occurred in village economies, family relationships, the life of an individual Tongan woman, and Tongan tradition.

The personal, economic, family, and cultural changes that you will see in these chapters have all occurred in the wake of migration, but it is too simplistic to say that migration directly *caused* all the changes. It is more accurate to say that leaving home and the changes that occurred at home are all part of one related process. Migration, and the forces throughout the century that lead to migration, have tied the villages that were left behind and the people who stayed to a global process that is changing their lives too.

Chapters 7 and 8 show what the money and goods sent back by migrants have meant to both the outward appearance of the village and the inner dynamics of families. Chapter 7 offers a closer look at a village economy whose subsistence base is eroding and which has come to rely heavily on remittances from overseas relatives. It offers a view of recent political and economic changes from the standpoint of daily life within a village and the concrete experiences that impinge on the lives of particular villagers.

The changes that migration has wrought in family life are seen intimately in chapter 8, where the relationship between villagers and their overseas relatives, home for the holidays in 1994–95, are explored. This is a chapter about Tonga's global families who are struggling with the contradictions caused by family members who have different economic means, different nationalities, and, increasingly, different cultures.

In chapter 9 the island side of Tongan migration is seen from the individual perspective of Finau, the eldest sister of Emma and daughter of Malia. When her family migrated in 1990, Finau stayed in Tonga. We will meet her as she was in 1991, shortly after the family left Tonga. You will hear her talk about her life memories and her decision, even after visiting in the United States, to stay in Tonga. You will meet her again, five years after the migration of her family, and witness her life in a seacoast village on Tonga's southernmost island.

In Finau's memories and current life experiences, we find many of the personal contradictions and pulls that exist in contemporary Tongan life. You will see a woman strongly committed to tradition, whose experience of growing up traditional awakened a strong sense of personal freedom and a need to break with authority. You will see a woman who opted for life on a small island in Tonga, and yet whose daily routine is so hectic that it resembles the busiest working mother's schedule in the States.

The final chapter in this section looks at the issue of "tradition"—at some of the guiding principles that define Tongan custom and identity—and the forces that are coming to influence tradition in the post-migration age. In a transnational context where families and economies cross national borders, tradition is an anchor of continuity and stability. But, as chapter 9 shows, this is also the reason why tradition must change.

⁙ We have *returned*, this section's title suggests, but the question is: to where? Although the chapters in "Returns" take you "home"—that is, back to the same Tongan village that Tongan migrants left, you may find, as I did, that there is no going home. Tonga, like the United States, has been transformed. It has become a transnational place—a theme I will return to in the last section—and that is why even in returning to a small Tongan island village, one encounters individuals and families, lifestyles and customs, that now belong to a much wider world system.

7

Going Home:
Tongan Village Life
in the 1990s

꙾ There were some good reasons to be in Tonga
in December 1994. A women's group in San Mateo, California, wanted to
exchange a shipment of manufactured goods plus $1,200 cash for woven
pandanus mats, a specialty of women from a far northern island. An exchange on the main island had been arranged with the northern island
group, and Malia planned to fly to Tonga and oversee the exchange for her
group. Most important, though, it was the hundredth anniversary of the village church, the oldest Catholic church in Tonga, and there would be big
goings-on in the village, including memorials to those in the village who
had died. We were both thinking that it would be a good time to remember Atu and to be together again in Tonga.

The family decided that even though little Lio would miss three weeks
of school, he should go too and meet his cousins in Tonga. His second-grade
teacher sent books and homework exercises, packed with her instructions
that he was to practice his reading if he were to keep up with his grade. Both
of Eseta's children—Alyssa at nineteen and Sara at twenty-three—planned
to make the trip. It would be the first ever for Sara, the second for Alyssa.
Chaperoned by their father's elder sister, they would stay in the new house
that Manu had built with his retirement money. Both young women were
prepared to join in the dances that would be held in the village during the
celebrations. Malia had instructed them in Tongan dancing and had already
sewn their elaborate dancing costumes. Sara would join the group sitting
dances and line dances. Alyssa would perform a solo dance called the

tauʻolunga.[1] Palu contemplated making the trip too, but in the end decided against it—because of her work, she said.

Malia and Lio had flown in earlier in the month, when my own teaching schedule would not allow me to leave. So I traveled alone to Tonga and prepared myself for the significant changes I expected to see. Through my reading I was aware that the 1980s had been a decade of major social and economic changes in Tonga, which included the stepping-up of external migration, the introduction of television, the electrification of Tonga's outer villages and islands, and the growing democracy movement among Tongan commoners.

The family had also prepared me for the material changes, particularly as the time of my visit got closer. "Tonga is really different from when you were here," Finau warned me. "There has been much progress, and you will not recognize Tonga. Nukuʻalofa [the capital] has many big buildings. There are electric lights on our street. And there is TV."

"Bring more money than you think," Malia warned.

Indeed, all of the changes they referred to had happened on some level. But, after a warm reunion, as I rode expectantly from the airport with Malia and Vei to the village, I was surprised not by Tonga's growth but by how little had appeared to change. The monumental alterations that were supposed to have occurred in the past seven years were not obvious to me.

The main road to the village was rough and pockmarked, as it had been a decade earlier. The village looked worn in places, but well kept. The main village street, once ground coral, was paved now, but all the familiar structures were there: the old church by the lagoon; the stone convent; the cooperative store in the community hall built by village women's development groups. All looked slightly more battered but were still functioning. The old "pool hall," a room-sized wooden building where mostly adolescent boys played billiards, was boarded up, but a new one—in block concrete—stood right across the path. The little village stores, some the size of a U.S. newsstand, still sold dry goods, bread, cigarettes, soda, and other items. Some were newer versions of those I had remembered with an expanded line of products that included disposable diapers and chocolate candy bars and videos.

Two things struck me as different about Tongan housing. I saw almost no thatched houses, which made up almost a fifth of the dwelling places in 1982. The kitchens, in thatch or bamboo, for openfire outdoor cooking which almost every household had had in my earlier survey were also gone.[2] There were new and bigger houses than I had ever seen before in the village. The able young man who had lived on the corner, and was educated overseas as an engineer, had returned to become head of Tonga's Electric Board. His well-apportioned, multilevel home sat on a groomed lot with a carport for his two cars, the property enclosed by a chain-link fence. His residence on the coral path that led to our house explained the electric street lights which illuminated our village side road.

But other houses looked shabbier, falling apart. Our house, as it turned out, was one of them. As we approached the third structure on the village path, the one that should have been the family house, I kept searching in vain for familiar signs. The house was not at all as it had been seven years earlier. The plot was overgrown and unkempt, the ground strewn with gum wrappers and cigarette butts. The wooden fence surrounding the property had broken, so that pigs came and went easily in and out of the yard, rooting up any remaining flowers. Several of the house's louvered windows had been shattered by storms. Unable to be replaced, they remained there with cracks or had been removed entirely, leaving gaping openings in the walls.

Inside the house, sheet vinyl, installed in do-it-yourself style, had replaced the layers of pandanus mats that had once been the flooring. A couch, a TV, a propane hotplate serving as an indoor stove had been added. In the kitchen, where several louvers had broken, the window area was completely covered over with boards, leaving the room dark even at midday. Everything was falling apart.

The sink in the bath area hung out of the wall at a forty-five-degree angle, dumping water onto the floor whenever the faucet was opened. The rain catchment tank in our backyard, which once held sweet rainwater funneled from the roof, now was an ugly open cement square sunk into the ground. It held three inches of filthy brown water into which broken plastic bottles, rusted cans, and other garbage were strewn. The piped water that the village pumped up from the local aquifer now ran twenty-four hours a day, but it needed to be boiled. The bamboo kitchen that the family had worked so hard to build was ramshackle now, the home of termites and spiders and the household pigs. A huge wooden box sat on the front porch, eating up half the sitting area.

However much I tried, I could not help but cringe at the sight of the house as it mingled with my memories of it. How well tended it had always been. How hard Malia had worked in her development group to build the kitchen. How Lio Sr. had worked to secure the loan, and mostly Atu's pride in his retirement as he was finally able to complete the house.

OUR HOUSE. Our house in 1995. The large box that sits on the porch is an example of one of the smaller containers that was shipped from the United States to Tonga.

☡ On the day of my arrival, I took a walk around the village, recording those first impressions that anthropologists say are so important before the scene becomes familiar. The Paepae craft center, which had been so much a part of village aspirations and efforts in the early 1980s, was no longer operational but literally falling down and overgrown with vegetation. Tourist busses had stopped visiting the center. The familiar posters announcing the Friday night movie at the women's hall were missing. "That's right," people told me, "and there are no more movies at the banana shack either. People watch videos or go into town." In the center of the village stood the same cement frame that had been erected for a two-story house and then abandoned by its owners, who had decided to stay permanently in New Zealand. Several of the Marist brothers who had lived at the area's Catholic high school on the border of the village had been reposted elsewhere; now only two remained. The "college" looked decidedly bedraggled without the constant and purposeful energy of a full live-in staff. The tapa-making houses had finally fallen down.

Despite the many public structures that seemed worn, the village appeared to have more money—at least individual households did. I could even see the prosperity in the village dogs. They were healthier, more full-bodied, and they did not seem to cower as much as those I remembered. There was an obvious proliferation of "things": refrigerators, washing machines, TV sets, VCRs, household furniture, manufactured toys. In the early 1980s motor vehicles were a rare luxury; now there were numerous cars, trucks, and vans sitting outside village houses, and the village road was almost busy with traffic. Large shipping boxes that had carried goods from overseas sat next to their houses of destination. Sometimes turned on their sides and used as a sitting room, they were all over the village. I was to see these, and larger containers the size of railroad cars, throughout Tonga—a ubiquitous reminder of the overseas presence in Tongan life.

Certainly, as the family had said, there were changes in Tonga. But the changes seemed to exist on a household-by-household basis. What I witnessed in the village were bouncing fortunes—mobility adjusted both upward and downward. I could see this in the outward circumstances of the ten families I had known most intimately from their diaries thirteen years before. Some had prospered: those with much help from overseas, farmers with their own land who had added borrowed or rented land to their holdings, and people on government salaries. Some had not been so fortunate: subsistence farmers, wage earners without good government jobs, people without land. Some had left for overseas. Thirteen years had made quite a difference, and few households were as I had first seen them. The bases of people's fortunes were transparent in the lives of two friends whom I met again in 1994 on this very first walk. They are women of approximately the same age, both with children, both married for twenty years or more, but whose fortunes over the previous ten years had sharply diverged.

Sālote and Moala

Sālote calls out from the women's hall. We embrace and talk awhile. She and several other women are making kava for a big kava-drinking evening (*faikava*) that she has arranged and is supervising. It is a family fund-raiser. She has bought the kava and has asked female friends and relatives to make it and serve it to the men who will pay to attend the kava-drinking evening. The profits from the event, after she has paid for the kava root and given gifts to the kavamakers, will be hers.

"You must see my house now, Kefi! I have a big new house with many nice things inside. It's so different from when you were here. And I have my own store," she beams.

For most of Sālote's twenty-one-year marriage, her husband has been a merchant marine. He works for an overseas shipping company and is away for long stretches, several months to a couple of years at a time. Among other places, his ship will travel this year to Philadelphia and Maryland, and then on to Argentina. Since he began working for a new company a year ago, he has managed to send home $1,000 per month. With his overseas salary, Sālote has built a modern new house and set up a little grocery store in the village. She is easily able to afford the up-front expenses of her profit-making kava evening. After many years of separation, Sālote hopes that her husband will be able to come back and live with her permanently by next year, or the year after. It is their hope that their savings and their little store will be enough to provide the basis for a living and capital for the rest of their lives.

"Come to the *faikava* tonight," she asks me. "You come and make kava for the men; it's my faikava tonight, OK?" OK, I tell her.

Moala's house is visible from the women's hall. It is clean and well kept but sparse and simple. It looks the same as it did ten years ago, only older. It is small, perhaps six hundred square feet, and wooden, consisting primarily of one large room with two small areas for sleeping. The latrine and thatched kitchen are outside. Nicely woven mats, which Moala made herself, lie in layers on the floor. A small standing wooden cabinet with a mesh screen is the repository for leftover food and ripening fruits, so that insects and animals could not easily get into it.

Moala is at the same stage of life as Sālote, only, as Moala herself would tell you, she has not been as fortunate as some. Moala and her husband have four children, ranging from their mid-teens to twenty-four. None of her children is working right now. The eldest, a son, had a wage job, but then the job ended. Another son has just finished teachers' preparation school but hasn't started working yet. He'll begin at the local high school next year. One child is still in school, and another, a girl, who has just finished school, says she will try to find work next year.

Moala and her husband have no overseas relatives to help them, and thus their whole income depends on their domestic enterprises. Manase grows their food and sells his small surplus locally. Moala has always been a fine weaver and basketmaker. She used to make money crafting tourist items—pocketbooks and laundry baskets—and selling them to tourists either in town or at the Paepae.

"How're your handicrafts going?" I ask.

"Oh, I don't do that much, now. It's been six years or so since I made a basket. Tourists are not such a big thing here anymore," she tells me. "Handicraft making has almost disappeared in the village. It's very slight compared to what it used to be."

"Then what do you do to make money?" I ask.

"Now I make mats and sell them to Tongans. I stopped making baskets," she explains, "because the money for weaving mats is so much better."

Her answer initially surprised me, but it explained more about the decline of the Paepae craft center. The whole focus of production had turned to overseas Tongans. Indeed, as I talked more generally to people in the village, they confirmed that they could get much more money from making traditional tapa cloth and mats for overseas Tongans than they could by making things for the tourists. Nevertheless, compared to the prospects of others in the village with overseas support or government jobs, Moala's fortunes had declined. Her hopes now centered on her children, and the continued possibility that they might get decent wage-earning jobs.

A Remittance Economy

What I witnessed in the village on my first day back were the tangible signs of the remittance economy, and the full grip it had on Tonga. Since the 1960s, when exports exceeded imports, Tonga's balance of trade had tipped in favor of imports, and the national debt had risen steadily.[3] The cost of overseas products—primarily for development and for consumption in Tonga—had come to outweigh by far national income through the sale of agricultural produce.[4] Part of the difference was made up through remittances—the money and goods sent to Tonga from Tongans overseas. Between 1970 and 1975, $10.7 million in remittances was sent per year, approximately 40 percent of the country's annual receipts during the same period and 60 percent of its export bill.[5] Between 1980 and 1985, annual remittances were double this amount. By 1989, despite burgeoning imports, an estimated 65 percent of Tonga's import bill was paid for by overseas money. Remittances brought in almost four times the revenues of exports and accounted for 45 percent of Tonga's gross domestic product.[6]

At the household level, a 1984 study reported that 28 percent of Tongan household income came from remittances, and that 90 percent of all Tongan households received at least some remittance income.[7] A 1991 study found that remittances accounted for as much as 42 percent of total household income.[8] This new source of income was apparent at the household level in the increased consumption of store-bought food, often imported, and in a new flood of household appliances and furniture.

Remittance money also translated directly into the new houses, the new cars, and the new businesses I saw in the village. Upward mobility was so

clearly a factor of remittances that the exception was notable. When I visited a friend in his two-story cement house, built ten years before, he was
quick to remind me proudly: "There's not a person in Tonga who's built a
house like this with money just from Tonga. All these new houses being
built—it's all with overseas money. But not a single overseas dollar went to
build this house. It was built from what I myself grew and sold."

In traveling throughout the main island of Tongatapu, and to one of the
smaller islands in the south, I was to witness the same remittance-related
phenomena in many villages: increased motor traffic, new and more opulent village homes, and more small Tongan-owned village businesses, from
a corner dry goods store to a sewing shop to a video store.

Kai, the cabdriver who drove me around the main island for a survey trip,
was one of Tonga's new entrepreneurs. He owned his own taxi service, consisting of two cars, which he planned on replacing the following year with
two new vehicles. He had bought the cars with the money he earned as a
tuna packer in American Samoa. For three and a half years he worked for
"great pay," in his words, putting tuna tins in boxes, earning as much as
$300 some weeks. When his father in Tonga became ill, he returned home
with savings sufficient to buy two used cars and begin his business. His father and younger brother now went to the bush every day to grow food for
the family, with a small amount saved for export. Kai's taxi business contributed to the family income. He told me that he made about $30 per day,
and that, although he drove both tourists and Tongans, the mainstay of his
business—like Moala's—was other Tongans.

So overseas cash flowing into the village from relatives or returning migrants had funded a new mobility for many. But the remittance economy
had also meant that those without overseas money, like Moala, or those with
only one overseas low-wage earner, like our family, were by comparison
poorer than they had been. These relative fortunes, and the reasons behind
them, escaped no one in the village.

Back at the House

Ever since the family had migrated and both of her sisters in Tonga married, Vei had remained alone in the family home. She cried uncharacteris-
tically as she talked about it to me: "Sometimes I come home and there is
no one here and I cry. I just sit in the house and cry."

Living alone is not considered a desirable arrangement in Tonga, and it was not surprising that, within a few months of Vei's lone residence, new configurations emerged. Kalo, the woman across the street, was a recent widow. Although she is not a "real" relative, her deceased husband was considered a distant relative of Atu. Everyone emphasized that connection when she and all her daughters moved into the family house to keep Vei company. Kalo's sons stayed across the street at their own house. Kalo cleaned and cooked and did laundry for the nine people living in the now joint household.

The scene at the house was hectic. Malia, little Lio, and I moved into the family home with Vei. Malia's other two daughters—Latu and Finau—and their children returned for the holidays as well. Latu, her three children, and her husband, Feleti, arrived from their residence at the Tongan seminary where Feleti was in school. Finau and her two children eventually came in from the southern island of 'Eua. To accommodate the influx of holiday traffic, Kalo and her daughters moved back across the street to their own house. Kalo's eldest daughter was preparing hurriedly for a holiday trip to visit relatives in the United States, while Kalo's son had come back to Tonga from New Zealand. Despite all of Vei's visitors, two of the neighbor's children also slept at the house, as well as the son of Atu's closest friend from another village. In all, the 850-square-foot dwelling housed nine children and five adults on most days.

Two boys carried in a refrigerator and plugged it in to the house's only outlet. It came from down the block, a favor to the household that had guests from the United States, including *palangi* company. Other households, both neighbors and kin, sent food: papayas and coconuts, green bananas, pineapples, and yams.

Malia had been in Tonga for two weeks by the time I arrived, and she was as busy as I had ever seen her. When she was not preparing food for the nine children in the house, she was checking to make sure that her American nieces (Eseta's children) were all right, that Lio had clean clothes, that the drink one of the children had spilled was wiped up. She was also busy sewing clothes for herself, including her outfits for the big dances in which she was participating.

"Why are you sewing clothes?" I asked her, knowing that she had already made her dancing costume, as well as those of Alyssa and Sara, and that Malia and I had jointly sent literally racks of clothes as presents for village friends in the huge box that sat on the porch. Shaking her head, she told me the story of the box.

It had arrived, she thought, on a Monday. By the time Malia's plane came in three days later, on Thursday, Vei had given all of the clothes away. "Who came to get things?" I asked Vei. "Everyone who could see the box," she said, "even people who weren't close."

"What about kin?"

"Some were kin, such as Salote, but mostly it was neighbors who could see the box sitting there. Relatives didn't know soon enough," said Vei.

Anticipating the demand of kin and friends for the crate's cargo, Malia had been smart enough to send a separate small package with her own clothes for the celebration and for daily wear while she was in Tonga. She told Vei not to touch it. "Wait until I come!" she told Vei by telephone. But by the time she arrived, all that clothing was gone too.

"It was funny," Malia told me. "I'd see the woman from the corner store walking in my skirt. 'There goes my skirt,' I thought to myself. And then I'd see someone else in the village with clothes made from the bolt of cloth I had sent. 'My new outfit just went around the corner,' I said. 'Vei, you gave everything away!'" Vei, hearing our conversation, came to explain further: "I couldn't stop people when they came. I really just couldn't. I told them to take what they wanted."

So when Malia arrived in the village, she had no clothes to wear except for the skirt she had traveled in. She had to sew all new clothes, including her outfits for the dance. Malia thought this more funny than upsetting because, as she herself would say, this is part of the Tongan way. It is how Malia herself operates, and how she wants her children to be.

Conversations on the Porch

The house sits on the corner of one of the walking thoroughfares of the village. The porch of the house—a cement slab shaded by an overhung roof—is a social gathering place. Neighbors, relatives, and other village passersby regularly come by to chat and pass the time, particularly because Malia is home.[9]

Many former villagers are back from Australia, New Zealand, and the United States for the centennial celebration and the Christmas holiday. The village is bustling. From the porch you can hear an outdoor bingo game on the corner. A man sitting under an awning calls out numbers to people seated on the grass. "O-52!" he yells. It costs twenty-five cents to play a round, and for each quarter, you get an old vinyl floor tile onto which someone has written the letters B-I-N-G-O with numbers in each of the letter columns.

Players look for little flat rocks on the ground with which to mark the successful numbers on their cards. It is a new thing in Tonga, people say, and there are big Bingo games in town.

Fefita comes by. She is one of those whose fortunes changed in the few years between 1980 and 1987. With the money from children overseas, she was able to upgrade her home and her lifestyle in Tonga. "Malia, I am so glad you are not like those other people who let strangers [non-kin] stay in their houses while they are overseas," she says in a low, confiding tone. "Do you see what some of these houses look like? Non-relatives don't take care of the houses in the same way that real kin would. And the village looks bad as a result! It is good for people who go overseas to only let their own children or relatives stay in their houses. Like you." Given the state of our house, and the family's very distant relationship to Kalo, I think she must be chiding us in a backhanded way, but no one seems to take offense at the remark.

Latu is doing laundry at the end of the porch with her "new" washing machine. The round machine with the electric wringer is actually a renovated washer from the 1950s. Imported mainly from New Zealand and the United States, these older machines work better in Tonga than their modern descendants, which require more electricity as well as hookup to a water source. One can pour water into the older machines, and use electricity just to agitate the washer and turn the wringer. These thirty- and forty-year-old machines with all-metal parts are sturdier and better built than their modern counterparts, which people complain break down so easily. Latu's one request from me was for such an old round washing machine to help her do the hours and hours of hand laundry for both her own family and others at the seminary where her husband goes to school.

Latu is on her third load of laundry. When she finishes washing and wringing the clothes, she hangs them on a long piece of barbed wire strung between two poles. As the wire and nearby fences fill with drying laundry, a neighbor comes by with her wash. She has already made arrangements to be the next one to use the machine. After she leaves, another woman shows up to use the washing machine.

Throughout the days, there is a steady stream of visitors who sit for a few minutes or a couple of hours while children run in and out of the house and laundry and sewing get done. There is an exchange of news—who's doing what in the U.S., who's doing what in the village. Who left, who came back, who got married, who died.

Latu's husband, Feleti, is busy fixing the household fence. With no materials to do it, he has taken the wooden shipping crate from the porch and broken it down board by board and nail by nail. He flattens crooked nails with a hammer so they can be reused and carefully stacks each board. The shipping box from overseas becomes our new fence, an apt metaphor, I think at the time.

Malia is doing some crocheting. The blanket she is finishing took her more than a month to make. She brought three of them, crocheted during her evenings at the convalescent home in the United States. This one is white and purple with raised flowers on each crocheted square. She will finish it tonight and bring it tomorrow to her son-in-law's sister as a gift. She has already given one blanket to the woman on the corner who was taken with the "American wealth," and who came back with pandanus mats to give to Malia in return. Malia also brought a blanket to a wedding recently of Lio's mother's relatives—what Tongans would call the *kavenga,* or obligations, of Lio. The fact that Lio's father and mother never married is irrelevant. Lio has obligations to both his mother's and father's relatives, even though he is only eight years old. When his obligations come up, as through a marriage or funeral, other relatives must help him to fulfill his *kavenga.* As Malia works, Kalo is sitting with her, talking. Moala, the ex-basketmaker, comes by to visit. Both women are fascinated by the American-style crocheting and watch Malia closely as we talk.

The conversation is about traditional wealth and exchange. The women are talking about the *village* end of the exchange network through which Tongan-Americans get their tapa cloth and mats. Last year both Moala and Kalo joined production groups to make traditional Tongan wealth—mats and/or bark cloth. Both women hoped to use some of the wealth in exchanges with overseas groups. Moala joined both a cloth-making group and a mat-making group. Her groups produced two big mats and three full tapa cloths for each woman in turn. The only problem, she says, is that it took her the entire year—working full-time—to make them. Moala barely had time to do anything else, and then, when family obligations came up, she used most of the wealth for family purposes.

Kalo also joined a tapa-making group last year. Although she planned on making two tapa clothes, she didn't have enough bark to make even one full cloth. She had planted mulberry in the bush, but, as often happens these days, it was stolen. Kalo had to buy bark to beat from the marketplace, a commodity that has skyrocketed in price.

Village women say that they like what the New Zealand exchange groups are now doing. They will exchange suites of furniture for tapa cloth. If you want a bedroom suite, it "costs" two tapa cloths. You can get a kitchen; you can get a living room set; you can get different kinds of "sets" for a specified amount of bark cloth. If you want to furnish your whole house, it's five cloths for every room in the house. Women can also sell their tapa cloths outright to buyers in the town market. Often the buyers are overseas Tongans who need a cloth for their relatives and are acting as brokers. A tapa cloth will sell for T$700 in April or May, up to T$800 in November, December, and January, when Tonga is inundated with overseas Tongans.

As we all talk, children run in and out, making constant trips to the little store during the holiday season to buy penny candy, gum, soda, and ice cream. There are clothes everywhere, most hanging on lines now, some dirty and doubling as rags to wipe up the floor or the baby before they are washed. Three times a day someone cooks for the household. People eat in shifts because serving all fourteen-plus at once would be difficult in the little house. Whenever a big Sunday meal is cooked in the underground oven, plates of food go out to other houses, and they come in on a regular basis from others. All day long children from other households also come in and out to put something on ice, or take it out.

Tongan TV goes on the air at 5 P.M. and runs till 10 or 11, and there is always a bevy of children in the house to watch the opening moments. Major sports and cultural events in Tonga are carried on Tongan television, but Tongan TV fare is largely U.S.-produced and distributed. There are only two operating channels, and the programming consists predominantly of half-hour sitcoms, religious programs, sports, and cartoons.

The religious programs are sometimes reenactments or mini-dramatizations of biblical stories. Much of it is what I would call "religious right" programming. In the United States, it would probably air on a cable channel targeted at evangelical or fundamentalist Christians. One segment that aired several times during a two-week period featured a male singer on the steps of the U.S. Capitol. The song asks, what has happened to America? The singer laments, sometimes with tears in his eyes, the degradation of U.S. life, depicted in images of gay pride parades, inner city scenes, drugs, and abortion. It is a very particular moral and political message.

I notice the commercials. They do not sell sex, like American TV; they sell a sense of finery, privilege, class. For the very best, go to ———. If you want the finest, then buy ———.

The kids watch everything, but they prefer videos. The videos available in Tonga are overwhelmingly action films. Watching a video is an "event," and other children from around the neighborhood come and watch together when a VCR and a movie are somehow procured.

With the children watching the TV and the refrigerator plugged in, the electric outlet in the house is full. The house, built with only one outlet in 1987, can no longer keep pace with the unanticipated use of appliances. To boil water at night in the electric coffeemaker from the United States, one must unplug the refrigerator. Vei cannot iron her clothes while Malia uses the electric sewing machine. Such scenes drive home a larger point: infrastructure has not kept pace with development. The same is true in a variety of spheres: the number of vehicles has grown faster than the development of roads; consumption of batteries, plastic, glass, and other manufactured products has outstripped the ability to dispose of the products; the water needs of homes and agriculture exceed the capacity of the village water system to deliver.

It is already almost 10 P.M. when yet another woman comes by to do laundry. She intends to run the machine by unplugging the refrigerator, but it is hot and we are afraid the food will spoil. She comes back with several extension cords that will be joined and then run to the house across the road. The washing machine will run almost all night.

I am sitting with a group of women looking at photographs of past celebrations. There is one of a recent twenty-first birthday. The young woman who is being honored lies stretched out amid her gifts of mats and tapa cloth wealth, holding up a small object that looks like a decorated Christmas tree. What is that? I ask pointing to the unidentifiable object in her hand. It is from her father's side, from relatives in New Zealand, and it accompanied the gifts they sent, I am told. It is a plastic tree. On each branch hang cutout photos, like ornaments, each the face of a different relative who could not be with the young woman on her special day.

As Moala gets up to leave for the evening, I ask her, "Would you still make a basket for me?"

"Sure I will," she responds, "but my weaving will be slow because I am out of practice."

My request, as I knew, came at an opportune time. Moala wanted extra money to prepare feast food for the celebration, and I could give it to her in time for the event, before the basket was made. The next day another woman—who heard that I gave Moala money for a basket—came by with mats to sell so she could afford the special food that each household would make for the upcoming centennial feast.

Getting Ready for the Celebration

Christmas came and went. It was not the focus of activity. Everyone was centered on the centennial that would occur two days later. The one hundredth anniversary of the church was an occasion of national significance that showcased the village. There would be two days of dancing and feasting attended by both the local noble family and other Tongan royalty, including the King and Queen.

The ostensible function was to raise sufficient money to restore the old stone Catholic church that sat near the lagoon. Restorations would include cleaning the stone and replacing broken stained glass lost in storms. But it would also serve other purposes: it would recognize the one hundredth anniversary of the church in the village and offer another public occasion to affirm the increasingly strained relationship between Tonga's churches and its monarchy. For the church, this was also a major opportunity for fundraising beyond the renovations, to bring in additional monies to the church coffers. For individual families, it provided occasions for memorials—to give funds publicly in the name of relatives who had died and thus honor them and the donating family.

Each household in the village was expected to make one *pola*. A *pola* consists of one's finest food—several roasted piglets, different varieties of yams, watermelon, fish, roast chicken, steamed lobster, packets of baked taro leaves stuffed with lamb or canned corned beef and coconut cream, fresh drinking coconuts, and other items—all set out on a twelve-foot-long wooden platform lined with banana leaves. For the first time, I saw liberal use of expensive cellophane wrapping to cover each dish, perhaps because of the many flies in the village. Over the top of the platform rose a series of arched trellises. These were draped in leis of candy and covered with mosquito netting to keep insects away from the food.

Formal printed invitations were given to each household that made a *pola*. Ten people eat at each *pola*. The household may invite five guests to sit and eat at its *pola*. The five other invitees must be members of the clergy or their guests. Most households gave their invitations to overseas relatives home for the holiday, to their eldest daughter, or to relatives from other villages. The rest of the family, who contributed to the *pola* and helped make it, would eat later, from the leftovers, after the *pola* was returned to the house.

Malia and Kalo made their *pola* together. Kalo provided the yams and pigs from her own stocks and our household purchased the remainder necessary for the *pola*. Most items could be bought from the village stores or from the fishermen who arrived in their open trucks bearing strings of fish. Melons and a few other items had to come from town. Produce was not available at the local stores this Christmas. Village farmers would lose too much money by selling their produce in the village, where kinship and friendship loyalties would bring down the price of their food.

The town market—where farmers brought their excess produce for sale in an open-air lot—was begun in 1970, when the customer base of non-farmers or part-time farmers had become large enough to justify its existence. In the early 1980s the town market sold primarily produce. The perimeter areas sold tourist items, such as Tongan jewelry, woven handbags, and T-shirts. There were some booths, or parts of booths, that sold imported items to Tongans: mainly toiletries, batteries, and school supplies.

In 1994 the market where farmers brought their produce had temporarily moved so that a new space could be built in the center of town. The temporary produce market was set up next to another market that was now of huge proportions. This overflowing new market was not for tourists; it consisted of budget import items for Tongans. What had been the periphery of the marketplace a decade earlier had burgeoned into a bustling and formidable market of its own. Stall after stall in this sprawling bazaar sold used microwave ovens, hair dryers, music tapes, T-shirts, shampoo, perfume, and other imported goods. The stalls were stocked with items sent by overseas relatives.[10]

Vei and I squeezed through the crowded market to buy the *pola* items we needed. Vei wanted a Coke, now readily available from scattered food and drink stands. She popped the lid and took a long drink and began walking with me. No sooner had she taken her first sip from the can than a Tongan boy came toward us headed in the opposite direction. "Give me my drink," he said softly as they passed each other. In an instant, her hand went out and he took the can and walked on. Neither looked back. "Who's that?" I asked Vei.

"I don't know," Vei said.

"Why did you give him your drink?"

"Because he asked," she said.

With students on school break, and with many returning Tongans in town, the produce section of the market was packed. Pineapples were in season, and many stands displayed small stacks of ripe pineapple. Lettuce, cabbage, and assorted vegetables, special offerings of the town market, were available to satisfy overseas and foreign tastes. Handfuls of beans and carrots were tied together in bundles and labeled with a price. Most plentiful were the big coconut-frond baskets of yams, green bananas, and taro that covered the dirt floor. There were 'Olungan people selling at the market. One woman, selling pineapples, had been a diary participant. "Come over here!" she signaled to us, and filled my arms with five sweet little pineapples. She would take no money.

We needed a watermelon for the *pola,* and we searched every stand that sold melon for the best one at the best price. The watermelon we bought cost $12. Baskets of yams were selling for $60 each. I was astounded at the prices, and I remembered Manu's comment to me that islanders will buy things at prices that overseas Tongans will not pay.

Even with some of our *pola* food coming from the bush, the *pola* easily cost $350—this for one meal, and then a day's worth of leftovers. I thought of the basket Moala would make for $90 that would take her almost two weeks to finish. The cost of the melon we bought was equal to a full day's pay for Vei. Malia and I talked about the tremendous differential between prices and earnings in Tonga. "How can islanders survive with these prices?" I wondered. "They can do it," she said, "but only with help from their relatives. It will be a sad day if relatives stop helping. Tongan people cannot live the way they're living without the remittances."

Celebrations and Frustrations

It was the twenty-seventh of December, the first day of the centennial celebration. Half of the village—literally all the villagers who lived on "our" side of the central road—went with their *pola* to the celebration. There were close to one hundred *pola* there. The king was in attendance as well as the local noble, the princess, and other notables. Villagers who had married and left the village returned for the occasion, and *pola* spaces were filled with visiting relatives from overseas.

An old friend of the family came in for the event, expressing his mixed feelings about the wonderful feast to come. "I came," he said, "but I don't want to go and eat the energy of the people." He explained, "The people are losing a lot. Everyone has things today for the celebration but what will they do tomorrow? They give everything to the celebration and the church, and then what? What will they eat tomorrow?"

What I heard from this man, I heard from many people, in different forms. His thinking is part of the changing sentiments of Tonga. Some Ton-

gans focus their criticism and dissatisfaction on the church, some on the no-
ble-run government, some on both. Some do not know, as yet, where the
responsibility lies.

For many, maybe most, young men, the immediate problem is land. This
was one of the topics discussed at the kava-drinking circle where I served
kava to a group of eight men in their twenties and thirties. They are entitled constitutionally to land, and yet there is no more land to be had. So
many young men work for low wages on the farms of others where there is
no future for them. Many know that they must migrate and work overseas
for a time, even if they would prefer to stay here.

But even migration, and hard work overseas, is not a panacea for one's
future, as Fonu's story reveals. Fonu was a farmer with a wife and ten children. Wanting to build a better life for his family, Fonu left to work in the
United States. He moved in with relatives in northern California and lived
there for four months. When he found steady work as a gardener in Berkeley, he got his own apartment. Fonu worked six days a week, sometimes
seven, taking home as much as $800 per week. He saved most of what he
made and worked for three years without seeing his wife and children.

When he returned home with his savings, he was able to build a fine
house of brick and wood with a tin roof for his family. He was proud of his
home, and happy to be back in Tonga, but he was troubled. What about the
future? There had been a loss of momentum. This is how he described his
predicament to me:

> Now, I've been to America and my thinking is open. [As he says the word
> "open," he presses his wrists together and makes a triangle outward with his
> hands.] And now I come back. [He makes an inverted **V** with his hands,
> pushing his fingertips together and indicating his sense of a narrowing hori-
> zon.] I don't know which way to go. I don't know which way to go for my
> family.
>
> Here I work hard and I go to the bush and I sell my produce. But I want
> my wife to have things and I think about my children in the future. . . . In
> America, you make lots of money. In Tonga, there's the family, there's help.
> If you don't have gasoline, you go next door and borrow money for gasoline.
> If you don't have food, you come to people and they give it to you. But it's
> not that way in America. Most of my family is here in Tonga. I don't know
> what to do.

Fonu is an example of how hard work and overseas labor pay off. Yet his
story also shows the continual pull that the differential between overseas

and Tongan earnings exerts. Even those who have migrated, worked, and saved will fall back down as their nest eggs deteriorate through inflation coupled with a dearth of new earning opportunities. And so they are confronted over and over again with the same dilemmas. There are few options: permanent migration, a greater dependence on overseas relatives, or new and risky money-earning entrepreneurial schemes. For people with land, like Fonu, the desire to stay in Tonga but not lose economic ground relative to others has led to a greater emphasis on commercial agriculture, particularly in growing lucrative but risky cash crops such as vanilla or, more recently, pumpkins (squash). Commercialization among small Tongan farmers is a response to inflation and the upward mobility of others.

Finding ways to be successful in circumstances of limited opportunities and rising expectations produces a palpable frustration. During my visit some of this frustration was directed toward the flies. Flies are always a fact of life in the dry Octobers and Novembers leading up to the monsoon season of late December. The flies seemed to linger later this year, and they were, indeed, noticeably bad. When we all went to the beach for a picnic, the flies were so thick and noxious that no one could eat. We had to pack up the food and take it home.

What anyone could tell you, though, is that the number of flies and that slightly putrid odor in the bush this year were because of the pumpkins. The pumpkin situation was talked about everywhere I went, even on other islands.

A Japanese firm had made arrangements with the Tongan government to have farmers grow a certain kind of squash. The government organized the growing effort, and arranged for the bank to lend farmers the capital necessary for fertilizer and seeds. At harvest, the plan was for farmers to sell the pumpkins to the government, which would pass them on to the shipper. Last year the program was a great success, and the farmers who participated made substantial profits. This year a different company made the same arrangement. When farmers came to bring in their pumpkin crop, the company had lowered the price at which it would buy. Tongans had overproduced, and the company had them over a barrel. Sell at the lower price or not at all, farmers were told.

The Tongan farmers appealed to the government for help, but the officials backed the exporter. Consequently, many growers had to sell their crop at a price that did not cover their expenses. Most of the farmers would not take the lower price, and let their pumpkins rot in the bush. Instead of the financial boon farmers had anticipated would help them keep pace with their neighbors, many had wasted the whole year's effort. Even worse, those who had taken out loans for their seed and fertilizer went into debt. The flies and the smell of rotting pumpkins became infuriating reminders of dashed hopes and falling aspirations.

The pumpkin incident fueled antigovernment feeling. For the first time since the upheavals of the nineteenth century, there was an overt act of political violence. A Tongan took a shot in the direction of a Tongan official, firing bullets at the Finance Minister's car. The pumpkin fiasco was only the most recent incident to provide fodder for the pro-democracy movement in Tonga. It fed the discomforting sense that a few profit while the mass of Tongan commoners have no place to go—but overseas.

꠸ The chapter of I. C. Campbell's (1992) history of Tonga that describes the decade from 1980 to 1990 is titled "The New Tongan Society." It was a decade marked by many changes, several of which can be seen in the incidents described in this chapter: increasing land shortages, migration, and social mobility; the emergence of an educated Tongan middle class; the rise of local entrepreneurship and commercialization in agriculture; the growth of democracy and inflation; and the questioning of traditional relationships and structures.

It is no accident that these forces inhabited the same historical space, and thus appeared in village life together in the 1990s. These were the interwoven threads of a larger fabric, fashioned by both indigenous and global capitalist forces that have been grappling in Tonga throughout most of the century. Some of the newest human dynamics in this system—the ones likely to affect the twenty-first century—are examined in the next three chapters.

8

Distant Family

᠃ Certainly there were overseas relatives who re-
turned home to Tonga during the holidays in the early 1980s when I was
living in the village. But that return was on nothing like the scale I witnessed
in 1994. It was a matter of simple arithmetic. The village, like the country,
had been losing villagers to overseas migration since the mid-1960s, but
Tongan birthrates were very high, and many migrants returned. As the migration rate quickened throughout the 1970s and 1980s, and as migration
became more permanent, the numbers of Tongans overseas began to con-
stitute an ever larger proportion of Tongan islander networks.

When I first went to the village, although migration was well under way,
Tongan-born people overseas equaled only about 18 percent of the population in Tonga. In family terms, this meant that approximately one in six
people in a Tongan family was overseas.[1] By 1990, closer to one in every
three or four Tongan-born family members was overseas.[2] When you add
in villagers' foreign-born nephews, nieces, grandchildren, and other relatives (another 14,500 in 1990), then overseas Tongans numbered more than
half the Tongan island population. By 1994, the year I returned to the village, the overseas population had swelled to 70 percent of the Tongan island population; one of every two or three Tongans in the world lived
overseas.[3]

What this meant in the village in 1994 was that, during the Christmas
holidays, well over half of all the households in the village had a visiting relative staying there—a New Zealand–Tongan, an Australian–Tongan, or an
American–Tongan. I had known many of these visitors when they were un-
hyphenated Tongans. People in the village no longer asked me what America was like as they used to ten or twelve years previously. Either they had
been overseas themselves or they knew what it was like from their relatives.

There was a much greater sense of extension, a sense that the news of interest was going on here as well as overseas, overseas as well as here. Village life was transnational.

The Celebration

As the big centennial celebration for the village church approached, the special role that overseas Tongans would have in the proceedings became apparent to me. Formal printed invitations were distributed a week in advance announcing the two-day program of centennial events, which included feasting, speeches, and group dancing, and during which donations of cash would be made to the church. Overseas Tongans were listed on the program as distinct dance groups, separate from island Tongans and from one another: the New Zealand group, the Australian group, the American group. They were prominent and conspicuous in the formal program, constituting the majority of honored dancers and performing groups. Of the five groups who would dance for the nobility and clergy during the two days of events, three were overseas groups whose costumes, choreography, gifts to the nobility, and donations to the church had been organized in their respective countries of residence.

Dress rehearsals were held in the village prior to the centennial event, led by older local men expert in the teaching of Tongan dance. They provided instruction, with accompanying drummers, to ensure that the performance of each group would be appropriate for presentation to the king and other nobility. The dancers in the overseas group were of variable skill and ability. Some of the participants had lived most of their lives in the village and knew the hand movements and steps to the group dances. Others were rusty, having been overseas for some time without frequent opportunity to perform. Still others, usually those raised overseas, watched and copied the dancers next to them. Their hand movements were often stiff and clumsy, and they struggled to keep up with the motion of the group. Once in a while an expert instructor would watch the group and, with a smile on his face, would tease someone, "You, there, you sit in the back row." The group would laugh good-naturedly.

At one rehearsal of the American group, as the instructors finished and were preparing to turn to the Australian group, one of the women shouted out, "So you leave us now and go to the *kau hala* Australia." *Kau hala* literally means "we of the same road," but it is how one talks about the different areas of the village, and the ways it is divided for political and administra-

A GROUP DANCE. This huge line of overseas dancers is performing for the royal family and the local nobles on the occasion of the centennial for the Catholic church in the village of 'Olunga. In front of the line is a huge tapa cloth that will be offered as a gift to the noble family.

tive purposes. "Yes," she continued as people laughed, "go to the Australians, those people of the lower road."[4] Her designation of the Australian group as "those of the lower road" prompted another good chuckle from the Americans, but it was a telling comment. It portrayed a vision of a great global village made up of all Tongans—the lower road in Australia, and the upper (and more prestigious) presumably in the United States.

꘍ The King, Queen, and royal family arrived from the capital in their minivan at midday. As is typical at Tongan events, royalty and nobles proceeded to a sheltered area, where they could view the performances. In front of them, and in open view of the presenters, sat *matapule*, "talking chiefs," who thanked the people for their gifts and commended good performances in the name of their chiefly noble.

After speeches of welcome and an opening prayer, the festivities on both days of the celebration consisted of a midday feast and then dances throughout the afternoon.

Each scheduled group staged two or three dances including a *tau'olunga*, an individual dance performed by an unmarried girl (traditionally high-

THE TAU'OLUNGA. In 'Olunga, a dancer does the *tau'olonga* to celebrate a twenty-first birthday. Around her, older relatives perform the strutting, often comic steps of happiness. The "leaves" hanging from the dancer's neck and sewn around her waist are Tongan currency bills which have been strung together.

born chiefly girls). Sometimes a speaker would walk up to the microphone and announce that the next *tau'olunga* dance would be dedicated to the memory of ——— or was in honor of ———, and that a donation of $500 or more was being made. The *tau'olunga* is a highly honored performance and, in fund-raising events, typically the major avenue through which a family makes donations. While a dancer performs, her relatives, friends, and supporters walk up and put money on her oiled body. Older women will often join and prance around her, doing a comic high-strutting dance of happiness and letting out loud hoots of mirth. A *tau'olunga* dancer from an overseas group had wealthy supporters, both overseas relatives in attendance and contributors from overseas who had sent money to be placed on her.

Alyssa danced in conjunction with the American group. Eseta and Manu had sent $1,000 for her dance, and many others came up and put money on her body. This donated money is often sewn together—literally made into leis of bills worth hundreds, sometimes even thousands, of dollars. The

dancer wears these around her neck while she dances and attracts more contributions during her performance. At the end of this dance, the money was
collected and given to the church.

After two days of dancing, feasting, and donations, the celebration ended. On the following day, when the collected money had been counted, the
church announced that a staggering $T66,000 had been raised at the sin-
gle event—this in a country where a day's wage had climbed since the 1980s
to $T12–15.

꣓ "It would have been a very short celebration indeed if it hadn't been for
the overseas Tongans," Malia said to Kalo. "They would have had a dance
and one feast and it would have been over."

"You know," Malia said to me, "they extended it because of the number
of people from overseas and the amount of money they were bringing in. It
would have been a poor showing if the people from overseas and their money weren't here."

The event underscored what was everywhere apparent: overseas money
and overseas Tongans kept Tonga feeling prosperous. "What will these little stores do without us?" I overheard one Tongan-American say to another. Another woman responded, "Tongans are really going to be up a creek
when the foreign Tongans leave. . . . all this money pouring into the economy! These little stores, they are really going to be poor when everyone
deserts." One heard the same conversation in slightly different forms
throughout the village.

In individual lives, as in public events, the economic role of overseas
Tongans was inescapable and apparent to villagers and overseas relatives
alike. Whether one was talking about money for the church, or expenditures in village stores, or contributions for the school auditorium, or the donation for the village water pump, overseas migrants had taken on the role
of family and village patrons. The privileged place of overseas Tongans in
village life followed from this patronage, and it extended from the ceremonial, as in the centennial, to the mundane. It explained why, despite a dire
land shortage, Tongan land laws honored the rights of overseas Tongans
holding citizenship in other countries to retain their land as absentee owners, or why Tongan police, who regularly stopped cars to make sure they
were registered, balked at pulling over a car carrying overseas Tongans.

Early in the migration process, an overseas relative sending remittances
home was a boon to the family. The family was fortunate, and lived better

than others because of this income. Increasingly, though, as the land base has shrunk, and as remittances themselves have driven up inflation rates, the differential between prices and income has diverged. Overseas money has become more of a necessity than a luxury, and the value of overseas relatives has become further exaggerated. As Malia explained, "Now, it's really true that every family *needs* to have someone overseas. Otherwise the family is to be pitied." As migration has proceeded, it is perhaps more accurate to say that what a family needs is two or three relatives overseas.

Expectations and Disappointments

As the importance of overseas Tongans to islander welfare has grown, so too have the stories of disappointments. Villagers talk about unloving relatives who have somehow changed or forgotten them; women talk about the husbands who left to contribute to the family and then abandoned them; farmers are disappointed when their plan for growing cash crops is foiled by landholding overseas relatives who will not let them use their land.

Scratch the surface of transnational families and there are indeed upsetting realities: families torn apart by distance, distressed by the failed generosity of their relatives, and wary of the foreign ways that may have led to their disappointments.

Moala, the weaver, is confused by her relatives. She has one sister overseas, in Hawai'i, who helps her older sister in another village but not Moala. Moala cannot understand it. "She doesn't answer my letters when I ask for help," she confides. "I wrote her a letter asking her to help me make my *pola* for the celebration and she didn't even write back to me. I don't know. Maybe she doesn't love me anymore."

"It happens all the time that a relative gives to some kin but not to others," Malia says to me, but really to comfort Moala.

Moala responds, "I don't pay attention. I'll just have my little family here and I'll try."

꙳ When Leona's husband, Maka, left for Australia to work, Leona stayed in Tonga to look after their five school-aged children. Once overseas, Maka met another woman and moved in with her. He had a child with her in Australia, but continued sending money home. Then he had a second child with the same woman.

It is common, the women say, for a married man to go overseas to work and then find another woman there. It happens a lot. Some stay and throw their wife away completely. That, they agree, is the worst-case scenario. Others might go and live with a woman, and even have children by her, but continue to support the family back home. This is acceptable, the women agree. After all, they argue, he is supporting the kids, and for love, they say laughing, a woman can go find someone else for herself in the village.

Leona's story was a relatively happy one. Her husband never abandoned her. And when Leona heard that the other woman was pregnant with a second child, she and her son left for Australia and persuaded Maka to return to Tonga. She and Maka and their children now live in the village together. Of course, the women say, there are some happy stories like this. There are also some men who work overseas, remain faithful husbands, and come back to their families. But the counterexamples, the women agree, are becoming more prevalent.

Foreigners in Tonga

A young man is yelling something. He is Kalo's twenty-two-year-old son, who has just returned from New Zealand. His long hair, worn in a pony tail, and his frequent use of New Zealand English slang signal his overseas experience.

"Can you believe these bush Tongans?" he yells to me in English from outside our pig fence. "What?" I say in English, thinking I have not heard him correctly. He repeats, "Can you believe these bush Tongans? They don't even know what shampoo is! Do you see that girl?" he asks as he points at Vei, who stands not far from either of us. "She doesn't even know what shampoo is."

Vei shakes him off, and as the young man walks past our fence, she motions for me to come closer to her. "I know what shampoo is," she says quietly to me when I am within range. "He used up all his shampoo and he has no more money to buy some. He says that to me so I will run and get my shampoo to show him. Then he will take my shampoo. That's why he says that."

That Vei would feel that she needed to defend her knowledge of shampoo to me is symptomatic of the power that the man's overseas experience holds over her. The man who made these comments was born and bred in Tonga, so there was still an element of shared assumptions between them, and of teasing based on those assumptions, that one did not see when wit-

nessing the interaction of islanders with those raised overseas. Perhaps because they foreshadowed things to come, the most revealing look at relationships between migrants and islanders involved the encounters between
those children and young people who were raised in Tonga and those raised
in overseas communities.

The overseas children in the village were easy to pick out. The young
ones were outfitted in matching shorts and shirts or skirts and blouses, and
they kept close to their parents. Parents spoke in English to them with a
thick Tongan accent, but the children's own English was distinctively New
Zealand, Australian, or American.

At the airstrip on the island of 'Eua, where local Tongan flights leave and
arrive, four siblings ranging from about age nine to fifteen, and clearly Tongan-American, sat in a row, talking and laughing with one another while
they waited for the small commuter plane to take them to the main island.
An open truck pulled up to meet an incoming plane, its flatbed filled with
local villagers, including several children. The Tongan children stared with
awe and curiosity at the American children. With their store-bought outfits
and their boisterous voices, they contrasted sharply with the silent barefoot
kids in homemade clothes who sat in the truck. The Tongan kids seemed
endlessly fascinated by their foreign "cousins."

Although I was several yards away from both groups, I could hear the
conversation in English among the American children. "Can you believe this
airport?" one child asked. "I never saw an airport this little in my life!" "I
thought we could get something to eat here," another complained. "I want
a hamburger," a young boy said. "You can't get a hamburger until you get
home," said his older sister.

When I walked over to talk to the American family, they seemed happy
to hear a fellow American. They readily commiserated. They had stayed in
the island's only hotel, a local guest house that had always catered to foreign tourists who came to hike in 'Eua's forest. Even the best lodging on the
island shocked them.

"There were only three things in the whole room," one boy told me, "only
a bed and a dresser and a mirror." "And we had to sleep two in a bed!" another chimed in. At home, in Utah, they explained, they had never had to
sleep two to a bed. Although they lived among some other Tongans in Utah,
this was the very first time they had seen Tonga.

"How do you like Tonga?" I asked.

"It's OK," the younger girl answered.

"I don't like the food," said the younger boy. "I can't eat Tongan food."

"What do you eat, then?" I asked him. His younger sister answered for him: "He only eats fruit here."

The eldest girl volunteered, "Tonga isn't what I expected."

"What did you expect?" I asked.

"I guess I thought it would be like the pictures in the travel brochures," she answered. "But it wasn't."

꙾ Back in the village there were many foreign-born children, including three within our own family. They had special status, coming from overseas, but an isolation, too, born of both respect and social distance.

"What is it like for the Tongan kids when foreign kids come here," I asked Vei. "The Tongan kids look up to them. At least in the beginning they do. And when they get used to each other, they can manage each other and they can eat the same food. They can eat *topai* and *lu* [Everyday "poor" food].[5] But some kids like Lio, they just like to eat ice cream, but we don't have ice cream all the time here."

In the village, as in San Mateo, Lio is caught in between worlds. Malia had packed Lio's schoolbooks and the lessons he was to complete, and would remind him from time to time of his promised schoolwork. Reluctantly, he would open his books, sitting on the floor as the other children slept nearby or played outside.

As I watch him, he is sounding out a poem that has rhyming words to help guide him to make the right sounds. He is easily frustrated by the exercise and continues his efforts only with adult feedback. Vei, a teacher, helps him for a while: "It's *frog* not *dog*." He repeats the correct answer. I try too. After a short while, he is done with the reading. He wants a drink. The other children laugh when he misuses a Tongan word, saying "coconut" (*niu*) when he meant to say "drink" (*inu*).

I ask Vei about Lio. "Lio should have come back to Tonga and studied about the customs. That's what I think—so he could still be related with us." "Is he really different from other Tongan kids?" I ask. "Yeah! He's different from Tongan kids. He can speak English. And his *anga* [way of being] is not much like Tongan kids. Tongan kids, they play together all the time with the neighbors' kids, but Lio, we have to ask him to go play with other kids. Only then does he go. And that's one reason I want him to come back to Tonga—to be friendly and . . . You know, he's not *very* different now because he's still too young, he's still growing up." Vei says this with the implication that he will be quite different later on.

"Are you Tongan or are you American?" I hear a young village boy ask Lio while they play together on the porch. Lio responds loudly, "I'm Tongan!" "So will you stay here or go back to America?" the boy continues. Lio says he wants to stay in Tonga. The conversation has now attracted more participants. Another older boy chides, "So you will stay in Tonga and you'll eat just taro? Is that OK? And you won't be able to eat candy anymore, OK?" Vei adds, "Yeah and you'll have to sweep the floor and the yard! And you won't be able to eat ice cream and all the things we buy for you now." Lio holds firm. He would stay in Tonga. Two days later, in the evening, Lio goes over to Malia and whispers quietly to her that he has changed his mind. He wants to go back to America.

⚬ Sara's first time in Tonga was not easy for her. She called it "culture shock." It was not so much the living conditions themselves, because Sara and Alyssa lived in the house that Manu built with his pension money. They spent most of their time there. By village standards the house was a showplace and a visible sign of an important family. Manu had sent the building materials, the furniture and appliances and other accoutrements from the United States in one of the giant shipping crates that dot the Tongan landscape.

A huge living room, lined with beautiful Tongan mats, held a couch and coffee table; its walls were decorated with imported prints and paintings. The bedrooms, each with its own set of screened windows and locking door, were built off the living room. They were furnished with the same dressers and beds with headboards that I had seen in Eseta's house. A short walkway led to a separate building that was as large as some of Tonga's smaller houses. This was the kitchen. The huge area, replete with kitchen appliances, was the cooking and food preparation area. Guests ate in a separate dining room in the main house. It was probably the finest house in the village.

Both Alyssa and Sara were heavily chaperoned.[6] They were taken from one place to another, shuttled primarily between their own house and that of their paternal aunt a few doors away. They met only a small circle of relatives. Sara's aunt counseled her continually on the importance of marrying a Tongan—so intensely, Sara believed, because she had recently been dating a white American boy.

Vei had met her cousin from the United States—Alyssa—on her first trip. She'd liked her but, as she admitted, she hadn't really seen her a lot. This

second visit was similar. Vei and her sisters saw their American cousins only
if they went to visit them at their own house. Their cousins did not come
by to eat or sleep or spend the day.[7]

Sara had made an effort to be friendly, but the responses she got from villagers confused her. As Sara walked chaperoned through the village, there
were a few young village men sitting outside her property, but they said
nothing. She expressly said hello to two local girls on the road, but they
didn't answer her. In her words, "They looked me up and down and saw
my dress and they decided not to answer." Maybe they were shy, I suggested, but Sara interpreted their response as closer to hostility. She was upset
enough about the exchange to ask her aunt about it. The girls were jealous,
her aunt told her.

"No Problem"

When the entire centennial celebration appeared on Tongan television,
the family and other onlookers sat glued to the television set, calling out
with delight the names of people we recognized. An overseas *tau'olunga*
dancer who attracted large donations appeared in close-up on the screen,
and I noticed her stiffness and lack of grace. "She looks like she's doing
karate," I blurted out. No one said a word. I turned to Vei. "What do the village girls think of this?" She answered me directly, "They get really angry
when they see that."

Vei's blunt comment was unusual. The occasional strain I observed between islanders and overseas Tongans in day-to-day events was not readily
expressed in words, except by younger Americans used to expressing their
opinions or by those close to me, if I pressed the point. If I asked less intimate village contacts whether there were points of contention between foreign and island Tongans, I got a stock answer: "There is no problem." If I
tried to get at the tensions another way by asking villagers whether they
were different from their foreign relatives, they would say "No, we are exactly the same." Exactly.

In general, differences were minimized, similarities were maximized.
Tensions went unacknowledged, or they were muted through silence, teasing, and humor.[8] As in the "global village" metaphor mentioned earlier in
this chapter, islanders and overseas Tongans were presented as one—simply as different "roads" of the same community, different branches of the
same family. Making this so became an active, creative process. This was as

true of the inventive global metaphor as it was apparent in the incident described next.

  A potential problem arose around Alyssa's *tauʻolunga* dance. A student of Malia's, Alyssa danced beautifully, and the family was authentically proud of her performance. Eseta and Manu had sent a cash donation to be placed around Alyssa's neck. The $1,000 contribution was to be made, her parents said, in honor of Alyssa.

Malia perceived a problem in this. "When they announce that this dance and this money is in honor of Alyssa, people will say 'Who is this little girl?' The family should dedicate the *tauʻolunga* and donation to Alyssa's grandfather," who had lived in the village and whom everyone in the area would know. "This is the Tongan way and the better way," Malia explained. "My sister," she continued, "is so long overseas, sometimes she doesn't have a good sense of what to do."

Malia spoke with the family in the United States and here. She was pleased that she could successfully negotiate a change. The dance performed by Alyssa would honor her paternal grandfather, an ʻOlunga man who had worked hard for the church for many years before he passed away. The change was announced on Tongan radio so that relatives and friends would know that the dance would be in commemoration of Alyssa's grandfather, Tau. After the dance, Malia described the event: "Tau had other grandchildren still in the village, and they were extremely happy to see their grandfather so honored. When Alyssa stepped on the field to dance, and the speaker dedicated the $1,000 gift to Tau, there were many proud and happy villagers in the audience who remembered their relative, their friend, and will remember the young American granddaughter who danced in his honor."

Malia skillfully brokered the right ending: a shared history, a global Tongan village, a geographically distant but otherwise close and connected Tongan family.

9

Finau, the One
Who Stayed

〰〰   Finau was born in 1966, the eldest daughter in the family, after the death of a girl (also Finau) born two years before her. She became the eldest child in the 1990s after both of her elder brothers died. Finau was outstanding in everything she did. In school she was consistently the first or second in her class; every year she was a class monitor, an authentic honor in the Tongan classroom. She was a leader in her youth group, in Girl Guides, and a beautiful traditional dancer.

She continued her education as far as one could go, earning highest honors and a place in the Tonga training college for teachers. Her first teaching placement was on 'Eua, a smaller island to the south of her home island. It was there that Finau became pregnant by her husband-to-be and eventually settled.

Finau's pregnancy was a time of great decision. Both her parents had recently migrated to the United States, and she was wrestling with the issues of her life and her responsibilities as a Tongan woman. Eight months pregnant, she got on a plane to America so that she could have her child in the States. It was the first time she had ever been to the United States. By the family's best accounting, she did this for several reasons: to be near her mother for the birth of her first child, to give her son or daughter the opportunity for dual citizenship, and to think about her life.

Her baby was born in Arizona, during the time she stayed at my home. Her mother, Malia, joined us, and we lived together during the first months of the new baby's life.

Her thoughts in the first half of this chapter date from this time. She begins by talking about America and why she chose not to emigrate. In the second half of the chapter, we meet Finau a few years later, when she is married with two children.

Finau on America

What do you think of America?

Thinking of America. It's different, eh? It's like going on steps. Tonga is right at the bottom. Then it goes Fiji, New Zealand, Australia. But for Tongans, America is on top. Because it is very important, and many people, lots of Tongans, they migrate to America. Most Tongans, they see America as plenty of money and many, many things. And everybody wants to come to America. And whoever has been in the States will come back to Tonga a "big" person. People will see that person as very rich. They will see them that way, even though they are not. It's like me—when I return back to Tonga, to 'Eua. I know my boyfriend will be jealous because many people will come for me. I am rich, they will think, even though I am just coming with a baby and nothing else. Oh, that girl has been to America, and she is a "big" girl.

Doesn't anyone explain about the expenses here—that it costs so much to live?

That doesn't matter. Just being in the States is a very big thing for Tongans. But New Zealand is small, like Fiji. If you come to Australia, then people expect more. Coming to America, though, is a very big thing.

Why have you chosen to stay in Tonga?

The first thing is my age. I'm over twenty-one, so I couldn't come together with the family on that visa. So, we knew we were independent. I like the idea of coming to stay here, but on the other hand, I look at Tonga—I have my job, and I have my boyfriend. I think the boys in Tonga will give me the respect I want. They'll show me that I'm who I am.

Tell me more about that.

I mean by our culture. Our traditions. Tongan boys who come to the U.S., they change. They are getting more Americanized. They do like what Americans do—the *palangi* way. The Tongan boys are different; they're sort of low, and they show respect. The boys who come, they see America is a higher stage, and their attitude of mind gets higher. They want girls who are very pretty and have better jobs. But these boys who want this are not so pretty themselves and they don't have good jobs. But because they have been in the States, they think they're a big person. And everybody who sees they were in the States thinks it's a very big thing, so whether they have a job or money or what, people see you as a big person.

How do these boys act?

The *palangi* way. In public, they just want to show their feelings for the girls—like kissing them in front of other people. Sometimes they say things straight and not like the Tongans that go roundabout when they speak. The Tongan boys who are educated act different. And the boys who are not educated, they are more tied with the culture. If they go to a girl, they ask the parents. They make the kava. And they used to come as a group, with cousins and uncles. The girl makes the kava, and they come in and you talk and talk. Sometimes, though, you want to spend time alone with the boy, but it's much better to have it as a group. Your cousins and your uncles will do the talking to the boy. They talk about arranging a marriage. The boys who come back from the States to Tonga act differently. They don't like to make the kava or drink the kava. They just go and make a date with the girl—come with me to the movies during the day—just run away and the parents do not know.

Do girls like these kinds of boys?

Some girls, they like it, and some they don't. Some girls who want to be American, they like it. So they dress like Americans and talk that way too.

Are women in the U.S. different too?

Yes.

How?

Women here are competitive, trying to do more, showing that they can do more than what men can do. Women in America are more active. They can strive for whatever they really want. Women in Tonga do not have all that courage to go for it. Women in Tonga, they only think of being good house people, and they're not very competitive.

But you were competitive!

Except today. Girls today, like me, they are educated and they are competitive. The young generation—the students of my age—most of them, the girls, they are applying for scholarships. They want to be lawyers. In this young generation, more girls are competing with the men to be lawyers. Their mothers are happy.

Life Memories

What are the first things you remember?

My earliest memory was being with my grandmother—my dad's mother. She spent a lot of time being with the queen and the nobles. We used to sleep together, and she would come in and tell me legends and myths, and she used to say that I must answer her by saying *iso, iso* [an old word that means "yes, yes"] to see that I am listening.

What legends did she tell you?

She talked about the king of Tonga. And sometimes about animals, and people who were monsters. I remember one of her stories about how people were treated badly to build up the terraced tombs in 'Olunga. If you were lazy, whoever was at the end of the rope would get killed. Everybody had to work hard 'cause the people were very very important people—the Tongans. And she used to talk about the tortoise that belongs to the king. My grandmother was very important for the scholars. They used to come to talk to her. Sometimes my grandmother didn't give out stories. She said, "I have the knowledge, and they want to get their degrees from my knowledge." And she sometimes give out lies—things that are not true. Because these people make a lot of money and yet they only bring her some cigarettes and sugar and bread.

I remember my eldest brother, Vili, when we used to go to primary school. My parents have to go to the bush to farm. Vili had to get up and do the mother's work and when we got home, he make the beds and clean the house and everything for us. As the eldest girl in the family, I just couldn't do anything like that. He used to braid my hair too.

One thing I remembered as I grew older, my father say, "As the eldest girl in the family, you have to be the captain of the boat—you have to steer the boat." So I remember that, especially during rainy days and storms. One day I was cooking some food for the family—it was raining—it was a Sunday. The others can't come out to help me. So when I was doing the cooking—I was lighting the fire in our open kitchen—suddenly this wind blows the house—the top—under the fireplace and the pot of food is blown away. It was Hurricane Isaac. And I sat down and cried and said, "Oh God, what did you do?" I was so tired trying to make the food for the family. But the others, they were smaller than me. 'Cause I was trying to be a good captain, but I didn't have the courage to steer the boat. It was very funny. . . .

I think I was brought up very strict. In the school and in the village, people were afraid of Atu, and even the boys that came to the house, they are afraid to come home because Atu will ask them all kinds of things. It happens that a boy wants to talk to a girl because he likes her, and it's tradition that he has to go and talk first to your father and ask him for permission to see you. . . . If a boy want to come to me to talk, his first response to the boy is: "What is your name? Who are your parents? Where are you from?" And all those things.

So here is one thing that happened. I was already twenty, and my sisters and I wanted to go to the dance after the school holidays, and he said, "No, you stay home." And we cried—we went to the room and cried and stay home. He just said no. You're not expected to get an explanation. No is no. Yes is yes.

Sometimes, I was feeling—when I learned history and I learned about Martin Luther King and Gandhi and all those people who fight for their rights, for human rights—when am I going to fight for my rights? At home, every time I know I was right and I started to speak, my father says, "Stop, just do what I say." He is a very strict person. And I always say to myself, he should allow people to stand for their rights. My eldest brother only used to fight for his rights—ever since he was a kid. Vili asked to go to the movie, and he'd say that he need some money, not only for him but for all his friends. And he say, "Look, I have four friends and I want to take them to the movies. I want you to give me some money!" It was fifty cents for one person! And Atu say, "No!" And Vili say, "How come this time you say no. Last time you say yes! This time you say no. What kind of a parent are you? I want some money now to take my friends to the movies!" [She laughs, thinking about his brazenness.]

Our ears got tired of hearing Atu's family—the *matapules*—say: "In our time, we never do this. In our time, when we go somewhere we always tell our parents where we are going! In our time we never come home late! In our time. . . ." And my sisters and I used to say [imitating them], "In our time, in our time. . . ." That was their time. This is *our* time. And we always laugh and say, "This is your time. This is our time now. We have different timing!" It was very funny. We say, "We can never go back into your time. This is our time."

My grandmother said the same thing, too. "In our time, the girls never go and wandered around." "Yes, Grandma, but this is our time." And she would say, "It's terrible. Your time is terrible." In her time, in the evening, there would be one place that all the young girls would come. They sat in a circle and they shine their body with *tuitui*.[1] And they stayed together and they sing together. And I think to myself, yes, the girls then didn't have homework to do. They go to their friends, and stay together, and oil their skins, and prepare themselves for their big day, their marriage. Now we have to go and ask our friends to help us with our homework. . . .

I remember another thing. Me and my three sisters—we were old enough to go out then, and we want to go to a dance. We were standing, lined up in the house. We were already dressed up. Our parents tell us, "Whenever you want to go to a place, you ask first for permission before you get dressed." But for us, every Friday or every Saturday, we get dressed before we ask permission. One day we come and say, "We want to go to the dance. Can we have some money?" And they say, "What? You already dressed, without asking permission first?!" This time they just sit there in the living room and say, "No, you go back to your bedroom and sleep!"

So, me and my sisters, we went out the window. We just stood there when they said, "You go and sleep." And we went to our room, and we went out the window. We went to our neighbor and borrowed some money for the dance because we had no money. After the dance, we came back. Malia and Atu already knew that we ran away, so they locked the windows and they locked the doors because they wanted to keep us out all night. We came and tried the windows. All the windows are locked, and then the doors—we knock, knock, and they didn't open. Lucky for us, we had a mat on the verandah, and we slept there. And we woke up and—the boys were inside that night, and they came out and laughed at us. So from then on, we didn't go out the window, but every time we ask, they say yes. They say, "Yes, go, but come back on time."

The one thing that will always stick in my mind happened last year, in 1990. When the family left Tonga. There's only me and my younger sister and my older brother in our house. And then my brother commits suicide. A funeral in Tonga is a very big occasion, so you very much need your parents. But I had to do the whole funeral with the aunties and the uncles. The priests and the nuns, they helped me a lot, too. They keep praying for me so that I have the courage. I did the whole thing.

I know that God wants me to do it, seeing that the three older than me are all dead. Walking from this side to that side. I stand between my mother's side and my father's side. It's very hard 'cause they all have different views of what to do. In a funeral in Tonga, there has to be ten days. So some of the views say to just do it three days or five days. And my father's side, they wanted it ten days. Probably because the father's side is the boss of the funeral. It depends on you. We did it ten days.

The family sent the money later—after the ten days of the funeral—but I have to find the way to do everything without the money. Well, my mother wasn't there. The aunties—there's some people we call a *fahu*, my father's sister and their children—they did everything. My dad's sisters were not all in Tonga, but their children and their grandchildren were here and they helped. Their children are like Atu's age. The mother's side, they did the cooking and those things. The *fahu*, they got all the gifts from the funeral. We killed two or three pigs each day for the feasts. I tell them that I have to be the mother and the sister of my brother. It was a lot of work. I tried.

When my eldest brother died and I spoke to Atu on the phone, I was cry-

ing because I didn't know what to do [about the funeral]. I remembered what
Atu said: "There's no need for you to cry. This is your day. Ask the Lord what
you can do. This is your day. You have a job, and there are people there who
you need help from—they will come." And it happened.

Finau, to Her Child

*What would you want your daughter to know about being a Tongan girl? (The
baby turned out to be a son.)*

It's important that you are being brought up with tradition—not Western-
ized. The parents are very conservative, and they care about you a lot. They
do whatever you like. As long as I remember, being a girl in Tongan society,
you are very important. You get all what you need—the good stuff—especially the love and the care of parents until you get married. Even though
you get married in your thirties or forties, you still be at home. I'm still in
my twenties, and I still feel like a child. I only know a little bit about life.

When you grow up, I think you have to be very responsible, *very* responsible. And if your parents are not there, you can do what your parents
can do. And with all these traditional things happening, and with your parents not there, it's OK because you have seen these traditional things happen before, so you know what you have to do. So, because you have a job,
you have the money, and you can do your mother's job, your father's responsibilities. I didn't know what I was doing, but when Atu came up for
Christmas last year, people talked to him. The people in the village told him
how wonderful I did their jobs [her parents' responsibilities at the funeral],
and they keep writing to me and say, "Thank you very much for doing our
jobs. We know you are working very very hard, and you did our jobs better
than we could have done."

Sometimes when things happen, my sister and I don't have the goods—
the tapa and the mats—to give away and do my parents' jobs. But we have
the money. Like funerals—their relatives' funerals. If the funeral is for my father's relatives, it's Atu's job to provide a pig or some kind of meat. So we
provide the money to buy whatever they need. The same with the mother's
side. No mats, no tapa—but we give them the money. It is much important
for them to have the money.

So relatives come to you now for help, eh?

They do! And sometimes it's a great bother to me, coming for money—a bur-
den. I think they shouldn't always come to me because I don't have a thousand dollar pay a month, but I do what they want. One reason why I chose

to go to the little island to teach is to get away from home. I want to take my mind away from [them]. I have only little jobs, little responsibilities, when I go to the other island. So in the island, I do nothing. I just save my money. But school holidays, when I get home for a week or two, *all* these uncles and aunties, they come for this and that.

Is there anything else you'd want to tell your daughter?

There are many other things, but maybe I'd tell her about planning one thing and doing a different thing. If you plan for something, you have to stick to it. And about being very independent. About being the eldest girl in the family.

Even though I was the eldest, I never felt that way, because I always knew I wasn't really the eldest girl. There were people older than me, but they're dead. And I always remember that. Maybe if you talk to some girls who were truly born the eldest, they will say something different.

I'm used to working very, very hard. And sometimes I complain to God, "Why do I have to do all this?" And I keep saying to myself, "Maybe one day, maybe one day!" I used to say that every time. And today, all those who are older than me—my two brothers and my eldest sister—they are all dead. With me in the lead. I'm not surprised.

I wasn't a very happy girl when I grew up. Because I was really the fourth in the family. There was two boys and a girl older than me, and the girl older than me died when she was three. And what was in my mind was my two elder brothers. They always make my parents very sad, and they are very smart—very good in school—but they never did their best. My father has to stop the boys all the time from drinking beer and going into the pool house [hall] instead of doing their studies.

So when the days come that they give out prizes at the school, the boys don't get what they deserve. I see that my parents are sad, and they cry. Other kids, the neighbors, they make their parents happy during the prize-giving. So, maybe I wasn't a very intelligent person, but I tried. And I said, "Maybe one day when I go to secondary school, I'll make my parents happy." So when I finish my level six class, I went up to secondary school. Then I started settling down and doing my work. So my first year in secondary school, I was the first in my class. And now I see the tears of my parents—not tears of sadness but tears of happiness. And I remember my father saying, you wipe our tears away. We are very happy.

My whole time in secondary school, I got top in class. Or if not first, then second and third. I get prizes for these places too. In this way I honor my parents—make them happy all the time. Both of my older brothers, they died now. Now there's only us girls in the family. Atu will be sad to have no sons, but the four of us—the girls—maybe will bring him home sons that will be much better than his own sons. And he knows that. That's what Atu said when I got here to America. He is not angry because I'm not married. God has taken away five children out of nine, and now he is paying us back and will bring us more children and grandchildren. They're happy. They keep talking about Samiu as if they knew him and we are married. They wrote to each other. Samiu wrote to Atu and Atu wrote back to Samiu.

A Tongan Woman

In 1995 Finau was already married to Samiu, the father of the son she had delivered in America. This interview took place at their home. Together Finau and Samiu were raising their two children—Tomasi, age three, who was born in the United States, and Losana, born a year later in Tonga.

Finau and Samiu, both in their twenties, were part of Tonga's new educated middle class. They were both teachers at the high school.[2] Samiu had also earned a certificate in law from the University of the South Pacific in Fiji, and had run twice for the Tongan parliament, coming in second in a large field by a slim margin. He planned on running again.

I came to Finau and Samiu's house during the Christmas break, a three-month hiatus during which school is not in session and Finau and Samiu had more free time to visit and entertain. As I arrived at their home, a basketball game was in progress on the village's grass basketball court which sat on Finau and Samiu's property. The December school holiday (which ran until February) was the time when the basketball season was in full force. Only girls play basketball, and this was serious business. There were three age-graded teams in the village, with regular practices, appointed coaches, intervillage matches, special village uniforms, and speeches following the games.

Hundreds of children and parents were in attendance for this first game of the season, which was followed by live music and feasting. The children screamed with joy as they recognized the next American song the band was going to play, and they danced a wild "disco" on the court where they had just finished playing basketball. Samiu and Finau were the sponsors of the village team. Finau had designed and sewn the forty-odd white and green basketball uniforms. After away games, the teams often returned to Samiu and Finau's house for "tea," a light meal of biscuits and jam or bread and butter with cocoa. As with other village events and projects, the resources they expended were considerable.

Finau and Samiu's house was one of the nicest in their village. I was stunned, in fact, by their prosperity. They were clearly people who "have things," in Tongan parlance: a new wooden house with cement foundation, indoor plumbing, and three bedrooms; a truck to transport people and bush food; a full complement of overseas-made furniture and appliances; and a pen filled with pigs. In their new kitchen was a stainless steel sink, a refrigerator, a gas stove, and a kitchen table. In the living room was a dining table, hutch, bookshelves, a TV set, and sewing machine—all important markers of middle-class life.

The couple's prosperity was due in part to their education and to the two salaries that their degrees brought. Finau made $220 per fortnight, half of which still went to pay off the bank loan for the tapa cloth and mats that she had bought for her brother's funeral five years ago. Half of Samiu's $306 fortnight salary went to the bank for their house loan. Samiu anticipated an upcoming promotion and pay raise. As Finau said proudly, "People would say that's very, very rich!"

Indeed, Samiu and Finau were treated by others on the island as "big" people, as patrons, as a couple who were going somewhere. Theirs was a delicate balancing act of time and resources—to be patrons without going bankrupt, and to build a middle-class lifestyle without slighting the needs, and hence inviting the ill will, of relatives. It took more, in fact, than the couple's combined salaries to accomplish these feats.

Samiu had family land, on which they grew their food, and many local relatives who provided a network of daily support. Samiu and Finau worked hard to grow sufficient crops both for food and for sale, so they could earn additional income from their land. They also received some assistance from relatives overseas. Most of the children's clothing and most of the furniture and appliances in the house came from Malia. Education, industriousness, land, overseas help, and the building of local patronage were all part of their formula for success.

This is how Finau described her life in Tonga at this time when she and her husband were building their future.

> During the school days, in the morning I have to wake up around 6 A.M. and I have to prepare food for the kids and dress them. The oldest kid has to go to his grandmother, and the younger one has to stay with the baby sitter [a young girl paid to look after the baby, the first time I had ever heard of a baby sitter in a Tongan village].
>
> I go to school. I teach twenty periods per week, fifty minutes each. There is six periods in a day, but usually I have two periods off each day. If my fifty-

minute free period is followed by lunchtime, then I escape and run home and see the baby and soak my laundry so that when I get home after school I finish it. Like that. I'm sort of busy in school because we don't only teach but there's other work, outdoor work. It's a new school. We clean up, and there's gardens to tend. After school we get right in the truck, get home, get changed, get the kids, and go to the bush. We go to the bush every Monday and Friday. We help with Samiu's work there. We do the bush work—hoeing and weeding and planting. The other days we stay at the house and do the gardening and clean up. Samiu does the weeding, and the kids help me with the garden. There's laundry. And dishes and cooking and so on. And then we eat dinner. I always prepare dinner, but sometimes when dinner is ready I'm tired and I don't eat. So when they all went to bed, I'll have my dinner by myself. Most days I go to bed after 1 A.M. or 2, because when they all sleep, I do the dishes and I clean the floors and ready the clothes for the next day. It's true, it's very busy. . . .

Even on Sunday. On Sunday, I get up early. We have to go to church on Sunday. In Tonga, if you don't go to church on Sunday, people say, "Oh, you're a bad woman." I prepare the food, breakfast for the kids, and I have to make the food ready so that after church we can come straight for lunch. And lunch on Sunday, they eat while I sit and stare. *Eat!* When they finish, they go to have a nap, and I come and eat. One day I told Samiu, "Can't we eat together sometimes?" They always rush to the table and eat, not waiting for me. Before I got married, I always had time to sleep. I don't always work. I sleep most of the day. Now, I always think of the next hour. Like mealtime, I have to get something for breakfast. As soon as breakfast is over, I have to think, what am I going to make for lunch? And then, oh, what am I going to prepare for dinner?

I know I have to try to do things. We often get late for school, because I have to make breakfast and get our clothes ready. When Samiu's ready, he gets in the truck and goes beep, beep, beep! and I say, "Wait, where's he going?! Where's my shoes?!" Sometimes I run into the truck with my shoes in one hand and my bra in the other hand and put the dress on without it. And when I get to school, I go into my room and take off my dress and put my bra on and get dressed again. Those kids make me late for everything! Late to school. Late to church. We always walk to church halfway through.

What's the best day for you? The most fun?

A day like today where we stay together and go to the beach. Often on Saturday we go to the beach and go fishing. We barbecue fish. We go out once a week fishing with the family. We all have a line. We catch some small fish and light the fire and put them in the fire and eat them. That's fun!

We sat in the living room talking until Samiu said it was time to turn on the radio. Promotions and teaching positions would be announced for the coming school year tonight. And, indeed, it was through the Tongan radio announcements that Samiu and Finau learned whether they were retained for the next year, where they would be teaching, and what their salaries would be. The news was good, as they had anticipated.

Tomasi came in the room with his ukulele, put off by something. "I'll shoot you!" he said, with pointed finger. Finau laughed. She said that the three-year-old is afraid of the police from watching videos. "Because some police in the video he watches, they kill. He sees blood. He gets afraid. And he says, 'Mama, they're going to shoot you!' Now, when he gets angry, he says that to me too: 'I'll shoot you!'"

On the walls in the living room and in several albums were pictures of Finau's family, many of those who had migrated. I noticed in particular the pictures that Palu (Emma) had sent to Finau. They hung in a prominent place on the wall. In one Palu was wearing a black evening gown, deep red lipstick, and very high heels. Her American date was dressed in a tuxedo. In another Palu was in a cocktail dress. She was heavily made up. It was Valentine's Day, and she was holding a heart-shaped box of chocolates and a dozen roses. A bottle of champagne figured prominently into the background. I was struck by the messages of elegance and the high life conveyed by the photos.

Do you have a lot of contact with Palu?

Some . . . I write.

Does she send you things?

Mostly she just writes. She will send things, but only if I ask. When I want something, I ask her and she sends it over. Like, I asked for a red pair of shoes. She sent a red pair and a black pair.

Does she send money?

No.

Are you happy that you stayed here and didn't go to America?

Yes. But I'm happy here and I'd be happy if I went to America.

Both?

Yes. For now, I'd like to go with the family to America for a visit. Maybe sometime we will want to live there. But I think if you have a house of your own, you want to stay at home.

10

Tradition

᠅ There was a man from a small village on the eastern edge of the main island of Tonga who drove a Lincoln Continental, the only one I had ever seen in Tonga. He had eight children, and every one of them lived in the United States. Most of them worked as gardeners. His wife had had a stroke and was permanently hospitalized in the United States. He lived alone in the village, and he had no land.

He was a happy man, by his own admission. He was considered fortunate by others because his children sent him good things and came often to visit. But consider the precariousness of his situation. If all his children had been in the United States and had lost touch with him, then his life would be considered tragic, and people would pity the man. Yet if all his children had stayed in Tonga and lived with him in the village, people might also feel sorry for him.

There was only one sure avenue to the good life in Tonga under the conditions of land shortage, few jobs, and limited economic opportunity which obtained in the 1990s. It was a paradox of sorts: you must have foreign family, but with Tongan ways of thinking; your relatives must go to America, but stay Tongan in their heart.

Staying Tongan

"Staying Tongan" means maintaining one's identity as a Tongan, but more important, it also means thinking and behaving in a Tongan manner—what Tongans call the "Tongan way" (*anga fakatonga*).[1] You should help your family and maintain an attitude of love and generosity toward them. You should know your "place"—high and low—within the social network and use your full resources to demonstrate your obligations to others. This includes having respect for your father's sisters and love for your brother's children. There should be "shame" between brothers and sisters, respect between children and fathers, love between children and mothers. You should feel an obligation to take care of your grandparents. For those who stay in Tonga, the "Tongan way" of their overseas relatives is what keeps support flowing in to the island, even when they are far removed.

But it is not just islanders for whom being and staying Tongan solves a problem. For Tongan-Americans, following the Tongan way is the vehicle to their retirement (perhaps in Tonga), their network of aid in the United States, and their assurance that children and grandchildren will be their support network as they grow older. Without "Toganness" and the network of support it affords, life in the United States would have been much harsher for first-generation migrants, and their futures would look less bright. I believe this is why most Tongan migrants spend considerable resources and energy in asserting their Tonganness and in imploring their children to do the same.

Eseta and Manu, for instance, did not view their migration as *leaving* Tonga. Their departure was intended to help their families, not abandon their families. They understood their life in America, in fact, as very "Tongan," as continuous with their lives in Tonga. As Eseta described it:

> The first time I start work was in Tonga. I get my money. The first thing I did was buy my mom false teeth. Then I pay for the kids' school fees. Today, I'm still paying school fees over there. I began in Tonga taking care of my family. And I'm still doing it. Once I came over here, I still worked for me and the rest of my family, still in Tonga.

Indeed, it was Eseta who shouldered the responsibility for the various obligations of the extended family. Eseta was the one to call a meeting to discuss how the extended family would meet its obligations of food or tapa cloth or money for an impending family occasion or a family member in need. If you asked Manu about the Tonganness of Tongan-Americans, he would tell you that the Tongan-American branch of the family was, if anything, "more traditional" than the islanders.

Like many other Tongan migrants in the United States, both Eseta and Manu strongly voiced their support for the Tongan way, and they taught their children its principles. They also encouraged their daughters to marry Tongan men, join Tongan groups, and visit Tonga on the holidays. The message they have sent to other Tongans is that even though they have left Tonga, they and their children have stayed Tongan.

The contradictions in this are not lost on the next generation. One Tongan-American youth put it this way: "My parents want me to mix only with Tongan kids, and go to only Tongan youth groups. But I have *palangi* friends too. If they wanted us to be so Tongan, they should have given birth to us in Tonga."

Migration and tradition, however, must go hand in hand. Tradition and the Tongan way are buffers that mitigate the problems caused by migration. Together, migrating and being traditional accomplish the impossible task of "leaving Tonga but staying there," an ideology necessary both to those who stay and those who have left.

Keeping Tradition: Three Examples

The Tongan way may seem like something inside the minds and hearts of individual people which is left to individuals to perpetuate. Some things, though, are not fully within an individual's powers. Tongan-Americans can continue to value and teach Tongan ways generation after generation, but their actions will be performed in a world of changing conditions. Teaching old ways under new conditions does not always reproduce old ways. In the remainder of this chapter, I look at three examples that entail principles central to the Tongan way: traditional wealth (*koloa*); customary duties (*fatongia*); and "love" (*'ofa*). Specifically, I examine the making of tapa cloth in Tonga; two ceremonial occasions, a funeral and a twenty-first birthday, in the village; and giving among Tongans born in the United States. In each case, I consider how customary relations and institutions—what I'd define as tradition—are undergoing transformation in the transnational context.

Making tapa cloth in Tonga. The manufacture of traditional wealth is as important as ever. As in the past, women make the necessary mats and tapa cloth for their kin obligations. But, as a result of large-scale migration and the attendant overseas demand for traditional wealth, the sale and exchange of such wealth items has become a lucrative avenue for getting cash and manufactured goods. On the surface, this is a case where the transnational context of production seems to bolster and vitalize tradition. This is only partially true, however. A closer look reveals a more complicated situation.

When Moala, the basket maker, talked about her past year (chapter 7), she said that she spent her entire time making cloth and mats. There were many other obligations that she had let slide in order to accomplish a three-mat, two-cloth production level. The intensity of her effort was related to her intentions to sell or exchange wealth, in addition to having a store on hand for family use. As we saw in chapter 2, since World War II the pressure to produce more cloth in less time has resulted in changes in the tapa production process. In the 1980s, the intensity of production was stepped up again by the burgeoning market for cloth and mats created by overseas migrants. In the 1990s, one sees the results: a radical innovation in cloth making.

A tapa cloth is made in two layers. The tapa maker must have sufficient mulberry bark and several weeks' worth of labor time to beat the bark. Mulberry is grown in the bush, and takes a minimum of two and a half years before it can be harvested. The best bark—the widest, whitest, and most hole-free—is used for the top layer. The bottom layer, or underside, of the cloth is made up of small, mended, off-color pieces joined together with a vegetable paste. It is considered uglier, as well as being more labor-intensive to mend and paste.

It is in making this bottom layer that a major production change has taken place. Tongan women now purchase a manufactured white sheet imported from New Zealand which has a texture and dye-holding quality similar to that of beaten mulberry, and which might be used otherwise for a good napkin or the facing material in clothing. Actual bark is used only for the top layer of the tapa cloth, while this fiber sheet provides the lower layer.[2]

The change saves material and time. With the ready-made bottom sheet, a woman can make the same amount of cloth in half the time and with half the bark. Or to put this in another way more relevant to women's goals for manufacture: in the same amount of time, and with the same amount of bark, a woman can produce double the cloth. The process, however, is now dependent on imported overseas materials, and hence on money.[3]

"We could join a *tou langanga* from America now," Malia said to me. What she meant was that we could "join" by buying the fiber layer for a tapa maker. A woman with only enough bark for one and a half cloths (three sheets) would be able to combine her bark sheets with three sheets of manufactured cloth, which we would provide. She would then be able to produce three full double-layer cloths, each with a bark and a fiber layer. She would send us one of the cloths and keep two for herself. The exchange would be worth it to the tapa maker, who otherwise would not be able to make two cloths, and it would be worth it to Malia, who otherwise would have to pay more than the cost of the imported sheet for a full tapa cloth.

The need for traditional wealth for traditional purposes in this case has translated into vast changes in manufacture and the possibility of even greater transformation in tapa-making institutions.

A Twenty-First Birthday and a Funeral. The strength of the transnational Tongan family has meant, for villagers, a stream of support for ceremonial obligations that would seem to bolster and strengthen traditional practice. However, as more and more villagers come to depend on overseas relatives, so do they become subject to the fluctuations of foreign economies and on the tastes and decisions of an ever distant overseas family.

The photograph on the next page shows the gift wealth displayed in the village on the occasion of a young woman's twenty-first birthday in the 1990s. With a number of relatives overseas, the woman had a fine and memorable celebration with many gifts, good food, and music. The pictured display of wealth, however, is noticeably different from what could be seen even a decade earlier.

The multi-level cake is a startling new village addition, paid for and arranged by New Zealand relatives. As in overseas events, the piles of mats and tapa cloth are substantial for a Tongan commoner, and reflect the financial means and sensibilities of the overseas connection. And if you look closely at the stack of wealth, you can see other recent developments. While you cannot detect the fiber layer on the bottom of some tapa cloth, you can perhaps see the dyed wool fringes on pandanus mats, or the crocheted blanket (the item with a series of zig-zag parallel lines) that has joined the store of wealth.

The content and form of village events changes as overseas Tongans give their support and participation but, ironically, it has also changed as they lessen their support.

Despite the intentions of overseas migrants to "help" their island relatives, the conditions that undergird their intentions constantly shift with global economic tides. In the 1970s it did not take much from a Tongan migrant with an overseas salary to support his or her family back in Tonga, to pay for school fees, or to supplement funeral costs in the village. Land shortages and inflation only bolstered the prevalence and importance of transna-

"TRADITIONAL" WEALTH. The wealth at this village occasion included pandanus mats and tapa cloth, crocheted blankets (sent by overseas female relatives), and a multilayered cake delivered from the capital city, paid for by relatives from New Zealand.

tional family connections, spurring more people to migrate in search of overseas wages. As inflation and land shortage have exploded since then, however, they have pressed the transnational family system to its breaking point. Inflation rates in Tonga, themselves a partial result of remittances, far exceed inflation rates in the countries where migrants work. This means that paying Tongan school fees or keeping one's island family in canned corned beef now takes a much larger piece of a migrant's salary. And with every passing decade, more Tongans go without land. Increased landlessness means that more families must pay for food and thus sustain higher monetary expenses for basic island living.

The effect of this transformation within the transnational family can be seen in Eseta and Manu's discussion of their own support relationships in the 1990s. Both landlessness and inflation translate ultimately into greater demands on the migrant end of the transnational family—demands that migrants are increasingly unable to meet.

Manu: Like my family and her family that are still on the islands. I send to my father every month $25. Every month.

Eseta: If you send $20 a month, that's enough. That's good enough.

Manu: Well, maybe not now. But before, it was enough. Now everything is so expensive. A basket of yams is $50.

Eseta: Yes but if you go to the bush, it's OK. That money will be enough if you grow your food. Then you can use your cash for soap, kerosene, and it's enough.

Manu: But now, the land is too little. More babies and more babies, there's no more room.

Cathy: Do you think after a while the people overseas will get tired of sending money back?

Eseta: Yes! They'll stop. Lots of our family ask, ask, ask. Sometimes I stop. I cannot afford to.

Manu: Sometimes we can give some money, and sometimes we can't. Because we get many bills here, too.

As the global economy shifts, supporting relatives in Tonga has become increasingly more expensive. Many migrants literally cannot afford their family obligations. Overseas migrants who continue to play the patron role to their relatives often bankrupt themselves in the process.[4] If one is to "keep the Tongan way" without going bankrupt, it means developing strategies of paring down. The options are apparent. One must either give to fewer relatives—contributing to smaller networks of mutual aid—give more intermittently, or give less than is needed or wanted. These strategies, in turn, have their effects on customary behavior in the village.

Shortly after the centennial celebration ended in 'Olunga, a man dropped by and told us that Mele, an old woman who lived at the other end of the village, had died. "How lucky she is!" someone said. Malia agreed, "Yes, how lucky." It seemed a strange thing to say at someone's death. "Had she been sick and in pain?" I asked. "No," said the messenger.

"Then why is she lucky to die?"

"Because she died when her relatives were here. She had many family members here from overseas who came for the celebration," Malia explained.

The "luck" that people perceived in the situation included the fact that the old woman would have a fine funeral, attended by and paid for by her overseas relatives. The old woman had had a brother in the village, but he had already died, so the "wealthy" visitors, although not very close relatives, would conduct the funeral. But these overseas family members had just *paid* for their own plane fare to the village, and made considerable donations to the centennial ceremony. They were to leave shortly and return to their lives in Australia, which, by Australian standards, were probably not opulent. Left in charge of the funeral, the overseas family did their duty, but within the context of their own conditions of practicality.

The funeral staged by these overseas relatives was not a ten-day funeral, as is customary, or even the abbreviated three-day shortened funeral that I had seen in the village in the early 1980s. They decided on a one-day funeral, the first I had witnessed for an adult. Mourning would begin at night, and last throughout the night, as is customary. The woman would then be buried the following day, after which villagers would come back and eat one meal.

"Things have changed," Malia told me. "People don't want to waste the time and resources to do a funeral over a ten-day period. A lot of times now, when someone dies, there's the night before [a set of mourning, singing, and gift-giving rituals held the first night of a funeral], and then the burial, and then they divide up the *umu* [food cooked in an underground oven], and then that's it. Now," Malia continued, "it's usually one person [not the whole family] who decides how long the funeral is, and it depends on that person's resources and energy."

At least in this case, a shrinking kin base in Tonga, coupled with the hefty demands on overseas kin, resulted in modifying a village funeral, one of the most important of Tongan traditions.

Giving in the United States. As I board a bus in Hawai'i, I see a teenage girl wearing a T-shirt with a big fist and a male Tongan face that says "Tongan Power." I am standing in the bus aisle, two people down from her, and I greet her in Tongan. She looks at me with a sour city face. "I'm sorry," I say in English, "I thought you were Tongan because of that T-shirt."

"I am, but I don't talk it," she says sharply and looks away. An American girl of Tongan descent, I thought: T-shirts but not language. "Identity," but what about remittances? I wondered.

Being Tongan in the United States is different from being Tongan in Tonga because Tonganness exists there in a different context. Talking to a stranger on a bus is appropriate in Tonga but not in the United States. Some Tongan values do not translate easily into American life. Tongan leisure can be understood as laziness; generosity can be seen as stupidity; prestige-seeking can be read as waste. When surrounded by a larger culture that does not share Tongan values, individuals can more easily evaluate the Tongan way within alternative frameworks, picking and choosing, preserving, modifying, or exaggerating what best suits their new lives.

Within a year after Malia arrived as a new migrant in the United States and had been able to observe Tongan-American ways for a while, I asked her to tell me what she had noticed. Using her own family as an example, Malia talked about Tongans and Tongan-Americans. Malia believed that many Tongan-Americans do in fact become different—a little in the first generation, a lot more in the next. This is how she described it:

Eseta came over a long time ago and she doesn't keep her way of thinking from long ago. She is loving, and she does many things for the family, but then she will say, "Enough." Eseta helped a lot of the family to come over. But when the children of her sisters come and ask for something, and she sees that they are too lazy to go to work, she says, "If I give you some money today, then that will be the only time, because if you come a second time, you will not get it. Go and work! When school ends, you just hang around. I don't like laziness and people coming and just asking and asking for things. You start working and then quit. It's OK for you to go to work."

The children who are born in America are different. The kids born here have a foreign "way" [anga], a way the same as palangis. Maybe it's because they go to school and mix with palangis.

How are they different from Tongan kids?

When I look at Eseta's kids, for example, I see that they are very nice indeed. But at the time that people come to their house, they seem like they want to leave—like they want to go stay in their rooms. They stay just a couple of minutes sometimes and then leave. This is not Tongan.

You know, Eseta's kids want to do the Tongan way. But they don't like lies. If someone says, "I'm going to take this and return it," but then they don't return it when they said they will, Sara gets very very angry. She thinks she has been lied to. She gets angry and will telephone the person to tell them to return the item. When she's angry like that, I realize that she has *anga palangi* [a foreign/white way]. If it was Palu, even if she was angry, she would never say anything.

Sara yells on the phone, "You come and bring me that thing! Go and get your own things." She said this to the children of her father's older brother. I told her, "Stop talking like that and we'll get it back!" That was me, because I am embarrassed for the family. But Sara says to me, "No, let them go get their own things!" There was a girl once who came and borrowed Sara's typewriter. When Sara came home from school and went to do her homework, her typewriter was gone. She was furious! And she telephoned the girl and told her to go to the store and buy her own typewriter. Her father heard her, but he didn't say anything. But me, I was upset with her foreign ways. They can't stop her anger. They know it's truly felt.

Sara doesn't like Tongan customs too much, really. She says you waste a lot—Tongan goods and things.

Do you think she'll teach her own kids Tongan ways?
No.

What will happen to Tongan traditions?
I don't know.

When I asked Sara these same questions, she closed her door behind us (although she did allow me to put her words in the book).

I get so angry! You know, in my family, my father isn't eldest.[5] So at events, my sister and I do all the work. Let me tell you, there is no joy in cooking all night and not getting anything out of it. We can't even eat the food we make! Why should I do this?

At one of the funerals here, I met some relatives from Tonga for the first time in my life. One of them comes over and says she is named after my mom. And you know what she says to me? She says, "I can ask you for anything because I'm your mom's namesake." These relatives know I have a good job so they ask me for all this stuff—like VCRs and TVs and Freedom phones.

I'm not used to it, and I have no shame in not doing it. I ask you, what's the point of getting a higher education anyhow if you can't do anything for yourself with it—if there's no room for your own growth? That's why I think Tongans don't go to college. What's the sense if you'll have nothing to show for it after the relatives are done with you? And if you do find a sense of independence, then you're a black sheep—like Emma. I admire her, though.

Sara's sister, Alyssa, came in the room. I said to both of them, "Some Tongans in the U.S. say they're *more* traditional than islanders, and that Tongan tradition is getting stronger." The tremendous show of wealth at Tongan-American events, the basis for this statement, held a different meaning for the next generation, as Alyssa's answer shows: "I like tradition," Alyssa volunteered. "But a lot of what happens here—it's not tradition. You should see the dances here. They're fashion shows. Every family is trying to outdo the other families. A lot of Tongan events, they're just competitions. There's no tradition in it. It's hard for us to want to do Tongan ways when it's like that."

"What do you think will happen in the future?" I asked.

Sara put it this way: "I have an American side and I have a Tongan side. But the American side, I think, is stronger. Put that in your book."

IV

TRAVELS AHEAD

〰 In this book we have seen a changing culture through the eyes of changing informants and a changing anthropologist. This is very shaky ground from which to arrive at "conclusions." So, I will not speak of results and conclusions in this last section of the book. Rather, I will talk about the insights we can glean from the Tongan case. What I hope to capture in this final section are moments within an ongoing process of change that perhaps hold some clue to how the process works and how it may further unfold.

In Chapter 11, we will look at the experience of Tongan migrants and what it might have in common with observations about migrants elsewhere. We will consider what Americans can learn about *themselves* from the migrant experience and then examine the four transformations under way—of economy, family, tradition, and identity—that stand to reconfigure our world.

How can anthropologists study peoples and cultures on a transnational planet? In Chapter 12, I will reflect on some of the questions raised by doing an ethnography of Tongan migration in the late twentieth century, and we will look at what those questions mean for doing social science in the next millennium.

IV

TRAVELS AHEAD

11

The Meanings
of Tongan
Migration

When foreign anthropologists contributed articles to a book of readings about the United States, they had some very interesting and provocative things to say about Americans.[1] Several noted how fervently Americans believe in the superiority of their country and consequently, in the premise that everyone, if they could, would be a United States citizen.

A Belgian anthropologist wrote about being grilled by an irate customs agent who thought that "everybody who comes here tries to immigrate into the United States" (Pinxten 1993: 93). A Swiss national wrote that Americans thought of him as a "refugee," assuming that he "had moved to the United States to escape a repressive society, to enjoy free enterprise, and to pursue 'the American Dream'" (Drechsel 1993: 129). A Polish anthropologist tells us that Americans seem to have "a very strong and blinding conviction that the American ways are much better than the ways of other countries and peoples. . . . Americans are friendly in the sense that they would sympathize with other people; they would pity them and give them advice on how they should elevate themselves . . . to become more American" (Mucha 1993: 24–25).

Without getting into a discussion of the merits of the United States versus any other society, what we could learn from these observations is that there is something about how we as Americans think that seems strange to outsiders. What is more, if we listen to our own thoughts and words, we can hear that our ideas about ourselves are linked with our ideas about migrants. Studying migration is in part, then, an exercise in reflexivity. By this I mean that to understand migration more clearly, we may need to do more than look at migrants. We may need to look more realistically at ourselves.

On Migration and American Mythology

If migrants are our idealizations of them, then so is America many things: a beacon of hope in a sea of desperation; a dynamic home for the talented, motivated, rugged individualists of the world; the land of opportunity. Yet, when we look at ourselves through the window that Tongans' and other migrants' experiences provide, a more complex, if not a completely different, picture emerges.

A beacon of hope in a sea of desperation. As we have seen, Tongan migrants did not leave Tonga expressly in order to become Americans. They did not sob at the sight of the Statue of Liberty nor reject the citizenship of their homeland at the earliest possible moment. From the vantage point of a village in Tonga, Tongans left Tonga to be better Tongans—to develop themselves and their families and to improve their lot and status among other Tongans. In the stories of migration told in this volume, most migrants believed their move was temporary. Even after twenty-five or thirty years, some still do. Their motivations for leaving the village were often economic, but not in the sense we might think. Migrants were much more likely to be helping family back home than pursuing an American dream of personal success; they were more accurately "experimenting" with their future than they were escaping from a life of destitution.

Throughout the world, emigration is not generally the path of the very poorest people, nor do mass migrations usually occur until *after* an internal development process has taken place.[2] The United States, then, is not as a rule the last hope of a desperate people. And Tongans, like other migrants, have many reasons for migrating other than economic opportunity or political freedom: helping family, seeking prestige or religious community, visiting overseas family, curiosity, marriage, even avoiding family demands.[3]

Emma's account of her migration and its meaning (chapter 5) probably comes closest to a classic migrant story as most Americans would perceive it. She is a woman who relates her personal development to her new nationality. Before she was "nobody," but now she is "somebody." She was searching for something that she found in her new name and new identity.

Emma was probably the most articulate about her reasons for migrating, but note the point in her life when these comments were made. Before her migration, and in early interviews after her migration, she did not express sentiments of this kind. It was well after her move to the United States that such thoughts surfaced in our conversations. Her reasons for coming to the United States were, in fact, an aspect of the text that Emma wished to "correct" after the fact. It was five years after her migration, and after reading her earlier comments on the subject, that she revised her story in terms of "personal growth" and widened horizons, in sharp distinction to her life in Tonga. These ideas about her migration were truly meaningful to Emma, but they were ideas that were cultivated and made articulate only in the social context of the United States.

Home of the talented, the motivated, the rugged individualists. Tongan migration is a family strategy that, just like marriage, can be vetoed or embraced by the individuals involved. In chapter 3 we saw that Eseta truly wanted to join her sister overseas, and she probably would not have gone to the United States if she had opposed the idea. But the reason why the family facilitated her migration—blocking her marriage in Samoa and paying her airfare—was that they wanted the marriage stopped and Eseta brought overseas. As many observers of migration have suggested, migration may not really be an "individual choice" at all.[4] As a result, the relationship of migration to internal motivation, to "rugged individualism," and personal choice is at best weak. The person who comes overseas may just as easily be the least "ruggedly individualistic" as the most.

Look again at the life stories of Finau and Emma (chapters 5 and 9), whose early histories you know in some detail. I believe that one would be hard-pressed to pick in advance the one who eventually migrated. Who had been the more ambitious, competitive, rebellious, individualistic? There is a plethora of personal factors that affect why some people go and others stay, and they do not neatly divide among migrants and nonmigrants.

There is an often-heard belief in the United States that America absorbs the most motivated and most talented from other countries, a position that is part of our national consciousness. The implications are not very flattering to nations that send migrants because it bluntly implies that the donor is stuck with the leftovers. Let us reconsider the donor-U.S. relationship in the Tongan case from a Tongan village standpoint.

A Tongan family may choose which individuals go overseas for a number of reasons: because they have no land, because they could not pass their school exams and have no promise of a good job, because they are unmarried, because they are eldest and there are younger children who can stay behind on the family farm, or because they are the child the family has decided is most likely to remit.[5]

There are some cases in which the better-positioned people in a village might not want to leave, or might not be encouraged to do so. The daughter in Atu and Malia's family most pressured to go to the United States was the one with the fewest prospects at the time. In Tonga there is still a little room for the cream of the rising middle class—the enterprising farmer with land, the overseas-educated professional, the technician or secondary school teacher, people like Finau and Samiu.

So it may, in fact, be true that Tongan immigrants to the United States are more "motivated," but only in comparison to other U.S. citizens. Like other migrants, they work longer hours and are willing to work at harder, dirtier, more dangerous jobs. But when you compare them to Tongan villagers, such comparative judgments are inaccurate.

As we saw in chapter 1, the villagers who do stay in Tonga work hard. For a Tongan commoner, it takes talent and energy to secure a good government job, to start a local business, or to run a successful farm. The premise, then, that the most motivated and successful always migrate is sometimes reversed.[6] That is, people with less assured futures in Tonga are sometimes the ones who set their sights for overseas. This is why Malia would recommend:

> If they're not good at school, they should try to go overseas and maybe they will do better than the ones who were good in school. Yes, it's true. The ones who come overseas—their lives will develop more than the educated ones who stay in Tonga. Because they will work and get good money and build a nice house, better than those who stayed and worked in Tonga. Not everyone, but people sometimes do.

This is also why, as we saw in chapter 7, the villager who had built a formidable cement house with money earned in Tonga was so proud. He knew that I would appreciate what it took to accomplish this, as opposed to the more common way of building a home with money earned overseas. We saw the same principle, only in reverse, when Finau described the instant popularity of boys who had been to America, even if just for short while. A boy who never had girlfriends before on his own merits would suddenly be inundated with interest. From this vantage point, America can be considered not so much a magnet for global talent as it is a great exaggerator of ability, a puffer up of importance, an inflator of prestige.

R. C. Jones reports that in Mexico, young people have little ambition for work or school in their villages because they know they will be going to the United States. There they will be bellhops or busboys or migrant workers, and they will probably end up making more money than those educated boys who stayed in the village. This is quite a different picture from the America in many of our minds. As Jones (1995: 87) observes, "Migration is the great leveler"—not, as we normally think, of differences of birth and circumstance, but of education, ability, and talent.

The land of opportunity. There is no doubt that new Tongan migrants to the United States make much higher wages than at home. But look at what was also true in the Tongan case: Seini, the nurse, became only a nurse's aide in the United States, Eseta taught school in Tonga but worked in a laundry in California. Simi, another teacher, worked in a warehouse. Atu, head of the national credit union, was hired to sweep floors. Malia never needed to work for wages in the village, but in California she worked twenty-four-hour shifts cleaning, cooking, and caring for elderly people in a nursing home.

In social terms, many Tongan migrants experience downward mobility. Other migrants report this phenomenon as well. Studies of immigrants in the United States show that they are in lower-prestige occupations, such as laborers and service workers, with lower earnings.[7] In personal narratives, Barbadian migrants noted their boring and dirty jobs, inferior schooling, and run-down housing compared to their homes in the Caribbean.[8] Although wages are higher, the dignity of living is not. In other personal narratives by Mexican migrants, a man tells disparagingly how, despite his education in Mexico, the only job he could get in the United States was as a farm worker. Another Mexican migrant—and successful entrepreneur—despairs that he must move his thriving U.S. business home to Mexico from the United States where, despite his success, people would always think of him as lowly.[9]

The work opportunities for Tongans in California have been in jobs that nonimmigrants would not take. Tongans work disproportionately as farm workers, laborers, drivers, movers, gardeners, tree trimmers, maids, janitors, building guards, and aides in health and elder care. Some are assembly workers and technicians. There was limited mobility to begin with in these jobs, and opportunity has worsened with the economic climate of the

1990s. As private, corporate, and government downsizing has occurred, all Americans have suffered, but especially the most vulnerable, such as immigrants and minorities.[10]

A week before Christmas 1995, Eseta lost her government job. She was one of the layoffs when the municipal budget was cut. Emma still had her mail-room job, but she made the same amount she did four years earlier. She saw no immediate opportunity for promotion from the mail room. Manu was "retired," in my estimation, when his employers saw that his health was failing and that he might need to draw heavily on company health insurance.

These are not horror stories, but they are not particularly hopeful stories either. The literature on migrants encourages us to put our hope for mobility in time and the second generation.[11] Tongans born in this country have higher rates of college enrollment than those who migrated here. They are better represented in managerial, sales, and office jobs, and there are fewer, proportionally, who do farm work or service jobs such as tree trimming and house cleaning. In Eseta and Manu's household, Sara's college degree would earn her a management position and Alyssa would set her sights on an entry-level management position within the same company. Even so, the road ahead is not clear.

Again, it is the shifting economy, and its attendant social climate, that dims a brighter prognosis. The mid-level jobs that provided stepping stones to mobility are being taken away as corporations replace people with technology and U.S. labor with foreign labor. In the three-year period from 1993 to 1995, the United States lost 1.6 million jobs through corporate restructuring and flight. This left fewer jobs that are good jobs by American standards, and increasingly these demand an ever higher educational level. Meanwhile, public funding programs for education, for job training, and for affirmative action are all under attack.

Recent studies of migrants suggest that things may be changing for the worse, and especially so for certain ethnic groups.[12] Compared to the situation in the 1940s and 1950s, the gap between U.S. natives and recent immigrants is greater in both wages and unemployment; migrant poverty has grown over time; and, since the 1980s, the average earnings of long-term immigrants may have stopped improving.[13] In California, it is immigrants who make up the state's growing poor population. One study notes that those immigrants of working age who arrived from 1985 to 1989 earned 62 percent less than U.S. born residents in the state. Three-quarters of those adult immigrants earned less than $15,000 in 1990.[14]

A Dominican immigrant community in New York was, a generation ago, heralded as an example of immigrant success. "But now," a journalist writes, "it is in danger of serving as a model of how newcomers can end up struggling with poverty on the margins of American society." The writer quotes a man from the community who left the Dominican Republic a decade ago: "It used to be that everyone counted on improving themselves when they came here. Now people can't find jobs. They don't have money. A lot of people are losing their hopes."[15] His assessment is strikingly similar to Eseta's comments in 1996, when she sought work after losing her job: "It used to be," she told me, "that if you wanted a job you could get one anywhere— in a day! Now, it is no longer so easy to find good work."

The situation of Tongans in the United States in the 1990s tells an important story. Although Tongans have done better the longer they have stayed in the United States, and they earn far more than they could make in Tonga, these relative statements mask certain truths about the promise of America. It remains the case that 60 percent of Tongans in this country are within 200 percent of the poverty level, and more than 20 percent live below the poverty line, most without any public assistance.[16] And, although many children of Tongan migrants work in better jobs than their parents, more than 50 percent of U.S.-born Tongans have remained in laborer and service positions. What does it say about America that a literate, healthy, hardworking population who came voluntarily to this country can end up with a median *household* income under $15,000, and with 60 percent of their families on the brink of poverty?

Hearing of the impressions and experiences of migrants in the United States, we must remind ourselves what keeps immigrants coming here. At least for many third world migrants, it is not so much the promise of lucrative jobs or unlimited mobility as it is the differential between what they can earn in the United States as opposed to the country from which they came. This difference is a legacy of colonialism. But today the difference really means that even if one has a low-paying, low-status job in the United States, one can still aspire to a better life—often, not so much in the United States as in one's home country.

The Transnational Equation

The savings or pension from two decades of work at a low-paying job in the United States would not go far after retirement in this country. In Tonga, the same U.S. pension made Manu a well-to-do man. A small pension or nest egg does the same in Thailand, in Sri Lanka, in Mexico, and a host of other nations from which migrants originate. It is no wonder that many first-generation migrants (especially those who came as adults to the United States) think of retiring in the country of their birth.

There is more to this transnational equation than money, though. Both the successful Mexican entrepreneur *and* the educated migrant farm worker cited in the last section returned to Mexico. It is in Mexico that the farm worker's education counts, where he can use his education to invest his earnings. It is in Mexico that the entrepreneur can spend his money as a model citizen rather than as a second-class citizen in the United States.

As many Tongans in the United States have discovered, even working two jobs will not allow them really to make it in their new country. They are educated but untrained for skilled labor positions; they are literate but speak with accents; and they are brown in a country that favors whites. As a result, many Tongans try to hoard a nest egg from a meager income by living as cheaply and sparely as possible in the United States, then funneling all their savings into retiring or building a house or a business back in Tonga. In Tonga, as in Mexico, most capital for private development since the early 1980s has come from overseas Tongans whose greatest hope is to come back with foreign money to their native land.[17]

There is a phenomenon that you will notice only if you keep crossing the ocean, as migrants do. There are Tongans who live in hovels in the United States, working one, sometimes two minimum wage jobs, subsisting on the bottom-most rung of America's economic and social ladder. A few even collect welfare. In Tonga these same people have fine houses and are important figures in the village when they go home for two or three months each year.

In such examples we find the real underpinnings of transnationalism, the pattern by which family, identity, and resources cross national boundaries and link together the country of origin with the country of settlement. It is the *differential* in both social and economic mobility that is the key to understanding transnationalism. This differential ensures that it is only in returning "home"—in transnational visits, investment, retirement, and remittances—that the real promise of the migration process can be fulfilled.

It is worth noting that the majority of academic studies on immigrants focus on the relationship of new migrants to the host culture. In the United States the topics that dominate our research concern subjects such as assimilation, adjustment, or stress—that is, questions of how well migrants are faring within American institutions and with other Americans.

In focusing research and questions this way, we miss certain crucial dynamics of the postcolonial world that are occurring in the "space between"—between the income and the status earned in host as opposed to home countries, between family members who migrated and those who stayed. It is in this transnational space that new social and economic structures of social mobility, development, tradition, remittances, and social identity are being wrought. It is here—in between countries, between relatives, and within the transnational family—that one can understand the transformations of the world system that will define the twenty-first century.

Tonga and the Space Between: Four Transformations

The Tongan case can offer insight into four transformations occurring in the "space between"—those of economy, of family, of tradition, and of identity—and the relationship among them. The migration process has moved each of these areas, from identity to economy, into a new transnational arena that both transforms them and binds them together in novel ways.

The first transformation is the development of economies based on remittances from migrants. Remittances are not only the lifeblood of small island nations. By the 1990s they had become the world's second largest trade item, surpassed only by oil.[18] More than thirty-eight nations in such diverse areas as the Pacific, the Caribbean, North Africa, eastern Europe, and South Asia depend on this wealth sent back through the family.[19] Tonga represents one of the prime examples of remittance economies in the world.[20]

The conduit for the new form of economy is a new form of family. When you ask children from Tonga (or, for that matter, from Central America or the Caribbean or most of the world's labor-sending nations) to name everyone in their close family, they will include people who live in another country. Conversely, many immigrants living in industrial nations consider themselves part of a family in another country—a transnational family. Between 1980 and 1990 alone, overseas phone calls from the U.S. quintupled—an indication of the raw size of the transnational family phenomenon. In one Dominican neighborhood in New York, a new industry started in the 1990s—telephone shops, where entrepreneurs set up stores that simply contain rows of telephone booths advertising cheap overseas calls.[21]

Transnational family patterns were evident in the many descriptions throughout this book of information, wealth, and visitors that went back and forth between Tonga and the United States, New Zealand and Australia. Tonga's peak (and most expensive) season for airline travel is now during December and January, the hottest and most uncomfortable time of the year, but the time when returning family, not tourists, fill the planes for the holidays. As we saw in the Tongan village, almost every household belongs to a transnational family, and in the 1990s, the same thing can be said about almost every Tongan-American household.

"Are you Tongan or American?" a boy in the village asked Lio. The dichotomous form of the question leaves no room for the new complexity of identities that can be witnessed, whether among Tongan-American youth or globally. American-born Tongans, like other American-born migrants, often report dual identities or confusion about being placed in either category. Increasingly, the population of the globe has a foot in more than one world. As people change countries, as families traverse nations and nations become increasingly multiethnic, their cultural identity, and the traditional symbols and practices around which that identity is built, take on new dimensions and new functions.

As Tongan migration has continued for three decades, new institutions have become entangled in the migration web. Tongan traditions and identity have become tied to remittances and the family in ways that they never were prior to migration. They provide a counterweight to migration—bearing new importance in connecting migrants to the culture they or their parents left. The question of "Tonganness" has become increasingly important to the maintenance of the transnational family, even as traditions and identities themselves are changing rapidly.

The re-formation of tradition and identity to address new contingencies is a familiar theme throughout the world. There is a worldwide reorientation of tradition and identity that has become the subject of anthropological inquiry.[22]

In the remainder of the chapter, I consider these global changes more closely, asking what are their implications for the twenty-first century. I use the Tongan case, and what we have seen in the preceding chapters, to make some guesses about these global transformations in the economy, the family, tradition, and identity, their relationships, and the prognosis for the future.

New remittance economies. Some of the most significant effects of migration throughout the world can be seen in the often "hidden villages" that make up the other side of the industrial world's immigrant wave. Our glimpse at a village in Tonga showed that the effects of the global migration system are far-reaching, leaving no untouched, "pristine" corner where everything stays the same. Migration out of Tonga has transformed the internal life of the village, and, in the Tongan case, we can see the complexities of this transformation.

If the Tongan case is characteristic, then the pattern of migration and remittances is making the nonindustrial world more prosperous and yet more dependent at the same time.[23] Over all, the Tongan village that we saw in the 1990s had a more opulent way of life than it had had fifteen years before. There was an increased level of consumption and an increasing range of imports—from plastic wrap, children's toys, videos, disposable diapers, furniture, and electric appliances to the imported fabric for "traditional" tapa cloth. Tongan villagers had better housing, more reliable piped water, more modern conveniences, and, for many, a general increase in social mobility.[24] These observations of elevated lifestyle and increased mobility are consistent with changes observed elsewhere in the world.[25] In Tonga the growing middle class—increasingly visible through its consumption—had strong connections to a developing pro-democracy movement.

There was also, however, another side to this prosperity and mobility. Infrastructure in the village had not kept pace with the changes in individual lives, a problem seen in everything from the dearth of electric outlets, to the condition and number of roads, to the amount of undisposed garbage. There was increased economic disparity in the village. In the 1990s, the people in the village who were poor were, relatively speaking, poorer than they had been a decade before.[26] There was a sense among villagers that their fortunes had "fallen" while others' had risen. Remittances had also resulted in more disposable income and higher prices, a cycle of inflation that hit 26 percent during the mid-1980s.[27] As a result, villagers felt pressure to keep up, and to keep migrating so that their own positions would not deteriorate. Migration in this instance cannot fairly be considered a simple "choice." It was the outcome of a deeper systemic transformation with its own dynamics.

At the local level, the upshot of the migration-remittance-mobility cycle appeared to be a new kind of dependency, both on continuing migration and on migrant relatives. Kai's (the cab driver's) business, which depended for half its revenues on Tongan customers; Moala (the weaver's) switch from making baskets for tourists to making mats for overseas Tongans; the burgeoning town flea market stocked with giveaways from overseas relatives— these examples were all symptomatic of this shifting economic connection to other countries.

Colonialism may have been mediated by missionaries, administrators, and traders from European nations, but the global transformations of the so-called postcolonial era were being mediated by overseas kin. Tonga's new economic reliance on remittances had brought about new family strategies for success. Mobility for a family required that some members must leave. But, as we have seen, migrants must also stay—at least in their hearts and in the sense of still being Tongan. The transnational family strategy depended on the contradictory principles of maintaining migration and at the same time maintaining Tongan identity and tradition. This quandary—with implications for change—became a built-in feature of the migration process.

New global families. On a structural level, remittances represent the flow of wealth to labor-giving countries from labor-receiving countries. But at a human level, a remittance economy is based on exchanges among family members who live in different countries. As we saw in the Tongan case, these are not one-way exchanges. There are responsibilities at both ends.

Those who stayed in Tonga must caretake the assets of those who left. They look after land.[28] They tend houses or care for relatives left behind. They send traditional wealth overseas, and they offer overseas kin a place of importance and comfort when they return to visit. They also receive the hundreds of children sent back to Tonga each year from the United States, New Zealand, and Australia.

Migrants shoulder different responsibilities. They must continue to send back money and goods to their island kin. They support village projects. They help other islanders to make the trip overseas, and arrange housing, sponsorship, and work for new arrivals.

For migrants, through relationships within the transnational family they maintain a place of security and importance in Tonga to which they and their children can return. For islanders, these relationships make possible a life of relative prosperity and mobility. Family relationships support the weight of the remittance economy.

How well are these relationships holding up in the Tongan case? On the economic surface, the remittance economy and the global family remain strong. Tonga has not yet shown the dramatic drop in remittances that has characterized many remittance-receiving nations. Some 90 percent of Tongan households received remittances according to a village study in the mid-1980s. In the 1990s, as much as a third of household income in some Tongan villages came from remittances. A reported 81 percent of migrants who had been away from Tonga for fifteen to twenty years still remitted, and this percentage increased for those away more than twenty years.[29]

Yet, when I examined the intimate relationships between migrants and islanders which undergirded this economic flow, there were obvious signs of stress. Tensions were apparent daily in the village in 1995. They surfaced as interpersonal problems, taking the form of everyday disappointments, resentments, misunderstandings, annoyances, betrayals, and anger. They were evident in the look on the face of a returned migrant who discovered the misuse of his village house and in the tone of the village woman who complained how migration was leaving the village unkempt and untended. Tensions appeared again in the cool distance between American-born Tongans and Tongan islanders of their own generation.

When Tongan islanders in the late 1980s were asked why their relatives had left for overseas, they answered that migrants had left for their families. When Tongan migrants overseas were asked why they had left Tonga, they said they had left for opportunities.[30] These different versions of what the migration process was about were reflected over and over again in the transnational families who interacted in the village in 1995.

"How can I keep give, give, giving?" one Tongan-American asked.

"I don't know, they just don't love me," said an islander.

Tensions were apparent in the United States as well. In 1996 the kava group who had sent money for the village water pump were concerned that the money they had sent had been "eaten." There were always accusations of people in the village "eating money," meaning that they were redirecting resources meant for the common good into private consumption. But the interpretation of the "eaten" water pump donation, as I heard it from one man, was different because it targeted islanders as a group rather than a specific individual or family.

"It happens a lot now," a Tongan-American contributor told me. The money that we send back for some purpose isn't getting used for what it was intended. You know what the problem is? People there want to develop and they have no money to do it so they steal. I think maybe the good people who think of doing good for their country are overseas and the bad ones, they stay there." It is a changing interpretation that reflects a changing relationship between islanders and their fellow villagers overseas. These are the attitudes and incidents, I believe, that foreshadow a change in remittance patterns.

For a time these rifts will go publicly unrecognized, and personal frustrations will be downplayed. They are, for now, covered over with an ideology of "no problem," in which people minimize their differences, asserting that they all are the same, all Tongan, and all people who love the "Tongan way." The divisions are bridged by a heightened sense of shared identity and tradition.

Ultimately, though, I believe that the ruptures in family life and the related decline in family-directed remittances cannot be mitigated this way for long. Remittances will eventually both slow and transform in kind, and both of these processes will have to do with the larger demographic and economic factors in which the global family has come to be embedded. Neither emphasizing Tongan tradition nor bolstering Tongan identity will keep remittances flowing or family ties strong, for the foundations of Tonga's transnational families and economy lie elsewhere—in global processes occurring outside Tonga.

It is easier to see this in concrete terms. When Eseta's steady government job ended and Manu was retired, they were both forced to take lower-paying employment. At the same time, the Tongan economy continued to inflate. Basic math shows that Eseta's contribution to her sister in Tonga will, in practical terms, decrease. Eseta will have less money to give, while at the same time the money that covered two nephews' school fees a decade ago will now not even pay for one. With no change in her sense of identity, tradition, and obligation, her contributions to her Tongan family will fade. The real source of declining remittances in this case is an American economic and social climate that determines Eseta's ability to get and keep a job that pays decently.

Continued migration has also altered the material and social relations between Tongan islanders and Tongans overseas. As overseas Tongans have brought over more family members, the locus of migrants' economic and social support network has moved slowly away from Tonga. For many U.S. migrants, it is other Tongan-Americans—both kin and non-kin—who are most essential to their daily lives, on whom they and their children depend, and with whom they interact. Conversely, their family ties with islanders are fewer and thinner, a process that will increase over time.

In 1990, decisions to remit, to visit Tonga, and to keep up with island family still fell to first-generation migrants with strong ties to Tonga. The average age of a second-generation Tongan in the United States was 7.4 years.[31] Over the next two decades these demographics will change. Even with continued high levels of immigration, American-born Tongans will make up an increasing percentage of Tongans living in the United States. I estimate that the number of Tongan-Americans born in the United States will exceed the number of first-generation migrants by the end of the second decade of the twenty-first century.[32] Tonga's remittance and family system will then depend on those whose cultural background and economic ties are more solidly in the United States.

As this occurs, the volume of remittances is likely to fall.[33] Where they continue, they are likely to be transformed in nature from payments based on emotional and social obligations to family to calculated investments. There are already indications that such a process is occurring. In explaining continued high levels of remittances to Tonga, two researchers write, "One possible explanation is that while remittances motivated by family consumption support might decline with length of absence, there is an offsetting increase in remittances motivated by the migrant's savings and investment decisions." Studies of Tongan remittance behavior in the 1990s showed that 13 percent of Tongan remitters were sending back money and goods for investment purposes. Moreover, this group had a higher propensity to remit.[34]

Over the next decade, relatives may attribute waning remittances or unmet demands to a loss of traditional values, but the factors most likely to affect remittance levels are the conditions that influence investment behavior: the health of the American economy and the flight of its corporations; U.S. receptivity to Tongan-Americans, including its degree of racism and xenophobia; the mobility of second-generation Tongan migrants in their home countries; and policies of the Tongan government to encourage migrant repatriation and investment. This last point is, not surprisingly, a goal of Tonga's sixth five-year development plan. If it succeeds and Tongan-Americans continue to supply the Tongan economy with money, they will do so less as relatives than as investors.[35]

New cultural traditions and identities. Over the past two centuries, social traditions and institutions in Tonga reinforced particular relationships of hierarchy and cooperation between commoners and chiefs, junior and senior relatives, males and females. They were relevant to the way Tongan society was structured and reproduced. But, as we have seen, in the latter twentieth century, Tongan tradition has become entwined with the processes of transnational migration and remittances. Tradition has come to buffer the global family against its own internal differences and to become the social cement that binds the community of Tongan-Americans together.

As this process has taken place, Tongan tradition has become an essential rhetoric of the 1990s. Visiting Tongan religious leaders in the United

States talk about the importance of maintaining Tongan values in America. (I have observed two such talks personally.) Tongan-Americans demonstrate their commitments to tradition by elaborate giveaways of traditional wealth, much more so than their island counterparts. Parents teach their children to honor the Tongan way. Children are sent to Tonga for holidays. They are urged to marry Tongan spouses, join Tongan youth groups, attend Tongan funerals, and learn Tongan dances.

These expressions of Tongan tradition, however, are no longer simply Tongan. Existing now in a transnational social space, tradition solves problems and belongs to a world system that it never did before. And in the process, tradition and identity are themselves transformed.

As we have seen, emphasizing traditionalism within new transnational contexts caused the institutions identified as "traditional" to change. With both migration and monetization as the backdrop, for instance, the expanded use of traditional wealth by overseas Tongans placed increasing pressures on tapa cloth producers, which in turn transformed the production process. Traditionalism thus changed tradition.

For Tongan youth growing up in an environment that differs markedly from that of their parents, the pressure on them to "be traditional" changes the meaning, and ultimately the form and effect, of tradition. A study of out-migration among youth on the Tongan island of Kotu actually showed the important role of traditional relations in pushing young men *off* their home island. The boys were essentially seeking to escape the onerous obligations to senior (higher) relatives by moving elsewhere, both to the capital and overseas. The study concluded that the outward push was related to convention rather than to changes brought about by modernization.[36] But, really, it was the interaction between the two that was responsible—the fact that "convention" came to be located in a larger global context in which modernization had occurred.

In this example, traditional demands on young people spurred their migration only at that historical point when small island life was steeped in a wider social environment that offered working in town or going overseas or attending college as possibilities, and where alternative models of social relations existed that seemed freeing to youth. Such a wider context for viewing tradition was what led Palu to reinterpret her own childhood as oppressive. It was only in the setting of an alternative American social system that Palu could become Emma and cast her experiences within her family in a new light.

These new frames—a product of historical changes worldwide—transform Tongan culture and tradition from a taken-for-granted reality to a set of practices and beliefs that can be evaluated from a vantage point outside itself. This is even more true for those Tongans raised in a different culture. Alyssa considers herself traditional, but she and her parents interpret the great expenditures of wealth at Tongan events differently. For her father, these shows of wealth translate into being "more Tongan." For the American-born, they signal opulent display, ugly competitiveness, and social climbing. Sara is struck by the "unfairness" of some Tongan traditions—cooking food that she will never taste, for instance. They offend her American sensibilities. She, like Emma, will pick and choose among the things she likes and doesn't like about Tongan tradition, and will decide what to embrace and pass on and what to discard. In terms of identity, Sara will talk about how she is part Tongan and part American (but mostly the latter). Many second-generation migrants understand themselves, like Sara, as having dual identities, or they report confusion about their identity, like Lio Jr.[37]

Tongan identities forged in the United States have also expanded to include new dimensions. Consider the notion of "Tongan power" that has developed among some Tongan-American youth. The T-shirts and the language that express this identity is recognizable to almost any member of our society. It is an "American" phenomenon, or at least a form of identification that is related to living in a large, multiethnic environment. "Tongan Power" T-shirts belong somewhere in between other T-shirts that say "Irish and Proud of It" and "Black Power." They are badges of ethnic identity appropriate for displays of ethnic pride and social solidarity in multiethnic industrial societies.

It is important to realize that it is not just among migrants that these new frameworks operate. "Tongan Power" T-shirts are widespread on the Tongan islands among youth who have never been overseas.[38] The Americans I met, in fact, had purchased them in Tonga. They are sold alongside other T-shirts, originally manufactured for the tourist market, with legends such as "Paris. Rome. Tokyo. Nuku'alofa" (Tonga's capital) or "Where in Hell is Tonga?" These two sets of T-shirts give different messages—the "power" shirts assert the importance of Tonga, while the others laugh at its insignificance—but both proceed from a vantage point in which Tonga is perceived and evaluated in terms of the larger world. T-shirts, as well as a plethora of other daily evidence, reveal that Tongans perceive themselves and their culture in a global perspective.

Even among islanders who, like Finau, are committed to the importance of tradition, "outside" eyes, developed through education and childhood during the 1980s, lead them to see some traditions as old-fashioned or inappropriate to the times. In chapter 9, Finau talked about her frustration with older people's refrain of how things were in "their time." As she says, "This is *my* time," and so there are ways in which she chooses to act differently from her elders, and to reject the customary behavior they endorsed.

Meanwhile, in the 1990s, American-born children returning to Tonga in order to become more Tongan and more disciplined bring their overseas socialization with them. One chiefly observer is reported to have said that overseas children are changing Tonga, not being changed by it. They bring their values with them, and so the "sending home" phenomenon teaches island children an alternative framework as much as it teaches foreign-born children to become more Tongan.

Given the many novel factors affecting this generation—from television to migration to the presence of overseas cousins in their schools—Tongan island youth in the 1990s have a keen sense of a moving, changing larger world that becomes a context for evaluating traditional life. The content of the evaluation varies as it did with T-shirts. From the larger global standpoint, village life can be seen as dead end, as it is to some Tongan youth, but it can also be viewed with the awareness that Tongan culture has distinctive and admirable qualities that should be touted. Both views are heard in village conversations. In school yearbooks, which included poems and stories by students, I was struck by the pervasive presence of overseas references in the writing. In one 1992 poem a Tongan teenager lauds the English language as a "friend to lean on" that will be there wherever one wanders in life. Another student writes anonymously: "Home is important to me because one day I may leave for another place but I will always bear in mind that I can still return. . . . I pity homeless people in Europe, America, Africa, and other places that face the same problem who need food, good shelter, water, and what I have plenty of . . . LOVE."

The result of these wider vantage points on Tongan tradition both in the Tongan islands and among overseas Tongans is a much greater flexibility of custom. People select, modify, and distill custom, with the result that "traditional" institutional forms—everything from funerals to tapa cloth making to obligations to toward higher kin—are rapidly changing.[39]

"Tongan tradition" as a generic concept seems likely to survive initially, perhaps even flourish, in its new contexts. But there are real questions about what "tradition" will mean. Tradition as the "Tongan way" and tradition as "Tongan power" are not the same thing. They do not have the same forces buoying them and reproducing them, and thus their historical trajectories are different.

Tradition is now (and perhaps always has been) a creative, ongoing, mutable result of wider social processes. As traditions become entwined with other social institutions and forces—such as the remittance economy, the community of Tongan-American mutual aid, or the demonstration of ethnic identity—traditions are destroyed and reified at the same time. This is why I say that tradition in a transnational context carries the seeds of its own transformation.

Beyond Tradition and Ethnicity: An Educated Guess about the Future

Anthropologists know full well that they cannot generalize their narratives beyond the village, or certainly the culture, on which the narratives were based. So please do not judge other anthropologists by what I am about to do—which is to suggest that what has happened in a Tongan village says something about the future of the world. Although an anthropological study of a village has no statistical weight outside itself, I believe that the intimacy and depth of anthropological case studies allow one to detect social processes and relationships that one might not otherwise see. It is at the mundane levels of daily events and interpersonal relationships that the mechanisms for larger social trajectories exist.

So if one had had access to the day-to-day events, the private thoughts, and the interpersonal relationships in a hamlet in mid-thirteenth-century Europe, one might have seen signs of the social dynamics that would lead to the Renaissance and the Reformation. A village ethnography at this time might have revealed pieces of a larger picture that an analyst could put together: the rising tensions between the plebians and the ruling aristocracies, the growing discord between Church and State, and peasant dislocation, with public discontent funneled into anti-Semitic, anti-Muslim, and anti-witchcraft outbreaks (perhaps not unlike the anti-immigrant sentiments of today). The clues would have been sufficient to gain a glimpse of a larger picture, and perhaps suggest empirical studies that might be done to flesh out its details.

Consider in this light some of the observations we can pull from the Tongan case that have resonance beyond Tonga:

• A process of mass labor migration from former colonies and protectorates to the industrial world is causing demographic and economic changes that affect even the smallest villages of the smallest countries.

• The remittance economies that developed as a result of migration have been associated with increased social mobility and the democratization of economic privilege. With this mobility has come an increase in local economic differentiation, together with a growing and more powerful pro-democracy middle class. Societies that, like Tonga, were based on kinship or rank now contain many more elements of class.[40]

- In host societies, most migrants are entering the labor force on the lowest rungs of the economic ladder, but with an eye toward mobility in the next generation. This mobility is often elusive, as it has been for Tongans and many other, particularly non-white and non-Asian, immigrants.[41]

- Migrants are establishing themselves more permanently in their new countries, realigning cultural, national, and family borders. More than ever before in history, families are divided by nation and, in second-generation migrant families, by culture and language too.[42] This realignment causes an upheaval of sorts in the symbolic and personal dimensions of self-identification, resulting in multiple identities, confusion of identities, and changing identities.

- Rapid changes are occurring in what constitutes the content and practice of cultural traditions.

What can be made of these disparate puzzle pieces? I believe that these are all related parts of a larger transformation of industrial capitalism. It is understandable that the first references to "transnationalism" in the academic literature appeared in relation to corporations. The internationalization of business has been the entree to migration and to the transnational changes in identity, tradition, and family which I have just listed. As capitalism has arrived at a new stage of global integration, other changes in social, political, and personal life are occurring which both facilitate and result from this shift. This is the story I think my ethnography foretells.

Global capitalism must be able to count on an environment of political stability and a labor pool unfettered by limitations on its movement. It is a system that works best in a political environment of democracy, in which the institutions of state protect rights to property, free trade, and individual freedom. Capitalism exploits cheap labor, often that of children and women, but its real money is to be made in nurturing and shaping a middle class that can consume its products. Throughout the world, from Tonga to Indonesia to India to Thailand, a middle class with a consumer appetite and pro-democracy sentiments is developing. Noticed more by business journals than social science journals, it is being tapped and expanded by American manufacturers of everything from cigarettes to shampoo and from potato chips to TV sets.[43] The values of such a system are less regional and culturally specific, more globalized and universal.

A class-based global society will cross-cut old social boundaries. Culture, race, rank, gender, ethnicity, religion, nation, even family will no longer serve as mutually reinforcing anchors of social and self-identification.[44] The disarticulation of family, ethnic, and national boundaries is part of a reformation of identity and culture. As it occurs, people will find increasingly more in common with those of a similar economic stratum, beginning a global class formation process that will play out over the next century.[45]

This is not to say that the old categories will simply disappear as social forces. Class formation is occurring in a world of historically potent categories that include ethnicity, rank, race, and gender, and these will all leave their legacy to the emergent class system. Lower-class ranks will be disproportionately composed of nonwhites, women, traditional nonelites, and cultures or migrants from cultures that were colonialized, facts already glaringly obvious in the United States among both its native-born and its migrants.[46] Conversely, the middle and upper classes on a global basis will be overrepresented by whites, traditional elites, and members of former colonizing nations. Moreover, the definition of middle- and upper-class life will be based on the values and characteristics of the social groups which have traditionally held power.[47]

The new global class system will not be understood simply by looking at industrial class development. There are new dynamics at work. Tonga's emergent class system, for example, will be profoundly affected by the fact that old social relations have affected new ones: that Tonga's new investors and capitalists, for instance, are likely to be its overseas relatives, or that its traditional chiefly elite will make up both its top eschelons of government and the bulk of its upper class. Such circumstances will create a different manifestation of class.

One of the most important questions social scientists can now address is how and to what extent the divisions that are so important in the colonial world—gender, ethnicity, race, nationality, or older cultural relations of rank and patronage—will articulate with the emergent global system of class. To find the answers to this question and others in our post-colonial world, social science must re-examine its methods. How will we answer the questions of the twenty-first century with the tools of a colonial past? We now turn to a consideration of anthropology and culture in the next millennium.

12

Anthropology in a Transnational World

~ Anthropology as a discipline was born into a colonial world in which the colonizing nations sought to learn more about the peoples they had subjugated. Anthropologists studied "over there," with an eye to understanding primarily the differences between themselves and the other. To do so, they employed a number of constructs—such as traditional/introduced, indigenous/Western, pre-contact/post-contact—that persist as important distinctions in the field today. These analytical constructs have been useful in understanding the impact of colonialism. Their continued usefulness, however, for understanding both the other and ourselves, is worth questioning.

We now live in a world in which there are no "uncontacted" people. Colonial contact is, for most cultures, beyond the time that generations now living can remember, even centuries in the past. The institutions, lifestyles, and ideas that now appear "traditional" bear only a limited resemblance to their pre-contact forebears. Traditions are, instead, a particular amalgam of indigenous and outside forces that has been forged over a number of generations. And recently, migration, from both villages to towns and from homelands to overseas, has uprooted a substantial percentage of the world's population from their natal homes. The once-colonized live among the colonizers, and even where this is not so, it is the people of former colonies who work in the factories or buy the cigarettes produced by the companies that fuel the economic and political engines of the industrial nations. In such a world, many of the assumptions on which anthropology was based are called into question.

Are you Tongan or American? Is that traditional or Western? Is it indigenous or introduced? In chapter 2 we saw the difficulties of trying to distinguish these bipolar concepts in a Tongan village in the 1980s. As the twenty-first century begins, the processes and issues that most affect our lives no longer separate out into these categorical units, and sorting them this way obscures our ability to understand the central issues of the day. It is clear that a number of the terms, labels, and analytical constructs that anthropologists use are not up to the task of studying the world today. Yet they are deeply embedded in the thinking of social science.

Timeless Anthropology in a Changing World

Many issues are capable of pointing out the dilemmas faced by anthropologists in attempting to analyze the contemporary world. I want to raise two that confronted me in the course of researching and writing this ethnography. In both cases, one can see how the increasingly global nature of our postcolonial world has come to challenge the validity of long-held assumptions.

The first is an analytical problem: What will happen to remittance economies when, as many believe, remittances stop? The answer for many social scientists hinges on the extent to which remittances are currently being used for investment as opposed to domestic or consumption use. The logic is simply that domestic uses of money—buying food, building new houses, giving money to the church, or funding ceremonies—will not provide the business base for an independent economy. Only if remittances are invested as capital and provide the basis of a profit-making enterprise can they offer people the means to survive on their own once remittances cease.

Or so the logic goes. When I examined this logic in the Tongan case, its limitations became clearer. The thinking behind this research is really an extension of familiar dichotomies that separate "traditional" from "Western" or capitalism from kinship when these categories are in fact merged. The assumption is that a store is a capitalist enterprise that earns money, and buying merchandise for the store is an investment. So are outlays for a melon plantation that a family cultivates for export. By contrast, buying beer and distributing it to friends or paying for ceremonies is clearly a nonproductive expenditure. A yam plantation from which the family eats is a "subsistence" arena. Expenditures for ceremonies simply consume resources. The store and the export crops are thus considered productive investments that will expand Tonga's economic base. The other activities are not. But is everything what it seems?

The Tongan village economy, as we have seen, is not so simplistically constructed and divisible. Research that separates activities in this way and then answers its own questions by looking at formal, macro-level data will not reveal the data necessary to answer its questions.[1]

Researchers will not see, for instance, that the subsistence plot of a village farmer provided the mulberry trees to make the tapa cloth that the farmer's wife gave to her overseas brother, who in turn lent his vacant agricultural plot in Tonga to his sister and her husband to plant melons for export. Which of these inputs was the "productive investment"?

The research itself will not ask what it took to maintain the overseas relationships that resulted in the remittance money that paid for the seeds for the melon plantation. Nor will it ask about the personal or ceremonial investments necessary to secure the goodwill of the village community that kept the local store afloat. Attendance at village funerals, the portion of remittance money given to relatives in the village, the beer bought for village friends, the money given for ceremonies are all parts of the equation that will be missed.

So what will happen to Tongans if remittances fail them? The answer, I believe, cannot be determined until the old categories that ground our theory are rethought.

🜄 The second issue involves one of the central principles of the anthropological approach: cultural relativism. Cultural relativism is a hallmark of anthropological method; it appears in every introductory textbook and in every manual on fieldwork. The principle of cultural relativism is that the anthropologist should try to interpret the behavior and beliefs of others in terms of *their* structures, traditions, and experiences. Conversely, it means suspending one's own judgments of right or wrong, refraining from imposing one's own standards on another culture.

Like most anthropologists, I am a true believer in the importance of cultural relativism. Yet, when Malia moved to the United States and tried to hide my religious affiliation from other Tongan-Americans, I felt differently. Her view, I thought, was grounded in a nineteenth-century missionary legacy of anti-Semitism, and I was not prepared to let this belief widely held in Tonga go unchallenged—at least not once Tongans were living in the United States.

I thought a lot about my changing stance on cultural relativism. This was not the first time I had expressed it. In my work on Thai refugee camp policy, coauthored with a Hmong-American anthropologist, I criticized the idea of always supporting cultural traditions, showing how such across-the-board commitments to "traditional authority" often compromise the position of women and ethnic minorities.[2]

Yet, it was my experience with Tongan anti-Semitism that made me understand most clearly the assumptions and structure underlying my stance on cultural relativism in Tonga. It taught me that cultural relativism—the "I'm OK, you're OK" philosophy that always seemed to exude equality and tolerance—was actually infused with power. Cultural relativism works most smoothly when the beliefs and practices we are "not judging" have no chance of influencing our life. When the other person or belief became a potential force in my own world, my stance became less "relative," more judgmental, advocative, and political.

I had already read Faye Ginsburg's ethnography about an abortion debate in a U.S. community. An excellent ethnography, it offers a rich and sympathetic portrait of women in the right-to-life movement. After its publication, many of Ginsburg's academic colleagues criticized her work on political grounds. How could she contribute to the "wrong side" of the abortion debate? Ginsburg wrote later, "Relativism has its limits, I discovered, especially when the subject is a controversial group from one's own society."[3]

I began to notice how often the issue of "relativism" was being raised in anthropological circles after a century of going unquestioned. Cultural practices such as clitoridectomy—the removal of a woman's clitoris, usually as a ceremonial part of an adult rite of passage—have increasingly been condemned by the anthropological community. What became clear was that, as the world has become smaller and more integrated, there has been a more general shift in anthropology from cultural relativism to advocacy. The shift embraces an idea, once so foreign to anthropologists, that there *are* certain principles—such as women's rights and human rights—that we should promote universally.

While the politics of these positions fit my personal beliefs, the implications of advancing them in anthropology give me pause. Should anthropologists study only that which they already believe in? Should they treat with respect or understanding only those people and perspectives with which they agree politically? Is this movement toward advocacy part of the trend toward universal standards, discussed earlier, that will integrate a new global class system in a cultureless (or lessened) world?

The wholesale adoption of advocacy raises the concern that social science will lose an important function. If we are advocates only for the good and the right (as all people, of course, think they are), then we are thrown into the world of good guys and bad guys for which U.S. culture is so infamous, and which should be the goal of good social science to dispel.

In the end, I am not prepared to overthrow cultural relativism. Rather, I return to it on a new footing which is tempered by an understanding of its capacity for patronization in a world where the "other" has no power, and of its price in a world where the "other" does. Navigating between advocacy and relativism is a difficult task, a Scylla and Charybdis of modern anthropology. The narrow strait between the alternatives is a path I choose for myself, one that, for lack of a better word, I will call compassion.

The Future of Anthropology

Is there a place for anthropology in the twenty-first century? If so, what should a science of culture be like in a global world, where almost all important social processes transcend national and cultural borders? What should anthropologists study, and how should their study proceed?

Some anthropologists would call these questions theoretical. Debates rage as to what theory or paradigms should guide anthropologists in the next century. In listening to these debates, I am continually surprised at how readily theory in anthropology is separated from and superimposed on its "practice," by which I mean the way anthropologists learn about and write about culture. Often, the things that allow anthropologists to arrive at their most meaningful insights about the contradictions and directions of the field involve its practice.

Let me illustrate from this ethnography. In writing this account of Tongan migration, I made a number of decisions that might be called theoretical. The review and editing of the manuscript by "informants," a chapter in which the ethnographer writes reflexively about herself; the inclusion of multiple voices addressing the same issues; the extensive use of people's own words to describe their lives: these are all approaches that some might say indicate a "postmodernist" theoretical orientation. But I am not a postmodernist, and the approach taken in this ethnography did not derive only—or even mainly—from a theoretical commitment.

Consider, for instance, the idea of collaborating with informants to produce parts of the ethnographic text. Probably the most important reason for my collaborative approach to certain chapters was that I had a fifteen-year relationship with my informants which I hoped would continue for the rest of my life. I did not want to embarrass them, to make them angry with me, or to create a situation in which they would be quoted without their knowledge on a touchy or contentious subject.

It was a change in writing form that emerged not only from discussions with colleagues about ethnographic authority but also from working out long-term social relationships with the people we anthropologists have called informants, in a world that has changed to make my informants my neighbors. There is a dialogue between practice and theory in anthropological fieldwork that allows the personal and the practical to become theoretical.[4]

There are many issues that fall in this personal/theoretical domain. The audience for whom I wrote this book is one of them. My writing up to this point had been directed toward my academic colleagues. But the more involved I became with the political issues of migration and the personal lives of villagers and migrants, the more I wanted to make this book interesting to nonacademics. I began to direct my writing to an educated public—both an American public who might be interested in understanding more about U.S. migrants and a Tongan public interested in a piece of their own history. Without any simplification, the tone, the writing style—that is, the formality, the amount of jargon—and the content all changed from the original to later versions.

Some issues are as yet unresolved for me, issues such as anonymity. When I asked Emma and Greg what they wanted to be called in this book, they answered by giving me their own names. The same thing happened when I approached Finau and Samiu. Alyssa and Sara similarly questioned why I could not use the name of their grandfather, to whom Alyssa's dance was dedicated. When I listed the potential problems (there's a lot of personal information that you might not want everyone to know; someone now or in the future might get angry about something you said), they replied that they knew what was in the book, and they still wanted their names to appear.

"We *want* people to know that we are in this book," Emma told me. "We're proud. How can people know it is us if you change our names?"

I thought, why should I be the only person in the book to use his or her real name? I decided to use the actual name of anyone who wanted me to.

Then, in the time after we talked but before the book was published, I thought and read more about my responsibilities.[5] There are deep issues of both ethics and accurate projection involved. What happens if the children of people who want their name used come to be affected later by their parents' decision? What if one person who does not use her name is exposed because someone else did? What happens if we all fail to anticipate an eventuality that will come back to haunt the speakers in the book? Once names are named, anonymity can never be recovered. I felt that I could not see the possible eventualities clearly enough, so I have retreated to convention and changed the names over everyone's protests. Yet, my personal experience leaves me questioning whether this hallmark of anthropological writing—anonymity—is appropriate.

In changing the name of the central village in this book to the pseudonym 'Olunga, I again bowed to anthropological convention. My pseudonyms, though, protect or mask very little. In our post-colonial world, available maps and censuses pinpoint the precise demography of villages and local oral histories, now published, allow even a tourist to match an ethnographic description of a village to its true name. The places anthropologists write about are readily identifiable to anyone in a position to affect them. I have engaged here, then, in offering an anthropological gesture that, in the end, is largely ceremonial—part of "the culture of anthropology" that, perhaps, bears re-examination.

In the end, I attribute many of my theoretical commitments and journeys to the process of doing anthropology in a changing world. When I think about anthropology in the next century, it is the process of anthropology—rather than simply its theory or appropriate topics of concentration—that comes to mind as a central part of its future.

Anthropological practice is grounded in certain distinctive properties. One of its crowning features (I'd even call it a saving grace) is that it is based on the "participant-observation" of culture over a long period of time, a process that involves long-term relationships with other people and extended immersion in other cultures. This means that many of anthropology's insights are based on relationships whose depth and honesty matter to understanding. It is a science that must attend carefully to its own capacity for intimacy, mutuality, and compassion—qualities for which the scientific community often does not especially select or prepare.

The world that anthropologists study is both the context and the subject of study. This is true for all social scientists, but it is particularly poignant for anthropologists because our research is not so easily separated from our lives during fieldwork. The relationships we have or do not have, the problems that occur in our lives, the reactions (bad and good) that we experience or provoke are often the result of the processes we are studying. If what you are studying is important in the culture, you will usually find it embedded in your relationships. You must look inside as well as outside, then, to understand the phenomenon you are studying. You must become "reflexive."

There is another important aspect of anthropology's legacy. It is heavily inductive. It is, in other words, "ground-up," moving more easily from the particular to the general and from the individual case to the universal than in the other direction. An inductive mindset was a good quality to have in a world where anthropologists studied "strange and different" cultural phenomena. It is a good quality to cultivate again in a world that is changing rapidly. The shifting nature and context of contemporary cultures make "experimentalism" in the ways that anthropological data are represented and analyzed timely.[6] We need more and different ways of seeing in order to piece together the nature of our evolving world.

It is my personal belief that anthropology is a science whose purpose is to represent richly and clearly the truths of the human condition. Anthropology must be a special kind of science, however, grounded in a practice that is compassionate, intimate, reflexive, "ground-up," and experimental. I believe that it is from such a cultivated practice that the most important contributions of anthropology will be made.

Journey's End?

Things change as I write. You already know that Eseta was laid off (really cast off) from her government job.[7] She now works the 10 P.M. to 6 A.M. shift at the airport packing airplane food for a minimal salary. Manu, forced to retire from his janitorial job, took part-time work as a night watchman. These have been hard times for the family. Eseta's elder daughter, Sara, though, has earned her college degree, and taken a job in a small family-run company. At age twenty-six, she lives at home to help the family and her sister Alyssa manage college expenses. Alyssa works part-time while she finishes college.

In 1996 Lio Jr. became one of the children who was sent back to Tonga. He lives now with his aunts and attends school in 'Olunga.

A young migrant woman from 'Olunga joined Eseta and Manu's household for a while. You met this woman briefly in Tonga in chapter 7, when she was leaving for a "holiday." Along with her sisters and her mother, she had been one of the women who slept in the house with Malia's daughter

Vei in Tonga and kept her company. Her story makes clearer how the transnational system of aid among Tongans has come to work. When she visited the United States, she stayed with Malia, who found her a job. Before it was time for her to return to Tonga, she eloped with a Tongan boy in the States whose family came from the same village. She is pregnant now and does not want to go home.

As for me, I am in Arizona, while most of the family lives in California. We call often, and visit when we can. By the time you read this, Emma and Greg will already have had their first child, and my next visit will be to see the new baby. My relationships have become progressively confusing. What's the news from Tonga? I ask. The answers I receive follow dual pathways in my consciousness, sometimes ending up with the everyday news of family and friends, sometimes feeding into some grander analytical scheme about migrants. I am often uncomfortable about the motivation from which my questions arise. Doing research has become an embarrassment of sorts.

Back in Tonga, Samiu has lost his bid for election to parliament. He came in second again in a large field, but he will try again. He is a scholar, and he writes asking me for books. In 1996 Samiu and Finau had their third child, a girl. Malia called me with excitement in her voice to let me know that they had named her Cathy Jr.

Latu's eldest daughter, Aleta, is ready for kindergarten. Latu wrote me that when Aleta saw her pencils and her school uniform and a notebook laid out for school, she jumped up and down and clapped her hands. She told me proudly that Aleta had won the children's competition at the church which tested preschool children on Bible passages. "She is smart," wrote Latu. "Thank God."

Vei, who lives alone now in the 'Olunga house, applied for a permanent visa to migrate to the United States. Right now she waits for word. I feel an uneasiness I do not share with the family about how the current mood of the country will affect immigration laws. I write letters to the American embassy to get Vei's visa through before the changes happen.

The details in these last paragraphs will have changed by the time you read this book, but the relationships will remain and the stories will continue.

⚬ In our global world, we are all participants in relationships we may not even know exist, in histories we neglected to study. Once you realize that, there is a new sense of connection, and also of debt, of destiny, of "karma"—

a word I use rarely. There is an incident I want to relate to explain this better. It is a small thing that happened in January 1995, when Malia and I were back in the village.

"I'm going to write that book soon," I was telling Malia when we were both in the kitchen of the house. "I'm not sure how many people will buy the book, but half of all the money from the book sales will go to the family. It's going to be about changes in Tonga and the migration of the family and . . ." A grandchild—I think it was Aleta—interrupted us, crying. When Malia looked back at me again, she said dryly, "You told me this before. You already talked to me about the book a long time ago."

"But now I have time to write it," I told her, a little ashamed of my slow pace. "I have a sabbatical," I say, struggling with the translation, "a year without working to write it."

"Good," she says, and nothing else.

There is a voice from another room, my sister Vei laughing as she yells, "I'll be glad to have that money!"

I've had pictures in my mind since that scene. I've thought of the finished book and the first check the family will receive, with my letter of thanks for all the years of answering questions that allowed me to get my degree and advance in my career. I think of the year 1906. A teenage girl is placed alone on a boat to Finland to escape the Russian pogroms. A young Austrian man leaves his country. He lives for weeks off bananas that fall from the South American boats that dock where his boat arrived; he will never eat a banana again. They both end up in the United States. I am their granddaughter.

It is ninety years later. I think of you buying this book, and the money from book sales going to Tonga. I know how the money would be used right now by the family, and I picture it. It would contribute to Vei's plane fare to the United States and to Aleta's expenses for school.

So I think of Vei in the United States and of you reading this book in the same thought. For you, reading this book might be part of a course, which is part of a general studies requirement, which is part of a college degree. I imagine you as an American with a college education, who might hire people or make government policy, or whose job it will be to make a corporation more profitable. One day, in these roles, you may meet Vei, a new immigrant in your country.

I think of the Tongans and Tongan-Americans who might read this book too—perhaps the children and grandchildren of the women I think of as sisters. If I have said, or not said, something that should have been different, I hope that they will forgive me. I hope that the grandchildren of these grandchildren will better understand why their ancestors did what they did—better than I understand my forebears, whose pictures still hang on my mother's wall but whose histories have been lost.

Our voyages together are not over. You and Tongans and me. Maybe you will hear the story of our voyage continue, with someone else from these pages telling the next chapter. In my mind's eye it is one of Finau's children, or perhaps little Aleta, who clapped her hands to be in kindergarten, who will write the story of what happens next.

A P P E N D I X

Tongan Population
and Migration
Estimates

~~~   Tongan population and migration figures presented in this text are estimates or projections, except where census population figures are used. The Tongan census, which tracks island population, is conducted at ten-year intervals, and population in other years must be estimated. The 1996 government census was being conducted while this book was being written, and was not yet available for review.

Reliable annual estimates of migration are also unavailable. The Tongan government has not kept formal records of migration and return migration in the past, so there are no official counts of the number of migrants living overseas. Estimates are often derived from indirect data or host country sources, which include only a fraction of the large number of Tongans overseas illegally, including those "overstaying" their visas.

In order to provide a consistent basis for determining population and migration in any given year, I constructed a dynamic model of migration, using an icon-based simulation program, Stella II. The model simulates migration by removing islanders each year to an overseas repository (Migrants). It attempts to model target population figures in Tonga accurately for years when the population of Tonga is known.

For instance, according to the Tongan censuses, between 1966 and 1976 the population of Tonga increased by 12,656, from 77,429 to 90,085, about 1.6 percent per year. Given its high birthrate and moderate death rates,[1]

---

1. Thirty-three births per thousand women and a death rate of 6.8 per thousand population.

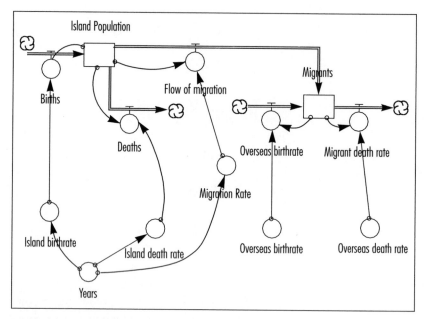

Icon-based representation of the population and migration model

however, the population of Tonga should have grown much more than this. By 1976 there should have been about 100,000 people in Tonga, a figure that the government, in fact predicted during the 1970s.

The difference between what the population "should have been" and what it was—about 10,000 people in 1966–76—is accounted for by migration. The model attempts to approximate this outflow by "migrating people out" each year at a graduated rate necessary to arrive at a population figure close to the 1976 census count. The model is capable of distributing this emigration from Tonga by years, rather than at ten-year intervals, thus approximating the yearly flow of emigrants.

The migrants removed from Tonga are placed in an overseas pool, where the total number of migrants, as well as the children born overseas, can be tracked separately. Demographics for the overseas group, including birth and death rates, can be manipulated apart from the island population.[2]

2. I used the birthrates of Tongan islanders to calculate birthrates of Tongans overseas to 1990, and then used a birthrate of 27/1,000 (the birthrate of Tongan-Americans in 1990) to calculate overseas birthrates, 1990–2000. (Although one would expect lower birthrates in industrial nations, this is offset by the fact that the population of migrants represents a greater proportion of people in childbearing age groups.) Birthrates after 2000 were calculated at a 2.5/1,000 level. A lowered death rate of 5.3/1,000 was used for the overseas population.

Using the model, population and migration can also be projected beyond current estimates further into the future. The model assumes a steadily declining birthrate (from 33/1,000 live births in 1966 to 25/1,000 by 1996), an island death rate of 6.8 persons per thousand, and an overseas death rate of 5.3 persons per thousand. The rate of migration is assumed to increase gradually between 1966 and 1990, and reach its peak by 1990. Future migration is assumed to level off at a moderate (late 1970s) level (1.8 percent).

A simplified visualization of the model is presented in the preceding figure.

This model tracks Tongan island and overseas population for a fifty-year period from 1966 to 2016. The projections of the model are presented in the table on the following page at two-year intervals from 1966 to 2016. Where cells are in bold and footnoted, the projections in the cells are compared with other estimates in the literature, or with census figures in years when these are available. Despite the specifics of the numbers, they are just rough estimates based on an assumption of continued moderate rates of migration. Changes in migration laws, shifts in the economies of Australia, New Zealand, and the United States, or improving opportunities in Tonga might all change these migration levels.

The following table presents projections of three population categories: (1) Tongan island population, (2) Tongan-born emigrants, and (3) second-generation Tongans (those born to Tongans overseas). Columns 4, 5 and 6 provide useful totals that combine one or more of these population categories. Column 4 (total overseas) figures the number of all those people of Tongan descent who currently live overseas, combining emigrants with second-generation Tongans. Column 5 (Tongan-born) figures the number of people who were born in the Tongan islands, combining the island population with the emigrant population. Column 6 (world population) combines the island population with emigrants and children of emigrants born overseas to determine the total number of people of Tongan descent in the world. These estimates provide a basis for statements made in the text.

Modeled population and emigration figures

Year	(1) Island population	(2) Tongan emigrants	(3) Second generation overseas	(4) Total overseas	(5) All Tongan-born	(6) Tongan world population
1966	77,429[a]	2000	0	2,000	79,429	79,429
1968	80,115	3380	156	3,537	83,495	83,652
1970	82,895	4793	417	5,210	87,688	88,105
1972	85,182	6818	800	7,618	92,000	92,800
1974	87,532	8874	1345	10,219	96,406	97,751
1976	89,946[b]	10,962	2065	13,027	100,909	102,974
1978	91,156	14,152	2963	17,116	105,309	108,272
1980	92,381	17,344	4127	21,471	109,725	113,853
1982	93,065	20,999	5550	26,549	114,064	119,615
1984	93,196	25,078	7285	32,363	118,274	125,559
1986	93,326[c]	29,100	9385	38,486	122,427	131,813
1988	93,177	33,153	11,790	44,944	126,331	138,122
1990	93,028[d]	37,130	14,587	51,718	130,158	144,746
1992	92,786	40,841	17,630	58,471	133,627	151,258
1994	92,452	44,282	29,877	65,160	136,735	157,614
1996	92,120	47,638	24,489	72,127	139,758	164,247
1998	91,789	50,537	28,476	79,013	142,326	170,802
2000	91,458	53,348	32,838	86,187	144,807	177,646
2002	91,312	55,889	37,236	93,125	17,201	184,437
2004	91,349	58,171	41,979	100,150	149,520	191,499
2006	91,385	60,379	47,077	107,456	151,764	198,842
2008	91,422	62,510	52,544	115,054	153,932	206,622
2010	91,458	64,561	58,394	122,956	156,020	214,415
2012	91,495	66,529	64,644	131,174	158,024	222,918
2014	91,531	68,410	71,308	139,719	159,942	231,251
2016	91,568	70,202	78,404	148,606	161,770	240,175

[a] This is the census count for 1966.

[b] The 1976 census counted 90,085. The model's projection of 89,946 comes extremely close.

[c] The original official census figure for 1986 population was 94,535, but it was later corrected downward to 93,049 (U.S. Bureau of the Census, International Database, Table 004).

[d] In modeling 1990 population figures, I used estimates available at the time of this writing. Unfortunately, the two estimates I worked with varied widely. According to an account by Campbell, who reported official estimates (1992: 223), the population was projected to fall 4,000 between 1986 and 1989, a population loss of about 4.2 percent. According to Ahlburg (1991), whose work has concentrated on estmating population and migration, the 1990 population of Tonga was about 96,000. I attempted to model a figure in between these estimates.

N O T E S

Part I. DEPARTURES

1. Stalker 1994: 169–70.

2. Although most migrants make more in wages than in their home countries, migrants are concentrated in lower-earning, lower-prestige jobs (Isbister 1996: 83). Many even report downward social mobility after leaving their native homes (Jones 1995: chap. 5; Gmelch 1992: 267).

3. Schlesinger 1995.

4. Reported in Stalker 1994: 82.

5. Except for a recent government scheme in which Tongan passports were sold to Taiwanese for $10,000 each.

6. Clifford (1988), *The Predicament of Culture*; Clifford and Marcus (1986). *Writing Culture*; Clough (1992), *The End(s) of Ethnography*; Brettell (1993), *When They Read What We Write*; Geertz (1988), *Works and Lives*; Van Maanen (1988), *Tales of the Field*; and Rosaldo (1989), *Culture and Truth*, to name just a few. I have been particularly influenced by the work of George Marcus, who, in addition to being a theorist of note, did some excellent ethnographic work in Tonga.

7. Some of the questions being asked include the following: Can we meaningfully talk about discrete, bounded cultures whose customs and traditions endure over time? Can culture be represented solely through the eyes of its expert "key informants" or its anthropologists? If not, whose voice(s) should be heard in ethnography? If customary ways are rapidly changing, then should we look at culture as a process rather than a repository of knowledge, institutions, and customs? In a global world, should anthropologists embrace "cultural relativity" when there are important human and political stances involved in remaining "relative"? Many such questions are being reexamined as the sensibilities of people change and our assumptions come in conflict with the shifting global scene.

8. Postmodernism critiques "ethnographic realism," a genre of ethnography marked by "the swallowing up and disappearance of an author in the text, the suppression of individual cultural member's perspective in favor of a typified or common denominator 'native point of view,' the placement of a culture within a rather timeless ethnographic present, and a claim (often implicit) for descriptive or interpretive validity based almost exclusively on the author's own 'being there' experience (field-

work)" (Van Maanan 1995: 7). Postmodern ethnographers, by contrast, write "messy" texts in which one need not see linear arguments or time sequences. People may contradict one another or interrupt one another in the text, and no one voice holds the premium on the truth. What is real or "true" is socially constructed and culture, like knowledge, is a product of social discourse. As a result, an ethnography will try to represent the range and sources of those different constructions, including the background of the anthropologist which has influenced how he or she constructs the text (reflexivity) and the different voices within a culture that express what is true (multivocality).

9. Marcus (1986) has argued directly that new ethnographic forms—such as postmodernism—are really attempts to grapple with the realities of the postcolonial world, to engage the complexity of twentieth-century relationships. I agree.

Chapter 1. Portrait of a Migrating Village

1. The history of the village is based primarily on information from two secondary histories of Tonga: Campbell 1992 and Wood 1932. The broad outline of Tongan prehistory is from Kirch 1984 and Bellwood 1987.

2. Proto-Polynesians probably traveled from the Admiralty Islands (off New Guinea) to the New Hebrides (Vanuatu) to New Caledonia to Fiji to Tonga.

3. Between about 200 B.C. and A.D. 1000 (Kirch 1984: 71), Western Polynesians began settling the rest of the Polynesian triangle, including the Marquesas, Tahiti, and Hawai'i.

4. By the time of the 1976 census, 64 percent of Tonga's total population resided on the main island. In 1939, 46 percent of the population lived on the main island.

5. Tonga, Census 1976.

6. The brother-sister relationship is a central part of Tongan social organization. Avoidance is one way of dealing with the fact that sisters in Tonga are considered spiritually higher than their brothers, while brothers are usually the heirs to family land and political titles. Much has been written on Tongan gender relations. For a good introduction, see James 1983.

7. On the basis of an earlier economic survey of the village, I had stratified village production into "types" (wage earner, cash-cropping farmer, and so on). I then chose households that were representative of these types and their concentration within the village, and approached households chosen to participate in the study. See chapter 2 for more detail on this process.

8. My earlier survey (1982) of wooden dwelling houses ($N = 161$) in the village revealed that almost 40 percent were older homes in visible need of repair.

9. In 1976, only 41 percent of eligible villagers held land in 'Olunga, compared to 35 percent of the eligible population in Tonga as a whole.

Chapter 2: Why Migrate?

1. In the ten years between 1956 and 1966, the village grew an astounding 37 percent. In the following ten years (1966–76), the village grew less than 3 percent.

2. There were 1,796 Tongans in my 1981 census. Correcting for foreign-born residents, including religious and teaching personnel, there had been 1,993 Tongans in the village in 1976 (Tonga, Census 1976, Table 2, p. 30). This represented a loss of more than 10 percent of the population in the five years since the last census!

3. The considerable movement of population *within* the village was eliminated from the statistics.

4. While ten people had moved out of 'Olunga to other Tongan villages, nine people had moved into the village.

5. Of the thirteen cases of overseas migration that occurred during the test year, six involved loss of a head of household; two involved loss of a grown unmarried child; four involved a parent and/or child(ren) joining the absent parent overseas; and one involved a complete family migration.

6. I tried to estimate what proportions of villagers' *closest* kin were being lost to overseas migration by determining the presence or absence of true siblings, the basis of the kin group, and their descendants. In 1983 I selected a small nonrandom sample of twenty-four adults ranging from twenty-one to eighty-two. They were asked to name all living siblings and siblings' descendants and their places of residence. Twenty-three percent of villagers' actual sibling network (including siblings' children and grandchildren, when applicable) were overseas, a figure that I used as a rough estimate of the proportion of close kin overseas.

7. For instance, there are textual references to tapa cloth being made of three layers rather than two. Older women reported to me that their grandmothers baked the finished cloth in an underground oven (which no longer is done). It is also reported that cloths were much wider in the past. A good history of the technical changes in tapa cloth is provided by Maxine Tamahori (1963).

8. Campbell 1992: 102–3.

9. George Marcus originally coined this term and has used it analytically to discuss the nature of change in Tongan institutions and culture (Marcus 1980; 1978; 1989: 197).

10. The diary project was very demanding and time-consuming. Each household was given watches and pads and pencils and was asked to write down their activities every hour. They were also asked to record any exchanges of food, money, or materials that occurred during the day and all income and expenditures on a daily basis. One family dropped out of the project before it was completed, and only six of ten households completed all the tasks every day. Still, I was pleased with the outcome. Almost all the participants completed most required entries on most days.

11. I defined "work" as agricultural, domestic, or other productive labor per-

formed for the benefit of one's household, as well as the travel done in connection with that labor.

12. Campbell 1992: 149.

13. This generational difference, which I noted from accounts of the era, is also noted by Campbell 1992: 159.

14. Tonga, Statistical Abstract 1983: 128–30.

Part II. ARRIVALS

1. In 1955, 345 migrants left Tonga, mostly for work or school in New Zealand (Campbell 1992: 186).

2. For a fuller picture of Mormonism in Tongan life and its role in migration, see Gordon 1988.

3. Campbell 1992: 197.

4. Limits did, however, remain in the form of quotas for the Eastern and Western hemispheres.

5. Reimers 1992: 64, 80, 92.

6. Mine is a conservative estimate, based on 1990 Census figures for the United States projected forward five years. This projection assumes that Tongan emigration rates remained moderately high (2.2 percent annually), that 45 percent of all Tongan emigrants migrated to the United States, and that Tongan birthrates of 27 per 1,000 and death rates of 0.68 per 1,000 obtained.

7. Only thirty-five Tongans were admitted to the United States as permanent residents before 1960. Approximately another two hundred became residents between 1960 and 1965 (Ahlburg 1991: 12). According to 1990 U.S. Census data, the number of Tongans in California who had migrated before 1965 was 269 (U.S. Government 1990c, Table PB01).

8. Forty-six percent of all Tongans in the United States resided in California. Computation made by author, based on U.S. Government 1990c, Tables PB01 (for California) and PB04 (for the United States).

9. U.S. Government 1990b, File 1C. Detailed Race for San Mateo County, California.

Chapter 3. Coming to America

1. I realize that the name "America" does not rightly apply to the United States, for it is a term that includes the North and South "Americas." I use the name throughout the book for two reasons: first, to convey its connotative meaning, and second, because Tongans use the Tonganized version of "America" (*Amelika*) to refer to this country.

2. About 10 percent of Tongan landholders were living overseas in 1984, according to an estimate by economist Feleti Sevele (Campbell 1992: 216).

3. Author's computation, based on U.S. Government 1990c, Table HB03 (for the United States).

4. Author's calculations, based on U.S. Government 1990a, Table 5, p. 171.

5. Author's calculations, based on U.S. Government 1990a, Table 5, p. 170, and Table 49, p. 49.

6. U.S. Government 1990b. Persons per family (for San Mateo City, Calif.).

7. U.S. Government 1990c, Table PB07 (for California).

8. According to Census figures, 67.4 percent fit these categories. U.S. Government 1990a, CP-2-1, Table 170, p. 336.

9. Author's calculations, based on U.S. Government 1990a, Table 4, p. 135.

10. Author's calculations, based on statistics for resident Tongans over twenty-five, U.S. Government 1990a, Table 3, p. 100.

11. U.S. Government 1990e.

12. These international exchange networks are not simply a product of migration. They are the newest versions of women's exchanges that have existed throughout this century, in which Tongan women exchange traditional wealth for wealth items from Samoa and Fiji. For more on this, see Small 1995.

13. Also typical is a severe racial bias toward Mexican-Americans and African-Americans. Many Tongan-born migrants believe that people inherit abilities and personal status in their "blood" (these beliefs explain, too, why the Tongan aristocracy are "higher" than commoners). American racism, including the selective and stereotypic presentations of these minorities in the media, feeds the conception, embraced by many Tongan migrants, that Mexicans and blacks in this country are a lower "rank" of people.

Chapter 4. One Family's Story

1. Making kava for a circle of men is a common courtship practice. Unmarried women make and serve the kava while a circle of unmarried men talk to, joke with, and sing to the kava maker, often providing presents of food.

2. This is a common occurrence: 24 percent of Tongans who migrate to Australia overstay their visas, the second-highest proportion of overstayers in the country (Stalker 1994: 186).

3. She did not use this specific term that Americans use to refer to a backwater. She named a small village where Latu's husband was raised. The tenor of Malia's comment, though, was that while the family would go to a "big place," her daughter was going to stay in the hinterlands.

Chapter 5. Palu, the One Who Left

1. She was embarrassed to supervise older people because age is respected, senior is considered "higher" than junior, and older people are expected to supervise younger people, not vice versa.

Chapter 6. An Anthropologist over Time

1. In the Tongan social system, one is "low" to the father's side of the family (lowest to the father's sister) and "high" to the mother's side (highest to the mother's brother). These status distinctions are expressed both in everyday life (one jokes with mother's brother's people but not with father's sister's) and in ceremonial events such as funerals. The "low" side of the family at a funeral are called *liongi*. The "high" side are *fahu*.

2. I might here be representing my own biased and limited conception of schizophrenia. He had delusions of God speaking to him and episodes of both violence and catatonia. He often spoke and wrote in verse. The first onset of real illness occurred in his early twenties.

3. Certain migrant groups are "making it" and others are not. There is some ethnic and racial basis for the distribution (see more on this in chapter 11, notes 12 and 13), and I find myself asking how much Malia's children's and grandchildren's brownness will matter to mobility in a country where racial prejudice runs so deep. What about Malia's halting English and thick accent in a national climate that is, at best, lukewarm toward immigrants? In the end, it is not clear to me how much my country will open its arms to the populations of countries that were once protectorates and colonies, or, in more abstract terms, how much of an unequal legacy colonialism has rendered.

4. It may occur to some readers that the appropriate thing for Malia or me to do would have been to tell him to get lost (or to put it in even stronger terms), but this is not appropriate behavior among villagers. Rudeness is simply bad form in Tonga, even in dealing with drunks.

Part III. RETURNS

1. Ahlburg and Levin 1990: 30.
2. JoAnn Cangemi, ed., *The World* (New York: Holt Rinehart and Winston, 1986), 367–71.
3. Ahlburg 1991: 1, 16. This 40 percent figure jibes with my own calculated percentage of Tongans overseas, but our numbers differ slightly. See Appendix Table for 1990. I estimated a Tongan-born overseas population of 37,130 and an island popu-

lation of 93,028. Ahlburg estimated 39,400 Tongans overseas and projected a Tongan island population of 98,500. If one includes children of migrants, then I estimate that the number of Tongans living overseas is equal to 55 percent of the island population!

4. Important changes were in progress throughout the twentieth century. Early in the century, customary behavior, both between commoners and nobles and within the hierarchies of commoner families, began to change. It "democratized," leading to a decreasing flow of resources and labor from those "below" to those "above." The education of Tongan commoners was another crucial twentieth-century development which greatly increased during the period 1947–65. During this time, numbers of students and government spending on education doubled (Campbell 1992: 205). Cash-earning ventures in agriculture have been growing throughout the century, encouraged by an increasingly enforced system of land reform that has allowed commoners permanent land tenure. In the 1970s, new land tenure laws were initiated, allowing land leasing and other arrangements that enabled more land to be consolidated for commercial growing.

5. The Tongan parliament works on a British model, in which there is an upper and a lower house, each with equal votes. In Tonga, the upper (Nobles') house, with nine representatives, is elected by the members of Tonga's thirty-three noble families. The lower (People's) house, also with nine representatives, represents the remainder of the Tongan population. Ministers and cabinet positions are appointed by the king.

6. Campbell 1992: 218.

7. Ibid., 219.

8. This includes *Kale'a,* an issues-oriented newsletter that regularly critiques government policy and practice, and two newspapers, *Matangi Tonga* and the *Times of Tonga.*

Chapter 7. Going Home

1. This is a special ceremonial dance of honor that unmarried women, traditionally high-born women, perform.

2. Part of the change in housing was due to Hurricane Isaac in 1982, which leveled some of the older homes. The replacement houses, part of a government aid program, were wooden.

3. Campbell (1992: 212) sets the date for this change in the mid-1960s. Tonga's 1975 Statistical Abstract (Table 59, p. 53) suggests that the last time exports exceeded imports was in 1960. It was not until the 1990s that new agricultural exports, notably squash, helped ease the trade balance. Hatcher (1994: 17) reports a 42 percent narrowing of the trade deficit in 1993, owing largely to squash revenues.

4. The highest price tags at the national level are for machinery and equipment, at the household level for imported foods.

5. Tonga, Statistical Abstract, 1975: 84–85, and Campbell 1992.

6. Ahlburg 1991: 18, Table 3.10.

7. Ibid., 25.

8. Faeamani (1995) studied four Tongan villages. In one village, where income from employment was high, remittances made up only 14.7 percent of total household income. In the other three villages, remittances as a percentage of total income were 30.4, 41.6, and 36.1 percent.

9. This section is an edited account of conversations that occurred between household members and visitors over a period of several days. For purposes of making a readable account without superfluous detail, I am not representing all conversations that occurred or the correct time frame of the conversations.

10. Brown and Connell 1993.

Chapter 8. Distant Family

1. See Appendix Table for 1980. Approximately 17,000 Tongan-born persons were overseas in 1980 and 92,000 on the island. Tongans overseas thus made up 15.8 percent of all Tongan-born persons in the world (109,000).

2. In 1990 the total estimated number of Tongan-born persons worldwide was about 130,000. Of this group 37,000 (or 28.5 percent) were overseas, approximately one in every three or four people born in Tonga.

3. I estimate that in 1994 there was an island population of almost 92,500 and an overseas population of 65,000. Of those overseas, almost 21,000 were born overseas. Forty-one percent of the world population of Tongans was overseas. See Appendix Table.

4. Lower and upper roads were not only geographic designations. They alluded as well to the lineages (ha‘a) from which chiefs of the area were descended, and to the genealogical relationship among lineages and their titles. "Roads" thus have both a kinship and a political dimension.

5. Topai is a type of boiled dumpling made from a mixture of grated coconut and flour. Lu is the cooked green leaves of the taro plant.

6. I asked Alyssa and Sara whether they thought they had more freedom in Tonga or in America. Sara thought that she had less freedom in Tonga because people watched her closely and reported back to her parents. Alyssa, by contrast, felt that she had greater leeway in Tonga. Her parents weren't as protective or worried about where she might go, and she felt that she could wander a little bit more in the village than at home.

7. I suspect this was because Vei's house was considerably less comfortable and more crowded than their own. Their paternal "aunties" set the itinerary.

8. I noted that the majority of overt comments and joking around dancing, for instance, were directed at overseas people who had been raised in the village rather than those who had been raised overseas. Although the crowd screamed with laughter when the New Zealand men could not get up and down easily in the sitting dance,

they knew that most of the men had grown up in the village. The target of comments such as "You, there, sit in the back" was usually a recent migrant, and she would not actually be the one to sit in the back. The people who genuinely did not know dances were people raised overseas. Nothing much was said to them.

Chapter 9. Finau, the One Who Stayed

1. Candlenut, a waxy, sweet-smelling seed that was formed into balls and used as a soap.

2. Finau and Samiu both benefited from Tonga's Fourth and Fifth Development Plans (1980–90), which enabled full training and certification of secondary teachers to take place within Tonga, at the Tonga Teachers' Training College.

Chapter 10. Tradition

1. For a fuller exposition of the "Tongan way," and its contemporary expressions, see Cowling 1990 and the recently released treatment of Tongan childhood and socialization by Morton (1996).

2. It is generally considered appropriate to replace the bottom layer with the manufactured cloth. Women say the cloth looks nice, it wears like mulberry bark, and it doesn't suffer from the damp as much.

3. The role of money in bark-cloth manufacture goes back further than the 1990s. What is new, however, is dependence on a foreign source for manufacturing material.

4. James 1991.

5. In Tongan custom the eldest is "highest," and this extends to his or her children. "Low" work, such as cooking, is assigned to the family's "low" side, yet it is the "high" side that gets to eat it.

Part IV. TRAVELS AHEAD

Chapter 11. The Meanings of Tongan Migration

1. I mention again that "America" is a misnomer. There are many countries in the Americas and many different nationalities who are Americans. I use the term to capture its colloquial use in the United States, in the knowledge that it is part of the mythology of which I speak in this section.

2. The poorest individuals are not generally the migrants (Stalker, 1994: 21; Portes and Rumbaut 1990: 12), and neither are the poorest countries the largest senders of migrants (Isbister 1996: 97). On the role of development in migration, see Stalker 1994: 26–28.

3. Adventure and "finding oneself" were identified as motives of Mexican mi-

grants (Jones 1995: 108). Barbadian migrants reported a desire to see the world (Gmelch 1992: 261). Perminow (1993), in a study of Kotu, a small island in the Tongan island group of Ha'apai, showed that young people sometimes left to avoid the demands of family, particularly those of "higher" father's side relatives, and of cross-sex avoidance relationships. I believe, however, that these seemingly different motivations share a theme, a derivative of the colonial past that makes industrial nations the source of prestige, power, money, an expanded horizon, or a more exciting world.

4. Stalker 1994: 33.

5. Gailey (1992) suggests that families prefer women to migrate because they are more likely to remit, and Perminow (1993) mentions that the family is likely to exert less resistance to the migration of children who have younger siblings.

6. Ahlburg and Levin (1990) present evidence for the opposite position—that there is a brain drain of Tonga's most skilled and best educated. Their study of migrants who were in the United States in 1980 found that the U.S.-Tongan population had a higher level of skill and education than the Tongan base population left behind. Their premise is that Tongan talent was drawn overseas to work opportunities that would allow them to use their skills and education. This assumption, however, does not jibe with more recent data, which suggest a substantial change over time.

The data that follow are my own comparisons derived from disaggregated data in U.S. Government 1990c, PB62. Of Tongan migrants who entered the United States before 1965, 100 percent of those who had a high school degree lived above the U.S. poverty level in 1990. Not a single Tongan with a high school diploma lived below the poverty level. Of those without a high school diploma, only 56 percent were above the poverty level. But among those who entered after 1965, education has played much less of a role in income and success. Fifty-three percent of those below the poverty level had a high school diploma. Education made only a small difference in poverty or success (28 percent of non-high school graduates and 18 percent of graduates were below the poverty level). Given this evidence, it is worth investigating whether, in the 1990s, a larger proportion of better-educated Tongans are still seeking employment overseas, where their education will now matter little.

7. Isbister 1996: 83–84.

8. Gmelch 1992: 267, 272, 264.

9. Portes and Rumbaut 1990: 2, Jones 1995.

10. With the downturn in the U.S. labor market, immigrants took a bigger hit in real dollar earnings than natives, losing 8 percent, compared to 4.7 percent for native-born workers (Isbister 1996: 85). In California, the gap between rich and poor widened even more than in the rest of the nation during the recession of the late 1980s, a fact attributed by one policy institute to the poverty of migrants (Marshall 1996: A13).

11. Among West Indians in the United States and Great Britain, Foner (1979) finds that the children of migrants are more likely than their parents to achieve white-collar positions. For most groups historically in the United States, earnings increase with length of stay (Chiswick 1978).

12. White foreign-born, black-foreign born, and Asian foreign-born new immigrants fared better between 1979 and 1989 than Latino immigrants (Sorensen and Enchautegui 1994). Chiswick (1978) found that the earnings of Mexican immigrants in 1970 did not increase over time, as did those of other groups.

13. Isbister (1996: 84–88). Borjas (1990) found that the wage gap between immigrants and natives (10 percent) disappeared after two decades among those who entered the United States between 1964 and 1968. Those who entered between 1975 and 1979 earned 21 percent less to begin with and after two decades would not be earning the same as native workers. (He uses these data to argue for a decline in the quality of the labor force.) The evidence, however, is not consistent. One more recent study (Sorensen and Enchautegui 1994) focusing on data from the 1980s showed that comparative earnings of recent immigrants have risen among certain ethnic groups.

14. Marshall 1996: A13.

15. Suro 1995: 8.

16. Only 7 percent of Tongans eligible for public assistance actually take it. Calculations by author from U.S. Government 1990a, Table 5, p. 170.

17. Campbell 1992: 212.

18. Stalker 1994: 122.

19. This statistic is based on the Global Economic Migration Table (Stalker 1994: app. 271–282) of sizable countries that are identified as either labor-sending or labor-receiving economies. It excludes small nations, under 200,000 people, such as Tonga. Of the thirty-eight nations cited, twenty-five exclusively send labor, while thirteen predominantly send labor but receive labor as well.

20. In remittance-based economies, remittances typically make up 25–50 percent of exports. Remittances in Tonga have made up as much as 65 percent of exports, and 40 percent of the gross domestic product (Brown and Connell 1993; Tonga, Statistical Abstract, 1983).

21. Stalker 1994: 32. A school principal from the New York–Dominican neighborhood reports, "We have students who go back and forth to the Dominican Republic every six months or every three months or when a parent loses a job or when somebody in the family gets sick" (Suro 1995: 8).

22. See, for instance, the work by Eisenstadt 1973; Fienup-Riordan 1988; and Portes and Rumbaut 1990: 136–39 on emergent identities, and Schiller et al. 1992: pts. 2 and 3.

23. There are sharp disagreements in the literature about the nature and implications of Tongan migration patterns and hence what policy should be (Connell 1983; Bertram 1986; Bertram and Watters 1985; James 1991; Connell and Brown 1995; Brown and Foster 1994, 1995; Marcus 1993; Miles 1992; Connell 1991; Ahlburg 1991). Most observers can see that Tongans have an increased level of consumption. The questions for researchers include, on the one hand, the "costs" of remittances (do remittances dampen production and motivation?) and their long-term consequences (is a remittance economy sustainable and desirable?). On the other hand, could remittances be fueling long-term growth and investment? In other words, is this a form

of dependence or of development? My position, based on ethnographic evidence in the village, is that it is both. See James (1993) for a good summary of these debates.

24. As elsewhere in the world, the largest single use of remittances is for housing (Stalker 1994: 126).

25. Similar evidence of mobility is reported among rural communities in Bangladesh (Gardner 1995), among migrants in the Zacatecas area of Mexico (Jones 1995: 72–73), among Thai villagers who have returned from work in Saudi Arabia (Singhanetra-Renard 1992), and among returned migrants in Barbados (Gmelch 1992: 306–7).

26. Income inequality was also reported by Hardaker et al. (1987) in his village-level study of Tonga, but the reverse was found by Ahlburg (1991: 41–42) in a 1984 Tonga household income and expenditure survey. The differences may be explained by the way researchers interpret economic "differentiation." For instance, Ahlburg looks at whether remittance income (when added to household income) brings those in the lowest income deciles closer to those in the highest deciles. My observations are longitudinal and nonstatistical. I state simply that a decade earlier there was not the same disparity in the lifestyles of the village's richest and poorest people. Many people have done better, and become middle class as a result of remittances, but those without substantial overseas income have seen their fortunes fall. Both of our statements may be true.

27. Fonua 1986: 29.

28. Ten percent of registered landholders in 1984 were overseas (Campbell 1992).

29. Ahlburg 1991, Faeamani 1995. Remittance patterns over time are based on surveys conducted between 1992 and 1994 in Brisbane, Australia, by Brown and Walker, reported in Brown and Foster (1995: 38).

30. Based on ethnographic work by Wendy Cowling (1990a) in Australia. See also Cowling 1990b.

31. U.S. Government 1990a, Table 1, p. 30.

32. This is a conservative estimate. See Appendix Table for estimates of Tongans (migrants and children) overseas, a figure projected to exceed the island population by 2013.

33. Second-generation migrants throughout the world remit dramatically lower amounts than first-generation migrants. This pattern is expected to hold among Tongan migrants as well (Brown and Foster 1995: 39).

34. Brown and Foster 1995. For more on Tongan remittance patterns, see Fuka 1985; Tongamoa 1990; James 1991; Brown and Walker 1994; Vete 1995; and Faeamani 1995.

35. The bid for an ongoing flow of resources from migrants to Tonga will likely be based on investment opportunities—the relative advantages in social and economic mobility that returning to Tonga, or returning wealth to Tonga, will provide. Brown and Connell's (1993) study of the Nuku'alofa flea market showed such a shift from remittances for family maintenance to business investment. One sees similar tensions between nationalism or cultural loyalty and capitalism in India (Lessinger 1992).

36. Perminow 1993: 118.

37. While some second-generation migrants develop dual or multiple identities, others report more of a confusion in identity. Wiltshire (1992) reports this confusion of identity among second-generation Caribbean migrants. Many Mexican-American youth perceive themselves as neither Mexican nor American or the dual Mexican-American but "Chicano," a new identity.

38. The exporting of a greater "ethnic consciousness" by migrants to their home countries was reported by Sutton and Makiesky (1975) in Barbados.

39. The list of changes is exhaustively long. See Tupouniua (1977) and Small (1987) for a fuller account of village-level changes in daily life. See Kaeppler (1978) for more on ceremonial changes.

40. That is, there have been increased economic differences between top and bottom echelons, a shrinking kinship base of cooperation and decision making, as noted in this ethnography and others (see, e.g., Morton 1987), and growing challenges to traditional authority.

41. Recent evidence about migrants' mobility shows a bifurcation of migrant *groups,* with some nationalities entering and staying at different ends of the economic ladder. See Isbister 1996; Portes and Rumbaut 1990.

42. Only 45 percent of second-generation Tongan-Americans over five years of age spoke Tongan in their home in 1990 (U.S. Government 1990a, Table 3, p. 100).

43. Selling to the third world, particularly China, is big business, largely through overseas affiliates. Investment in such overseas affiliates tripled between 1990 and 1995, while annual sales of foreign-owned U.S. companies are double the value of exported goods and services from U.S. soil (Zachary 1996: 1, A6). Four out of every five television sets are now sold overseas. To offset the loss of smokers in the United States, tobacco companies have increased smoking in Asia by 33 percent since the mid-1980s (*60 Minutes,* August 18, 1996). The selling of toothpaste and shampoo in rural India (Jordan 1996), the growth of shopping malls in Tangerang, Indonesia (Mydans 1996), and the recent proliferation of credit cards in rural India (Sharma 1996) are but a few of the economic changes now occurring on the global scene.

44. Only one-quarter of all marriages in the United States now occur between people of the same ethnic background (Schlesinger 1995), a statistic that would no doubt stun our great-grandparents. They might also find surprising 1990 U.S. Census data on ethnic identity, showing that 40 percent of the entire U.S. population identified itself as being in more than one ethnic category or in none at all. More than 55 percent of Californians self-identified this way, perhaps a harbinger of things to come (U.S. Government 1990b, Table 142, p. 166).

45. There is already a "metropolitan culture" developing among the well-to-do both within the U.S. and internationally. The elite of many countries now speak English, they vacation at the same places, shop in the same stores, enjoy the same international cuisine and art. One or two generations ago, upper middle class Japanese and American women would not have been carrying the same Italian handbags.

Racism slows class identification among minorities in the United States, but, even so, important class-based changes are afoot. Good discussions of the articulation between class and race in the U.S. appear in Steinberg 1989; Zweigenhaft and Domhoff 1991; and Menchaca 1995.

46. Persons of color in the United States—including blacks, Native Americans, and other nonwhites—have three to four times the poverty rates of white Americans. In the United States in 1989, at least one-third of all nonwhite and non-Asian households had an income under $15,000. (Among whites and Asians, the proportion of households at this income level was one in five.) The institutional means available to equalize these statistics across racial lines—such as public education—often fail, reproducing the same inequities over generations (Kozol 1991). See U.S. Government 1990a, Tables 48, 49, 94–98.

Among migrants, fortunes seem to be diverging along lines of ethnicity, national origin, and gender (Portes and Rumbaut 1990: chap. 3; Isbister 1996: 83–88). Racism and sexism, however, do not fully account for the data. Success by race varies widely between native and foreign-born blacks, who fare much better, just as gender differentials vary significantly by race and ethnicity (U.S. Government 1990a, Table 48, p. 48). For more on the complexity of the picture see Steinberg 1989 and Portes and Rumbaut's (1990: 85–93) discussion of contexts of reception.

47. "Acculturation" in the United States, as Menchaca (1995) points out, is power laden and thus requires minority populations to become more like dominant populations. The English-only movement is a good example of this "melting pot" process, which insists that minorities adopt the ways of the majority. It is within this social framework that I interpret the language of younger Tongan-Americans, who refer to Tongan nobles in this country as being "whitewashed." There is an association here between being more "American," being less Tongan, and being more "white" which captures some of the minority experience in the United States.

Chapter 12. Anthropology in a Transnational World

1. See Brown and Connell (1993), Brown and Foster (1995), and Brown (1995) for critiques of the formal means of remittance measurement, in which goods in kind and money that enters through informal channels are lost. James (1993) points out the difficulties of macro-analysis in understanding the Tongan remittance system and development.

2. Cha and Small 1994.

3. Ginsburg 1993: 172.

4. The anthropological term for this relationship is *praxis*.

5. In particular, Brettell (1993), *When They Read What We Write,* and Hopkins (1993) "Is Anonymity Possible?" raised many important questions.

6. I attribute this notion of "experimentalism" in my thinking to the work of Marcus and Cushman (1982; 1986).

7. Former labor secretary Robert Reich has suggested using the word "cast off" rather than "laid off," which incorrectly suggests that the worker will be rehired (*Wall Street Journal,* February 13, 1996, A1).

BIBLIOGRAPHY

Ahlburg, D. A. (1991). "Remittances and Their Impact: A Study of Tonga and Western Samoa." National Centre for Development Studies, Australian National University.

Ahlburg, D. A., and Levin, M. J. (1990). "The North East Passage: A Study of Pacific Islander Migration to American Samoa and the United States." Pacific Research Monograph no. 23. Canberra: Australian National University.

Ahmed, A., and C. Shore, eds. (1995). *The Future of Anthropology: Its Relevance to the Contemporary World.* London: Athlone Press.

Appleyard, R. T., ed. (1988). *International Migration Today.* Volume 1. Nedlands: UNESCO and The Centre for Migration and Development Studies, University of Western Australia.

Bellwood, P. (1987). *The Polynesians: Prehistory of an Island People.* London: Thames & Hudson.

Bertram, G. (1986). "Sustainable Development in Pacific Micro-Economies." *World Development* 14 (7): 809–22.

Bertram, G., and R. F. Watters (1985). "The MIRAB Economy in South Pacific microstates." *Pacific Viewpoint* 26 (3): 497–520.

Borjas, G. (1990). *Friends or Strangers: The Impact of Immigrants on the U.S. Economy.* New York: Basic Books.

Brettell, C. (1993). "Whose History Is It? Selection and Representation in the Creation of a Test." In *When They Read What We Write: The Politics of Ethnography,* ed. C. Brettell, 93–106. Westport, Conn.: Bergin & Garvey.

——, ed. (1993). *When They Read What We Write: The Politics of Ethnography.* Westport, Conn.: Bergin & Garvey.

Brown, R. P. C. (1994). "Migrants' Remittances, Savings and Investment in the South Pacific." *International Labour Review* 133 (3): 1–21.

—— (1995). "Hidden Foreign Exchange Flows: Estimating Unofficial Remittances to Tonga and Western Samoa." *Asian and Pacific Migration Journal* 4 (1): 35–54.

Brown, R. P. C., and J. Connell (1993). "The Global Flea Market: Migration, Remittances, and the Informal Economy in Tonga." *Development and Change* 24: 611–47.

Brown, R. P. C., and J. Foster (1994). "Remittances and Savings in Migrant-Sending Countries." *Pacific Economic Bulletin* 9 (2): 27–34.

—— (1995). "Some Common Fallacies about Migrants' Remittances in the South Pacific: Lessons from Tongan and Western Samoan Research." *Pacific Viewpoint* 36 (1): 29–45.

Brown, R. P. C., and A. Walker (1994). "Determinants of Remittances by Pacific Island Migrants: Results of a Sample Survey among Tongan and Western Samoan Migrants in Brisbane." ILO Report (Bangkok). Brisbane: University of Queensland.

Campbell, I. C. (1992). *Island Kingdom: Tonga Ancient and Modern.* Canterbury: Canterbury University Press.

Cha, D., and C. A. Small (1994). "Policy Lessons from Lao and Hmong Women in Thai Refugee Camps." *World Development* 22 (July): 1045–60.

Chiswick, B. R. (1978). "The Effect of Americanization on the Earnings of Foreign-Born Men." *Journal of Political Economy* 86: 897–921.

Clifford, J. (1988). *The Predicament of Culture.* Cambridge: Harvard University Press.

Clifford, J., and G. Marcus, eds. (1986). *Writing Culture: The Poetics and Politics of Ethnography.* Berkeley: University of California Press.

Clough, P. T. (1992). *The End(s) of Ethnography: From Realism to Social Criticism.* Newbury Park: Sage.

Connell, J. (1983). "Migration, Employment, and Development in the South Pacific." Country Report no. 18 (Tonga). Noumea: South Pacific Commission.

—— (1991). "Island Microstates: The Mirage of Development." *Contemporary Pacific* 3 (2): 251–286.

Connell, J., and R. P. C. Brown (1995). "Migration and Remittances in the South Pacific." *Asian and Pacific Migration Journal* 4 (1): 1–34.

Cowling, W. (1990a). "On Being Tongan." Ph.D. thesis, Macquarie University.

—— (1990b). "Motivations for Contemporary Tongan Migration." In *Tongan Culture and History,* ed. P. Herda, J. Terrell, and N. Gunson, 187–205. Canberra: Australian National University.

DeVita, P. R., and J. D. Armstrong, eds. (1993). *Distant Mirrors: America as a Foreign Culture.* Belmont, Calif.: Wadsworth.

Dreschel, E. J. (1993). "A European Anthropologist's Personal and Ethnographic Impressions of the United States." In *Distant Mirrors: America as a Foreign Culture,* ed. P. R. DeVita and J. D. Armstrong, 120–45. Belmont, Calif.: Wadsworth.

Eisenstadt, S. N. (1973). "Post-Traditional Societies and the Continuity and Reconstruction of Tradition." *Daedalus* (Winter): 1–28.

Faeamani, S. (1995). "The Impact of Remittances on Rural Development in Tongan Villages." *Asian and Pacific Migration Journal* 4 (1): 139–56.

Fienup-Riordan, A. (1988). "Robert Redford, Ananuugpak, and the Invention of Tradition." *American Ethnologist* 15: 442–55.

Foner, N. (1979). "West Indians in New York City and London: A Comparative Analysis." *International Migration Review* 13 (2): 284–297.

Fonua, P. (1986). "Inflation Slams Tonga." *Island Pacific Business* 12 (January 1): 29.

Fuka, M. L. A. (1985). "The Auckland Tongan Community and Overseas Remittances." M.A. Thesis. Auckland: University of Auckland.

Gailey, C. W. (1992). "A Good Man Is Hard to Find." *Critique of Anthropology* 12 (1): 47–74.

Gardner, K. (1995). *Global Migrants, Local Lives.* Oxford: Oxford University Press.

Geertz, C. (1988). *Works and Lives: The Anthropologist as Author.* Stanford: Stanford University Press.

Georges, E. (1990). *The Making of a Transnational Community: Migration, Development, and Cultural Change in the Dominican Republic.* New York: Columbia University Press.

Geschwender, J. A. (1978). *Racial Stratification in America.* Dubuque: William C. Brown.

Ginsburg, F. D. (1989). *Contested Lives: The Abortion Debate in an American Community.* Berkeley: University of California Press.

—— (1993). "The Case of Mistaken Identity: Problems in Representing Women on the Right." In *When They Read What We Write: The Politics of Ethnography,* ed. C. B. Brettell, 163–76. Westport: Bergin & Garvey.

Gmelch, G. (1992). *Double Passage: The Lives of Caribbean Migrants Abroad and Back Home.* Ann Arbor: University of Michigan Press.

Goldberg, B. (1992). "Historical Reflections on Transnationalism, Race, and the American Immigrant Saga." In *Towards a Transnational Perspective on Migration: Race, Class, Ethnicity and Nationalism Reconsidered,* ed. N. G. Schiller, L. Basch, and C. Blanc-Szanton, 201–16. New York: New York Academy of Sciences.

Gordon, T. G. (1988). "Inventing Mormon Identity in Tonga." Ph.D. diss., University of California, Berkeley.

Hardaker, J., Delforce, J., Fleming, E. and S. Sefanaia (1987). *Smallholder Agriculture in Tonga.* Armidale: University of New England.

Hatcher, C. (1994). "Tonga on the Move." *Pacific Business* (April): 17.

Hopkins, M. (1993). "Is Anonymity Possible? Writing about Refugees in the United States." In *When They Read What We Write: The Politics of Ethnography,* ed. C. B. Brettell, 121–30. Westport, Conn.: Bergin & Garvey.

Isbister, J. (1996). *The Immigration Debate: Remaking America.* West Hartford: Kumarian Press.

James, K. (1983). "Gender Relations in Tonga." *The Journal of the Polynesian Society* 92 (2): 233–43.

—— (1991). "Migration and Remittances: A Tongan Village Perspective." *Pacific Viewpoint* 32 (1): 1–23.

—— (1993). "The Rhetoric and Reality of Change and Development in Small Pacific Communities." *Pacific Viewpoint* 34 (2): 135–52.

—— (1994). "Tonga's Pro-Democracy Movement." *Pacific Affairs* 67 (2): 242–64.

Jones, R. C. (1995). *Ambivalent Journey*. Tucson: University of Arizona Press.

Jordan, M. (1996). "In Rural India, Video Vans Sell Toothpaste and Shampoo." *Wall Street Journal,* Jan. 10, 1996, B1–2.

Kaeppler, A. (1978). "Me'a Faka'eiki: Tongan Funerals in a Changing Society." In *The Changing Pacific: Essays in Honour of Harry Maude,* ed. Niel Gunson, 174–202. Canberra: Australian University Press.

Kirch, P. V. (1984). *The Evolution of the Polynesian Chiefdoms.* Cambridge: Cambridge University Press.

Kozol, J. (1991). *Savage Inequalities: Children in America's Schools.* New York: Harper Perennial.

Lessinger, J. (1992). "Investing or Going Home? A Transnational Strategy among Indian Immigrants in the United States." In *Towards a Transnational Perspective on Migration: Race, Class, Ethnicity, and Nationalism Reconsidered,* ed. N. G. Schiller, L. Basch, and C. Blanc-Szanton, 53–81. New York: New York Academy of Sciences.

Macpherson, C., et al., eds. (1978). *New Neighbors: Islanders in Adaptation.* Santa Cruz: Center for South Pacific Studies, University of California.

Manning, P. K. (1995). "The Challenges of Postmodernism." In *Representation in Ethnography,* ed. J. V. Maanen, 245–72. Thousand Oaks, Calif.: Sage.

Marcus, G. E. (1978). "Land Tenure and Elite Formation in the Neotraditional Monarchies of Tonga and Burunda." *American Ethnologist* 5: 509–34.

—— (1980). "The Nobility and The Chiefly Tradition in the Modern Kingdom of Tonga." *Polynesian Society Memoirs,* no. 42, Wellington.

—— (1986). "Contemporary Problems of Ethnography in the Modern World System." In *Writing Culture: The Poetics and Politics of Ethnography,* ed. J. Clifford and G. Marcus, 165–93. Berkeley: University of California Press.

—— (1989). "Chieftanship." In *Developments in Polynesian Ethnology,* ed. Alan Howard and Robert Borofsky, 175–210. Honolulu: University of Hawaii Press.

—— (1993). "Tonga's Contemporary Globalizing Strategies: Trading on Sovereignty amidst International Migration." In *Contemporary Pacific Societies,* ed. T. Harding and B. Wallace, 12–33. Englewood Cliffs, N.J.: Prentice-Hall.

Marcus, G. E., and D. Cushman (1982). "Ethnographies as Texts." *Annual Review of Anthropology* (11): 25–29.

—— (1986). *Anthropology as Cultural Critique: An Experimental Moment in the Human Sciences.* Chicago: University of Chicago Press.

Marshall, J. (1996). "Income Gap Widens Fast in California." *San Francisco Chronicle,* July 15, 1996, A1, A13.

Menchaca, M. (1995). *The Mexican Outsiders: A Community History of Marginalization and Discrimination in California.* Austin: University of Texas Press.

Miles, R., M. Alam, P. Wickramasekara, and T. Larhed (1992). *Employment in Tonga: Present and Potential.* Suva, Fiji: ILO/UNDP/AIDAB.

Morton, H. (1996). *Becoming Tongan: An Ethnography of Childhood.* Honolulu: University of Hawai'i Press.

Morton, K. L. (1987). "The Atomisation of Tongan Society." *Pacific Studies* 10: 47–72.

Mucha, J. L. (1993). "An Outsider's View of American Culture." In *Distant Mirrors: America as a Foreign Culture,* ed. P. R. DeVita and J. D. Armstrong, 21–28. Belmont: Wadsworth.

Mydans, S. (1996). "For Indonesian Workers at Nike Plant: Just Do It." *New York Times,* Aug. 9, 1996, A4.

Perminow, A. A. (1993). *The Long Way Home: Dilemmas of Everyday Life in a Tongan Village.* Oslo: Scandinavian University Press (distributed by Oxford University Press).

Pinxten, R. (1993). "America for Americans." In *Distant Mirrors: America as a Foreign Culture,* ed. P. R. DeVita and J. D. Armstrong, 93–102. Belmont: Wadsworth.

Portes, A., and R. G. Rumbaut (1990). *Immigrant America: A Portrait.* Berkeley: University of California Press.

Reimers, D. M. (1992). *Still the Golden Door: The Third World Comes to America.* New York: Columbia University Press.

Ritterbusch, D. S. (1988). "Isle Young Find Problems as Emigrants." *Pacific Magazine* 13 (July 1): 46.

Rosaldo, R. (1989). *Culture and Truth: The Remaking of Social Analysis.* Boston: Beacon Press.

Schiller, N. G., L. Basch, and C. Blanc-Szanton, eds. (1992). *Towards a Transnational Perspective on Migration: Race, Class, Ethnicity, and Nationalism Reconsidered.* New York: New York Academy of Sciences.

Schlesinger, A. M., Jr. (1991). *The Disuniting of America: Reflections on a Multicultural Society.* Knoxville: Whittle Direct Books.

—— (1995). "The Disuniting of America." Eleventh Annual Community Lectures in Humanities, Northern Arizona University, September 29, 1995.

Sharma, A. (1996). "India's Public Increases Use of Credit Cards." *Wall Street Journal,* Aug. 2, 1996, B4B.

Singhanetra-Renard, A. (1992). "The Mobilization of Labour Migrants in Thailand: Personal Links and Facilitating Networks." In *International Migration Systems,* ed. M. Kritz, L. Lim, and H. Zlotnik, 190–204. Oxford: Clarendon Press.

Small, C. A. (1987). "Women's Associations and Their Pursuit of Wealth in Tonga: A Study in Social Change." Ph.D. diss., Temple University.

—— (1995). "The Birth and Growth of a Polynesian Women's Exchange Network." *Oceania* 65 (3): 234–56.

Sorensen, E., and M. E. Enchautegui (1994). "Immigrant Male Earnings in the 1980s: Divergent Patterns by Race and Ethnicity." In *Immigration and Ethnicity: The Integration of America's Newest Arrivals,* ed. B. Edmonston and J. Passel, 139–61. Washington, D.C.: Urban Institute Press.

Stalker, P. (1994). *The Work of Strangers: A Survey of International Labour Migration.* Geneva: International Labour Office.

Steinberg, S. (1989). *The Ethnic Myth.* Boston: Beacon Press.

Suro, R. (1995). "The Decline of Washington Heights." *Washington Post National Weekly Edition,* July 2, 1995, p. 8.

Sutton, C. (1987). "The Caribbeanization of New York City and the Emergence of a Transnational Socio-Cultural System." In *Caribbean Life in New York City,* ed. C. Sutton and E. Chaney, 15–29. New York: Center for Migration Studies.

Sutton, C., and S. Makiesky-Barrow (1975). "Migration and West Indian Racial and Political Consciousness." In *Migration and Development: Implications for Ethnic Identity and Political Conflict,* ed. H. Safa and B. DuToit, 113–44. The Hague: Mouton.

Tamahori, M. J. (1963). "Cultural Change in Tongan Bark-Cloth Manufacture." M.A. thesis, University of Auckland.

Teu, A. (1978). "Tongan Communities in California." In *New Neighbors: Islanders in Adaptation,* ed. C. Macpherson, B. Shore, and R. Franco, 44–46. Santa Cruz: Center for South Pacific Studies, University of California.

Tonga, Government of (1966). Census of Population and Housing. Nuku'alofa: Government Printing Office.

—— (1975). Statistical Abstract. Nuku'alofa: Statistics Department.

—— (1976). Census of Population and Housing. Volume 1. Nuku'alofa: Government Printing Office.

—— (1983). Statistical Abstract. Nuku'alofa: Statistics Department.

Tongamoa, T. (1990). "International Migration, Remittances, and Tonga." *Review* 18: 12–18.

Tupouniua, P. (1977). *A Polynesian Village: The Process of Change.* Suva: South Pacific Social Sciences Association.

U.S. Government (1990a). Census of Population and Housing. United States Summary: Social and Economic Characteristics.

—— (1990b). Census of Population and Housing. Tape File IC.

—— (1990c). Census of Population and Housing. SSTF5: The Asian and Pacific Islander Population in the United States.

—— (1990d). U.S. Census Data. Database: C90STF3A.

—— (1990e). U.S. Census Data. Database: C90STF3B.

—— (1990f). U.S. Census Data. Database: C90STF3C1.

—— (1996). U.S. Bureau of the Census. International Data Base.

Van Maanen, J. (1988). *Tales of the Field: On Writing Ethnography.* Chicago: University of Chicago Press.

—— (1995). "An End to Innocence: The Ethnography of Ethnography." In *Representation in Ethnography,* ed. J. V. Maanen, 1–35. Thousand Oaks, Calif.: Sage.

Vason, G. (1810). *An Authentic Narrative of Four Years' Residence at Tongataboo.* London: Longman, Hurst, Rees, and Co.

Vete, M. (1995). "The Determinants of Remittances among Tongans in Auckland." *Asian and Pacific Migration Journal* 4 (1): 55–68.

Wiltshire, R. (1992). "Implications of Transnational Migration for Nationalism: A Caribbean Example." In *Towards a Transnational Perspective on Migration: Race, Class, Ethnicity, and Nationalism Reconsidered,* ed. N. G. Schiller, L. Basch, and C. Blanc-Szanton, 175–88. New York: New York Academy of Sciences.

Wood, A. H. (1932; reprinted 1978). *History and Geography of Tonga.* Canberra: Kalia Press.

Zachary, G. P. (1996). "Major U.S. Companies Expand Efforts to Sell to Consumers Abroad. Many No Longer Consider Emerging Nations Merely Sources of Cheap Labor." *Wall Street Journal,* June 13, 1996, A1, A6.

Zweigenhaft, Richard I., and G. William Domhoff (1982). *Jews in the Protestant Establishment.* New York: Praeger.

—— (1991). *Blacks in the White Establishment.* New Haven: Yale.

I N D E X